THE
Ambush of SS Persia

THE
Ambush of SS Persia

VOICES FROM A LOST LINER

ALAN WREN

© Alan Wren, 2020

Published by Alan Wren

All rights reserved. No part of this book may be reproduced, adapted, stored in a retrieval system or transmitted by any means, electronic, mechanical, photocopying, or otherwise without the prior written permission of the author.

The rights of Alan Wren to be identified as the author of this work have been asserted in accordance with the Copyright, Designs and Patents Act 1988.

A CIP catalogue record for this book is available from the British Library.

ISBN 978-1-8380408-0-2

Book layout and cover design by Clare Brayshaw

Cover based on the picture *PERSIA (1900) leaving the Thames* after a 1913 painting by Charles Edward Dixon.

© P&O Heritage Collection www.poheritage.com

Prepared and printed by:

York Publishing Services Ltd
64 Hallfield Road
Layerthorpe
York YO31 7ZQ

Tel: 01904 431213

Website: www.yps-publishing.co.uk

Contents

Foreword	ix
Working Notes	x
Preface	xi
Troubled Times	1
Descent into War	13
Blockade and U-boat Backlash	16
Armed Response	21
Lieutenant Commander Godfrey Herbert	24
Kapitänleutnant Max Valentiner and U-38	32
Great Orme to *Baralong*	36
The *Arabic* Pledge	41
U-boats – The Unwilling Exodus	45
SS *Ancona*	50
The December Departure of SS *Persia*	54
Marseilles and Malta	64
Colonel Lord Montagu and Eleanor Thornton	81
The Maharaja Enigma	87
Last Days, Hours and Minutes	92
Tiffin Torpedo	97
Battles for Survival	104

Four-and-a-Half Lifeboats	110
HMS *Mallow*	116
Half-Afloat	122
The Lottery of Life and Death	126
Why *Persia*?	139
What Became of Godfrey Herbert?	142
What Became of Max Valentiner?	146
What Became of some Survivors?	150
War Crimes or Warfare?	159
SS *Persia* Remembered – 1966 and 2016	163
Acknowledgements	186
Maritime Epilogue	189
Postscript	195
Glossary	196
Bibliography	202
Index	209

In remembrance of everyone aboard the SS Persia in late December 1915 and in tribute to the gallant crews of HMS Mallow and SS Ning Chow for their rescue of Persia's survivors from dangerous waters.

Foreword

The events of the First World War produced so many stories reflecting the best and the worst of humanity that it is not surprising the tale of the SS *Persia* has been largely forgotten. She is but one figure in the statistics of a conflict in which the human losses are too great to comprehend. But for those of us descended from the passengers and crew who were on board the *Persia* when she was torpedoed by German U-boat 38, this story has a special place in our family annals. My grandfather, John Montagu, was one of those who survived to tell the tale, whilst his personal assistant, Eleanor Thornton, travelling with him, was one of the casualties.

A hundred years on, in 2016, a gathering to unveil a memorial to all those who perished underlined how this appalling act of war is still remembered by the descendants. Whilst we all had some knowledge of the incident, the details had become somewhat blurred by the passing of time. This work by Alan Wren, which presents the context of the attack seen from both the British and German perspectives, puts that right. Mr Wren is to be congratulated on tackling this subject, undertaking so much detailed research and providing us with an account which covers every aspect of the SS *Persia*, the U38 and all those connected with these vessels. The questions surrounding the incident which have lingered in the minds of many have now been answered and finally laid to rest.

Ralph Douglas-Scott-Montagu, 4th Baron Montagu of Beaulieu

Working Notes

Some historians and publishers suggested that the telling of this story was not worth my effort. Their view was that the event was of no great interest. However, my main purpose was to create a permanent memorial to all those aboard the ship, naming everyone and telling some of their stories. As for significance, the ship was carrying bullion and jewellery valued at one million pounds in 1915. Early twenty-first century valuation calculations range from fifty-nine million to ninety-eight million pounds, so not insignificant. A submerged U-boat torpedoed the ship without warning, but if its crew had stopped and searched the SS *Persia*, what a prize they would have found!

I have used place names, job titles and other terms from those distant days. Examples include Bombay for Mumbai, Calcutta for Kolkata, Queenstown for Cobh and Burma for Myanmar. The term lascar for an Indian seaman, now deemed pejorative, was correct for the period, and is used now for historical accuracy. I apologise if it causes any unintended offence. Wherever the words 'mile' or 'miles' appear, they mean nautical miles, about 15% longer than statute miles.

Photographs are invaluable when describing people, objects, and events from the early part of the twentieth century. I searched long and hard to find appropriate images for this book, then worked to identify copyright owners, seek permission to use pictures and make proper acknowledgements in the captions. Where exhaustive searches failed to trace ownership, or where research indicated that images are in the public domain, I decided to use them because of their importance to the narrative and apologise unreservedly if I have erred in so doing.

AW

Preface

On Monday 30th December 1915, it was time for lunch aboard the *Persia* as she steamed south-east of Crete at about 15 knots towards Port Said, just over a day away. A westerly breeze chased her, ruffling the wave crests and strewing foamy white feathers along the surface. Aboard, waiters sounded gongs at 1 pm, one outside the First Saloon beneath the ship's bridge and another outside the Second Saloon down by the stern. Eighteen children and infants had already eaten and returned to their cabins for a nap or perhaps a story or lullaby from a nurse or ayah. Adults headed for their tables to dine in child-free relaxation, but as they settled to order they heard and felt a violent blow. *Persia* shuddered; waiters staggered; crockery, cutlery and glassware fell to the deck. Many guessed correctly that the risk of torpedo attack had become reality. A second explosion followed in seconds. Some of those in the saloons likened the following moments to the end of a church service as people stood and filed out quietly and in turn. *Persia* listed rapidly towards her port side and in about five minutes she sank, not too far from the Pliny Trench, some 4,400 metres (14,400 feet) deep, taking at least 334 innocent lives with her. It was five minutes past one o'clock. Nearby, Kapitänleutnant Max Valentiner, commander of the submerged U-38, scanned the blackened flotsam and bobbing heads through his periscope before turning away in search of his next target.

So that is the SS *Persia* story – the bare bones of the what, when, how, who and where of the attack. Important but unanswered questions remain. Hundreds were killed and thousands bereaved. Who were they, where were they going at Christmas and why? Why ambush a passenger liner without warning when Germany had recently promised not to sink passenger liners without warning? She was actually carrying tons of mail, Christmas cards, gifts and other cargo of no military significance that any legal U-boat 'stop and search' could have found.

In the weeks that followed, brief and angry outbursts continued in some newspapers, but by Friday 10th March 1916, the *Dundee Courier* was just one of those telling its readership that the Board of Trade would not hold an enquiry into the loss of the *Persia*. After all, she was a workhorse rather than a thoroughbred and lacked the enduring glamour of a *Titanic* or *Lusitania*. Fish and chip shops across Britain soon found use for the newspapers that had covered the sinking and she faded away, except in the hearts and minds of her bereaved. If the public had known then that part of her cargo was a million-pound fortune, she might have been remembered for a good while longer.

Much information about World War 1 at sea has simply disappeared under the Atlantic, the seas around Britain and in the Mediterranean, some by accident and more by design. Blame the fog of war, secrecy, censorship, domestic and military decluttering and the need for life to move on. During my years of solo research, I struggled to resolve gaps in *Persia*'s story and answer the 'why' question. Gaps remain and always will, but as I joined dots together a theory evolved – what professional historians might call a hypothesis. American historian Victor Davis Hanson summarised such difficulties well:

> *'In history, one gathers clues like a detective, tries to present an honest account of what most likely happened and writes a narrative according to what we know and, where we aren't absolutely sure, what might be most likely to have happened, within the generally accepted rules of evidence and sources.'*[1]

My collection of factual and circumstantial evidence gradually flowed together, gathering flotsam and jetsam, pieces, fragments and strands of information which entwined into a theory that I believe gives a credible answer to the question 'Why *Persia*?' Why did a U-Boat commander hide underwater to sink a harmless mail liner? Why was it so easy? What errors and attitudes allowed it? What decisions, policies, strategies and crimes enabled, provoked and triggered the vengeful series of murderous events that eventually led to the ambush of the SS *Persia*?

Her story is not just about a moment in time, but originates in an era when populations welcomed war which, once started, quickly turned merciless. At sea, the sinking of RMS *Lusitania* led to a breakdown of the mutual respect that had existed between the Kaiserliche Marine and the Royal

---

1   Victor Davis Hanson Quotes. (n. d.). BrainyQuote. com. Retrieved January 31, 2017, from BrainyQuote. com Web site:

Navy. As recently as 1911, 165 Royal Navy vessels had lined up for King George V's Coronation Fleet Review at Spithead alongside 18 warships of foreign navies, which included the German pocket battleship, SMS *Admiral Graf Spee*, and the ultramodern and supremely fast battle cruiser, SMS *Von der Tann*. Only four years later, naval attacks between those same navies were killing many innocent civilians after the sinking of RMS *Lusitania* led to revenge and retaliation which eventually ensnared the innocent SS *Persia*. Warships should have operated under international law, known as the cruiser rules, until some in command of warships chose to turn blind eyes to those rules.

Two such men, one a U-boat commander, son of a pastor from Prussian-occupied Denmark, and the other a British Q-ship captain, son of a Coventry solicitor, figure in my hypothesis. Both came from modestly privileged backgrounds. Both would face accusations of war crimes but would avoid trials. They were Kapitänleutnant Max Valentiner of the Kaiserliche Marine, commander of U-38 that would sink the *Persia*, and Lieutenant Commander Godfrey Herbert RN, commander of the British Q-ship HMS *Baralong* since 5th April 1915. Enraged by the 1,198 deaths on the RMS *Lusitania*, his crew killed, allegedly murdered, Valentiner's cousin.

I soon realised that my attempt to find out what happened and why needed to begin before 1915 in order to understand causes and circumstances that emerged during those days of the late nineteenth and early twentieth centuries when Britain really did rule the waves. During this period, decisions, conferences, strategies and attitudes shaped the early twentieth century at sea. Britain's dependency on its navy was based on two long-held convictions; the first that no other country, or group of countries, would be capable of matching the Royal Navy's power in the foreseeable future and the second that submarines and torpedoes were under-developed novelties, unlikely to be any serious threat. By 1914, Britain had the world's largest submarine fleet, intended only for defensive use. Most of its leaders failed to comprehend its stealth warfare capabilities. It seems not to have occurred to many politicians and military men that anyone would be so unsporting as to remain hidden beneath the sea to fire torpedoes at surface ships, particularly merchantmen.

The Buck Stops Here

I am not a historian and my lifelong love of history is not a qualification. Four years ago, after failing to find a single book about SS *Persia*, I set out to learn enough about her to close the book-gap, more like telling her story than history. It became a labour of love, buoyed up by those who believed in me, hindered by limited research resources and experience. As an amateur undertaking the very serious role of writing about past events, I sifted through a vast amount of information about what happened to and around the *Persia*. Some of this was 'hard' evidence, some fragmentary, some from opinions, letters, diaries and distant memories. Despite all the valuable help and support I received, all errors and omissions are mine.

People and sources still differ over exactly how many people were aboard the *Persia* and, crucially, how many died. This number varies between 334 and 343 but remains unresolved. I also set out to record the names of all who died and all those aboard who survived but whose lives were traumatised by the events of 30th December 1915. I hope I have included everyone and accurately recorded the correct form of every name. My story is a further memorial to them all.

AW

Preface

Buckler's Hard SS Persia Memorial
© *Alan Wren 2016*

Troubled Times

In the late nineteenth century, much of the world was unsettled. Industrial nations competed over lands in the undeveloped world, seeking to possess all forms of wealth, foodstuffs and raw materials. The people of colonised lands suffered the rule of invaders. Empires needed people, supplies, communications, munitions, law-enforcement and defence garrisons, all brought by ships, defended by warships. The pace of change in building bigger and better warships, submarines and weapons left international maritime law trailing in its wake, permitting circumstances in which the eventual killing of civilians at sea would become routine and seemingly easy to excuse. By the early twentieth century, Britain still ruled the waves with the Royal Navy pioneering the Dreadnought Era, while Germany struggled to keep pace but developed excellent submarines. Merchant ships also evolved to satisfy demand for ships that could carry the many people, exports, imports and large volumes of mail needed to manage distant empires. SS *Persia* was to be one of those ships and U-38 to be one of those submarines, forever after to be known as U-boats.

1881

Sir John Colomb, MP, a former Royal Marine Artillery officer, foresaw the need to arm British merchant vessels in any major war at sea. In a lecture delivered at the Royal United Services Institution in May of that year, he had predicted:

> 'that the exigencies of maritime war will necessitate our arming not merely a careful selection of the best, but every ocean-going British steamer. We must prepare in peace to give them, at home and abroad, armaments and trained instructors, and then on the declaration of war bid them follow their avocations

and let our enemies know that we mean to carry on our sea trade 'in spite of their teeth', under the banner, if you like, of 'Defence not Defiance'.'[2]

1889

As the nineteenth century approached its final decade, Britain paid close attention to France and Russia, seen as her most likely future enemies. Britain's naval strategy had relied on the informal 'two-power standard', the ability to out-gun the world's next two largest navies if they joined forces against her. In 1889, this was formalised into the Naval Defence Act. With a budget of £20m (perhaps £2.3bn in 2015), the Royal Navy commissioned ten new battleships, thirty-eight cruisers, several fast gunboats and motor torpedo boats[3]. However, as Britain's navy modernised and expanded, it should have been no surprise that those of France, Russia and Germany did so also. Britain was not the only nation in pursuit of Empire. When, in 1894, France and Russia formed an alliance to counter Germany's growing power, it reacted by strengthening its alliance with the neighbouring Austro-Hungarian Empire.

1897

At a meeting between Sir Francis Bertie, of the British Foreign Office, and German Diplomat Baron Hermann von Eckardstein, the Baron mentioned that his Emperor was thinking of sending German troops to assist the Boers in the Transvaal. Bertie countered that Germany must be aware that Britain would not hesitate to repel any German intervention and that if this led to war, the Royal Navy would blockade Hamburg and Bremen and annihilate German commerce on the high seas[4]. Over the next seventeen years, Britain planned and refined blockade variations, but if a war with Germany happened, a blockade would both be an early response and vital element.

1898–1900

Germany's First Naval Law authorised the building of a new German navy capable of competing with France and Russia. It planned to build nineteen battleships, eight armoured cruisers, twelve heavy cruisers and thirty light

---

2   Hurd, Archibald (1924). *History Of The Great War, The merchant marine* Vol. II. London, John Murray
3   Sondhaus, Lawrence (2001). *Naval Warfare, 1815-1914*. New York: Routledge, 2001
4   Clarke, Christopher M (2009). *Kaiser Wilhelm II, A Life in Power*. London: Penguin

cruisers by 1904[5]. Then, in 1900, the Second Naval Law came into force with the ambitious aim of challenging the supremacy of Britain's navy. The new Imperial Navy would have thirty-eight battleships, twenty armoured cruisers and thirty-eight light cruisers.

At the dawn of the twentieth century, one-third of the world's merchant ships were British, carrying half the world's cargoes and contributing a huge amount to Britain's earnings and exchequer. Financing and insuring this trade created jobs and earnings in Britain too. Growth in manufacturing, commerce and services spread across the globe. In 1912, British shipyards completed 920 new ships totalling 2 million gross tons[6]. International shipping traffic grew in three areas – freight, mail and passengers. Ships to carry all three gained wide appeal. The era of the passenger liner had dawned, with companies including Cunard, White Star, Orient Steamship Co, P&O, and Hamburg America Lines among the leaders. Thousands of Europeans relocated overseas, creating a need for carrying even larger volumes of mail and cargo quickly and regularly. Peninsular and Oriental Lines (P&O) secured much business including mail contracts on the Empire Run to India and beyond to Australia. Clyde shipbuilder Caird and Company helped P&O meet this need.

1900

Through the advent of the twentieth century and beyond, the Peninsular and Oriental Steam Navigation Company was just one company expanding its merchant fleet in recognition of the need for new, flexible, multipurpose vessels, the passenger–cargo liners that would help prepare the world for the opportunities of the twentieth century. One of these ships would be the SS *Persia*.

John Caird founded Caird and Company of Greenock in 1828[7] and engaged bright young family member James Tennant Caird as an apprentice in 1831. James was destined to become one of Clyde shipbuilding's greats. His enthusiasm and hunger for innovation helped Caird develop into a world-famous shipbuilder. As a measure of Caird's success, the Peninsular and Oriental Steam Navigation Company became its principle customer after 1870 and would eventually order eighty-five ships. In 1900, SS *Persia* became the fifth and last member of P&O's Egypt Class which included the

---

5   https://www.naval-history.net/WW1NavyGermanyOrganisation.htm
6   https://www.gracesguide.co.uk/1912_Shipbuilding_Yards_listed_by_Tonnage
7   https://www.gracesguide.co.uk/Caird_and_Co

vessels *India* (1896), *China* (1896), *Egypt* (1897) and *Arabia* (1898). *Persia* was the company's largest ship to date and, at £260,290, its most costly (perhaps £29.9m in 2015[8]). *The Shipping World & Herald of Commerce*, Vol. XXIII, No. 367, London, 31st October 1900, announced her launch.

'Quietly and without ceremony, the latest and largest to the P&O fleet was put into the water at Greenock on the 11th inst, the ship and her propelling machinery having been designed and constructed throughout by Messrs. Caird and Co. With a length of 500 ft, a beam of 54 ft and a depth of 37 ft 6 in, the Persia has a gross tonnage of close on 8,000 (to be exact 7,992) tons and is fitted with machinery designed to give her a speed of 18 knots. The vessel is built with poop, top-gallant forecastle and long bridge-house amidships, and has two masts and two funnels. There are six decks, boat, hurricane, spar, main, lower and orlop; and accommodation is provided for 320 first saloon and 230 second saloon passengers on the hurricane, spar, main and lower decks, all the cabins being large and well ventilated, and fitted with Hoskins' patented iron berths with spring mattresses. Each cabin is very completely fitted with furniture of dark mahogany. The first saloon is on the main deck, well forward of the boiler space and will seat 250 passengers. The framing is painted white with plaster panels above the dado by Messrs. Jackson and Sons, by which firm the roof panels and beam covers were also supplied. The whole of the saloon is furnished in white and gold, the furniture being of dark mahogany, with revolving chairs of a handsome design.

An easy and commodious staircase leads from the music room and spar decks to the saloon and is of dark mahogany with substantial but elegant balustrades and handrails. The music room on the hurricane deck is a large and lofty apartment. The panelling of this room is of polished African mahogany, inlaid with various designs in boxwood, the frieze and ceiling being in plaster, specially designed by Messrs. Jackson. An oval opening in the centre over the saloon is surrounded by rails and balustrades corresponding to those in the companion, and the skylight over the music room is filled with stained glass of an artistic character. The companion abaft the music room on the hurricane deck is a handsome and lofty apartment, with wood panelling painted cream and white, and a plaster ceiling. All the sofas and chairs in the music room and companion are of a most comfortable description, and the carvings are of a very handsome material and tasteful design.

---

8   Historical UK inflation rates and calculator; http://inflation.iamkate.com/

The second saloon is situated on the spar deck aft and is panelled in dark polished mahogany with a ceiling of Messrs. Jackson's plaster. The sides also have Tynecastle tapestry panels between the ports. The furniture here is also of dark mahogany, and there are revolving tables and chairs for 120 passengers; the sofas being covered with the best moquette. In addition, there are 66 seats on the lower deck for the second saloon passengers. There are smoking rooms for first and second saloon passengers that for the former is on the hurricane deck, and panelled in oak stained green, with numerous paintings in frames and having a plaster ceiling. The second saloon smoking room is in the poop and is panelled with dark polished mahogany the ceiling being of Tynecastle tapestry. The sofas in both these rooms are so arranged as to form most comfortable lounges. Marble baths are provided for all the passengers, and each is fitted with a wave, douche and spray arrangement, and supplied with hot and cold water. There are cage and shower baths also for gentlemen. The arrangements for the pantries and bars, which belong to the Purser's department, are of the most comfortable character. The very complete outfit of cargo gear and hydraulic warping capstans is worked by a hydraulic power plant specially designed and fitted by Messrs. Armstrong Whitworth & Co of Elswick-upon-Tyne.

The steam steering gear which is placed in a house on the after part of the poop is by Messrs. Brown Bros., Edinburgh, and will be worked by telemotor from the bridge.

The life-saving appliances are ample for the number of passengers and crew carried by the ship. There are fourteen boats in all, ten of which are lifeboats, and one a steam launch, besides four collapsible boats on Berthon and Chambers principles.

The ship has been built to Lloyd's rules under special survey, and all requirements of the Board of Trade for passenger certificate have been fully met.

The main propelling machinery consists of a set of compound triple-expansion engines, with four cylinders working a single screw and capable of indicating 11,000 h. p., which will drive the vessel at 17 to 18 knots at sea.

There are three double-ended and three single-ended boilers fitted with Howden's forced draught, capable of supplying an ample amount of steam to the machinery. The screw propeller has four blades of manganese bronze. All the auxiliary machinery is of ample character to meet every emergency. The Persia is expected on her maiden voyage to Bombay early in November. (1900)'

The SS *Persia* thus embarked on her first outward 'Empire Run', a route on which she would continue for fifteen years, sailing close to one million nautical miles for P&O. She sailed into a troubled era when seismic pressure for change was creeping and then sweeping across Europe and beyond. What did the future hold for countries such as Great Britain and Germany, both so reliant on stable ship-borne trade, not only to feed their populations and supply their factories but also to fuel their participation in the modern world's first major arms race?

1903

Four years into the new century, there were serious concerns about the impact of war on how long British food supplies might last once any conflict started. The Royal Commission on the Supply of Food and Raw Material in Time of War, appointed on 27th April 1903, examined the Royal Navy's responsibility for the security of British ocean-borne trade. It eventually reported in 1905. Its terms of reference were:

> *'To inquire into the conditions affecting the importation of food and raw material into the United Kingdom of Great Britain and Ireland in time of war and into the amount of the reserves of such supplies existing in the Country at any given period; and to advise whether it is desirable to adopt any measures, in addition to the maintenance of a strong fleet, by which such supplies can be better secured and violent fluctuations avoided.'*[9]

The Commission's working assumption was that 'strong fleet' meant that Britain would maintain its two-power standard and avoid challenges to its naval supremacy. The possibility of an effective blockade of the United Kingdom by an enemy navy does not seem to have been a concern. The Commission commented on the protection of merchant shipping that:

> *'It has sometimes been assumed that protection can only be given either by sending a number of cruisers to protect the trade routes or by a system of convoy.'*

Members expressed their opinion of the need to improve the protection of commerce in other ways. They recorded that command of the seas was

---

9   Royal Commission on Supply of Food and Raw Material in Time of War (1905). Report of the Royal Commission On Supply of Food And Raw Material In Time of War: With Minutes of Evidence And Appendices. London: Printed for H M Stationery Office, by Wyman and Sons, Limited

essential, was Britain's primary aim and showed unquestioning reliance on the two-power strategy, concluding:

'It follows from this that concentration of our forces will be the most effective protection that can be given to our trade from attack by the regular men-of-war of the enemy during, at any rate, the initial stages of a maritime contest and that the policy of an organised attack on our commerce, if adopted, is not likely to meet with any great measure of success.'

The mention of 'regular men-of-war' might suggest that some of them had taken peripheral notice of submarines, if only because of their novelty value. However, the Royal Navy decided not to use convoys and other forms of close protection of merchant shipping if it had to go to war soon. With the advent of armed submarines, this one-dimensional strategy would soon become dangerously dated. Britain had the world's largest submarine fleet, developed for coastal defence, and no one seems to have seen its use beyond that. Britain would operate any blockade of Germany by surface ships, so paid little attention to the attack potential of submarines.

1904

Britain's long-running antipathy with France relaxed when, on 8th April 1904, they reached agreement after settling some of the contentious issues between them. They gave each other a free hand – for Britain in Egypt and for France in Morocco. This 'Entente Cordiale' enabled diplomatic cooperation to counter German pressure, but it was not an alliance, nor did it involve obligations towards Russia. It was a friendly understanding between two neighbours, former enemies who shared a common concern. During the gradual emergence of this relationship, Germany's anxiety grew, as she saw herself surrounded by increasingly powerful potential enemies. Britain operated the world's most formidable navy, while France and Russia also had strong fleets. Previously, Germany had concentrated on building the world's most effective army, but strong land forces were no longer enough for the Kaiser, who set out to build a great navy.

Five of Europe's strongest nations had now joined two opposing groups. This did not in itself start a war but raised the temperature and the hyperbole. The idiom 'be careful what you wish for', sometimes followed by the explanation 'for you might get it', seems to have implanted itself in the minds and hearts of many of Europe's political leaders and newspaper editors, many of whom seem to have spent much of the Edwardian era urging a violent showdown between the Continent's great powers.

1905–6

A serious and vastly expensive arms race gathered pace. In 1906, Germany boosted naval expansion by passing its Third Naval Law, proposing six more battleships. However, Britain's First Sea Lord, 'Jackie' Fisher, played his ace with impeccable timing. His brainchild, HMS *Dreadnought*, appeared almost overnight, in that same year. The dockyard workforce in Portsmouth built her in record time and great secrecy. She was launched on 10th February 1906 and the Royal Navy commissioned her on 2nd December. Her design, specification, heavier armament, improved fire control and steam-turbine-powered speed made existing capital ships across the world obsolete. Two Dreadnought battleships had fire-power equivalent to five pre-Dreadnoughts, with greater range and accuracy, thus nullifying Germany's newly built warships at a stroke. When the Imperial Germany Navy sought additional money to build six battleships to match Dreadnought specifications, the government refused to budget for this and its navy had to settle for six cruisers.

Britain and France held conferences to discuss military cooperation if they were to go to war with Germany. Charles Ottley, Director of Naval Intelligence, suggested the two key roles for the Royal Navy were:

1. Seizure of German merchant ships

2. Blockading ports to disrupt Germany's commerce and industry and pressurise her Battle Fleet to leave port to do battle with the Royal Navy.

1908–9

By 1908, the Admiralty had revisited blockade planning and while some doubted whether it would work, others sought a more effective approach. Variations of blockade plans came and went right up to 1914, not about whether Britain would blockade Germany in any future war, but how.

For several centuries, rules about war at sea had evolved. These covered, among other events, attacks on and capture of merchant ships. Many rules survived from days when the wind in their sails propelled ships. Seamen and lawyers referred to them as 'prize rules' or 'cruiser rules', deriving the term 'prize' from the practice of capturing ships and cargoes as prizes and 'Cruiser' as a general term for warships. The rules were also concerned with blockading coasts and ports to prevent ships delivering or leaving with cargo that might be contraband, that is anything that might help an enemy. The Declaration of

Paris of 1856 and the Hague Conventions of 1899 and 1907 included a series of international agreements. Many countries regarded the cruiser rules as international law but they lacked universal acceptance and lawmakers needed more discussion, negotiation, clarification and agreement to ensure that the rules kept pace with the development of modern naval weapons.

After the International Naval Conference lasting from 4th December 1908 to 26th February 1909, the Declaration of London attempted to provide a widely agreed modification of law covering war at sea. It covered blockades, contraband and prizes, mainly by restating existing rules and conventions, but it also paid more regard to rights of vessels of neutral nations. Most of the great powers of the day, the United Kingdom, France, Austria–Hungary, Germany, Italy, Japan, Russia and the United States, signed the Declaration, together with the Netherlands and Spain. Was a workable agreement in sight?

In Britain, Parliament introduced a Naval Prize Bill based on the Declaration of London, only for the House of Lords to reject it. The Marquess of Lansdowne claimed that the government lacked solid support. He pointed out that the nation's Chambers of Commerce and representatives of Britain's shipping industry were against the Bill and that many in the Admiralty believed it could disadvantage the Royal Navy in any war. The House of Lords voted 145 for rejection of the Bill against 53 in favour. In consequence, no other state ratified the Declaration and it never came into force. However, a large number continued to believe that the rules meant that enemy or neutral merchant ships must stop and submit to search by warships. If a searching warship found contraband, it could capture the vessel as a prize, or sink it if a seizure was impractical. A preliminary draft of the Declaration had stated that signatory powers agreed that the rules it set out *'correspond in substance with the generally recognised principles of international law'*[10]. It is important to note that warships and troopships had never been protected by the cruiser rules and could be attacked at any time without warning.

An Order-in-Council of 20th August 1909 announced that Britain had adopted the unratified Declaration of London and put it into force. The Declaration defined contraband in three groups, 'Absolute', 'Conditional' or 'Free'. Absolute included any form or component of possible military equipment, including arms, projectiles, explosives, warships and aeroplanes[11]

---

10 Boyle, Francis Anthony (1999). Foundations of World Order – The Legalistic Approach to International Relations 1898-1922, Durham, North Carolina: Duke University Press
11 Royal Proclamation, 4th August 1914

and this was subject to seizure or destruction if it was on its way to any destination in enemy territory. Conditional included foodstuffs, forage and vehicles. Free items were those not liable to capture or destruction. Some items, notably cotton and rubber, were originally on the Free list but advisors quickly moved them to the Absolute category as cotton was usable in the manufacture of explosive guncotton, and rubber in the manufacture of all sorts of tyres, including those for military use. The decision on cotton caused great anger amongst growers in the United States.

After troopships were requisitioned from the mercantile marine into the Royal Navy, a new threat would evolve. No one seems to have noticed or mentioned the risk initially, but some U-boat commanders might claim any merchant ship they sighted to be a troopship, thus nullifying any protection provided by the cruiser rules – no need to warn; no need to stop – sink on sight, destroy all evidence.

The emergence of submarines as warships would launch a new and dangerous form of stealth warfare on an unsuspecting world. Submerged submarines were slow and invisible but relatively safe until their air supply ran out when they had to surface. For example, in a Kaiserliche Marine Class 31 U-boat, toxic gas emissions from batteries powering the electric propulsion motors limited dive time to only two hours. Submerged speed was below 10 knots, but when surfaced and diesel-powered, a very respectable sixteen knots was possible, equal to or faster than most merchant ships. Typical practice for U-boats would be to cruise on the surface, keeping a sharp lookout from their low viewpoint while maintaining batteries on a full charge. If lookouts spotted approaching smoke, they would dive quickly, with four practicable options – submerge deep and hide, hurry away, wait and watch for an approach, or take up an interception course. In the last two cases, they would maintain watch through a periscope and determine what action to take, if any. It was much easier to see a large ship through a periscope than it was to see a periscope from a ship, particularly when wind and rain ruffled the sea.

However, under the cruiser rules, a submarine was supposed to forego the protection of invisibility and surface, instruct a merchant vessel to stop and send a boarding party. If a cargo included weapons, ammunition or any other war-making items, or anything thought or known to be contraband, such as pack mules and even cotton, it would usually result in the U-boat ordering the ship to lower its lifeboats, evacuate its crew and any passengers and pull away to a safe distance. The boarding party would return to their vessel and gunners would bombard the vessel until it sank. While this was much cheaper than using a torpedo, a type U-31 u-boat carried 300 shells but only 6 torpedoes. An even lower-cost option was for the boarding party to scuttle the vessel by opening valves allowing water to enter the hull before escaping in their own small boat. Commanders of submarines would probably consider capturing a prize-ship as an unrealistic option.

A U-boat commander had another option, that of staying submerged and firing a torpedo, without warning. This would probably contravene the Declaration of London, recently signed by great powers and others; the never ratified but de facto rules. While this might seem easier, there was no absolute guarantee of success. Getting close helped, but also raised the likelihood of a ship's lookouts spotting a periscope, unwittingly inviting a possible counter-attack by ramming, or an attempted escape. In order to chase an escaping ship, a submarine would have to surface, switch from battery to diesel propulsion and then take up the chase. Most U-boats could make 16 knots (19 mph, 30 kph) on the surface, considerably quicker than many merchant ships which were designed for capacity rather than speed. Submarines of all belligerent nations were only likely to maximise their potential through stealth warfare, doing what their designers had intended, attacking from under the sea without warning, described by Admiral Sir Arthur Wilson, VC, as *'underhand, unfair and damned un-English'*[12].

1913

One British Admiral stood apart from many of his colleagues concerning threats to British ships from German U-boats. He was Admiral Lord (Jackie) Fisher, naval reformer, champion of the Dreadnought battleship and one of the few to foresee the potential of torpedoes and submarines. He had summarised his views in 1913, in a memorandum to Winston Churchill:

> *'The submarine cannot capture the merchant ship; she has no spare hands to put a prize crew on board; little or nothing would be gained by disabling her engine or propeller; she cannot convey her into harbour; and in fact, it is impossible for the submarine to deal with commerce in the light and provisions of international law. There is nothing else the submarine can do except sink her capture, and it must therefore be admitted that this submarine menace is a truly terrible one for British commerce and Great Britain alike, for no means can be suggested at present for meeting it except for reprisals.'*

---

12   Roskill, Stephen W.(1968). Naval Policy Between the Wars. Vol 1 P.231.

The former First Sea Lord had raised the merchant-raiding potential of submarines as a 'What if?' question well before the outbreak of war. His vital wake-up call went unheard or ignored.

1914

At Germaniawerft, Kiel, a type 31 U-boat, U-38, was launched on 9th September and commissioned on 15th December. She was just one of a class of eleven ocean-going diesel-powered torpedo attack U-boats, faster on the surface than most ships and heavily armed. U-38 would put to sea as part of II Flotilla under the command of Kapitänleutnant Max Valentiner before transferring to the Pola Flotilla in November 1915, operating out of Cattaro into the Adriatic and Mediterranean, where SS *Persia* and many other ships sailed regularly.

Descent into War

Through 1914, international relations across Europe become so strained that peace wobbled on a fraying tightrope. Audiences in several countries cheered in expectation of a lurch into war, widely perceived as a solution rather than a problem; hope rather than dread. It was almost as if a potential aggressor had removed the lids from an international collection of firework boxes, waiting, even hoping, for sparks. Europe did not stumble into an immediate war because of Gavrilo Princip's assassination of Archduke Franz Ferdinand and his wife, Sophie, in Sarajevo on 28th June. Instead, reactions smouldered for thirty-four days before the conflagration burst across much of Europe and many of its people celebrated the arrival of war.

After the German declaration of war on Russia on 1st August 1914, critical events followed across Europe, like dominoes tumbling. On the tower of U-9, on surface watch on the first sunset of the war, Kapitänleutnant Otto Weddigen remarked to his watch officer, Johannes Spieß (Spiess):

> *'Spieß, look how red the sky is. The whole world seems to be bathed in blood. Mark my words – England will declare war on us.'*[13]

His prophecy would come true just three days later, on 4th August, following the German invasion of Belgium on the night of 3rd August. Great Britain had guaranteed Belgium's neutrality as long ago as 1839 and affirmed this in 1870. Prime Minister Asquith sent an ultimatum to Germany that would expire at midnight on 3rd August, their time.

As clocks in Berlin chimed midnight, Winston Churchill, First Lord of the Admiralty, recorded the scene:

---

13   His Imperial Majesty's U-boats. https://uboat.net/history/wwi/part1.htm

'It was eleven o'clock at night – twelve by German time – when the ultimatum expired. The windows of the Admiralty were thrown wide open in the warm night air. Under the roof from which Nelson had received his orders were gathered a small group of admirals and captains and a cluster of clerks, pencils in hand, waiting. Along the Mall from the direction of the Palace, the sound of an immense concourse singing "God save the King" floated in. On this deep wave there broke the chimes of Big Ben; and, as the first stroke of the hour boomed out, a rustle of movement swept across the room. The war telegram, which meant, "Commence hostilities against Germany", was flashed to the ships and establishments under the White Ensign all over the world. I walked across the Horse Guards Parade to the Cabinet room and reported to the Prime Minister and the Ministers who were assembled there that the deed was done.'[14]

The hell to come was unrecognised, so decisions to go to war were welcomed with jubilation by large numbers in some of the countries involved, though not in Belgium. Each of the belligerents thought that God was on their side, their side was assuredly right and that right would triumph quickly.

Chief of Staff Alfred von Schlieffen had first developed Germany's strategy for a future war for the Kaiser in 1903. He based it on the assumption that Germany's large professional army would defeat France in a few weeks and before her ally, Russia, could mobilise and move her vast armies over an inadequate railway system. There was a genuine belief in Germany that a war against France would be over quickly, even before Christmas. However, Belgium lay in its path and Britain had promised to defend Belgium under the Treaty of London of 1839. Germany issued an ultimatum to Belgium insisting on unhindered passage and Britain issued one to Germany to withdraw from Belgium. Both recipients declined. The massive German army attacked through Belgium expecting quick capitulation, but this didn't happen. The Belgians resisted fiercely, but against overwhelming power. Britain declared war and sent the small British Expeditionary Force to support Belgium and the French, who resisted valiantly. The Entente forces halted the Imperial German Army's attack in the Battle of the Marne on 15th September 1914. Soldiers started to dig the first trenches. Four years of slaughter and stalemate would follow. The Schlieffen Plan, the short war, had failed. A vast war on land, at sea, and soon in the air, had started with

---

14   Trueman, C N. *The British Declaration of War.* The History Learning Site, 31st March 2015. 6th April 2019. https://www.historylearningsite.co.uk/world-war-one/causes-of-world-warone/the-british-declaration-of-war/

a powerful German army on one side and the mighty Royal Navy on the other.

The war had brought enemies with very different capabilities head-to-head. The Entente had massive collective sea power and France's large army, pitched against the Central Powers with Germany and Austria–Hungary's huge, well-trained and experienced armies and capable naval power. Britain, with only a modest-sized professional army, relied on sea power, capable of winning major sea battles if opportunities arose, but happy to play the long game, pinning the Kaiserliche Marine in the North Sea and starving Germany to its knees. The long-established blockade plan gave Britain an initial advantage, while Germany's wealth of natural resources worked in her favour.

Both sides relied on uninterrupted imports from similar sources, many of the needs of both coming from North and South America. Each had to feed its population and supply raw materials and fuel to war industries and ships. Unfettered access via Atlantic routes to and from home ports was vital to both. Although their armies would slaughter each other in between a series of standstills along the Western Front, control of the seas and the resulting starvation had the potential to decide ultimate victory. The power of U-boats in commercial warfare had yet to surface in the minds of most strategists. One exception in the Central Powers' hierarchy was Vizeadmiral Hugo von Pohl, Chief of the Imperial Navy Staff, a strong supporter of unrestricted submarine warfare and advocate of abandoning the cruiser rules. When he eventually took command of the German High Seas Fleet in February 1915, he put these policies into effect. He went on to command the fleet only until January 1916 when he became weakened by liver cancer and died a month later. However, the seeds he had sown in the fertile minds of both senior officers and U-boat commanders were to flourish.

Blockade and U-boat Backlash

Britain implemented its planned blockade of German ports from the outset, so that the Royal Navy's Northern Patrol effectively reduced German access to the North Sea, while its Dover Patrol strangled the approach through the English Channel. However, although the blockade had been in Admiralty plans for some time, the Northern Patrol had not been equipped well. Known as the Tenth Cruiser (or Training) Squadron, it consisted of eight outdated Edgar-class protected cruisers, in service for some twenty years and not well suited to the task. Its inexperienced crews got ready for the Northern Patrol between Iceland and the Norwegian coast, north-east of the Shetlands. HMS *Crescent* and HMS *Edgar* went on patrol, ready and waiting, by 6th August.

By September 1914, the Royal Navy had ordered minesweeper HMS *Dryad* and armed merchant cruisers *Alsatian* (formerly Allan Line) and *Mantua* (previously of P&O), to join the patrol, making the strength up to eight old cruisers, two armed merchant cruisers and a torpedo gunboat[15].

The Northern Atlantic and Dover Patrols both intercepted merchant ships heading for Germany and escorted them to ports where they could unload any 'contraband' including food. Once cleared of any contraband, the searchers released ships and even escorted them through British minefields to enable them to reach their destination ports in Germany. This alienated many of Germany's international trading partners and quickly threatened starvation to Germany, which did not have a large enough fleet of capital warships to tackle the Royal Navy head-on. Germany had to fall back on its small U-boat fleet. Despite early losses, the number of operational U-boats

---

15 http://www.dreadnoughtproject.org/tfs/index.php/Tenth_Cruiser_Squadron_(Royal_Navy)#December.2C_1912

would increase to twenty-eight by the end of 1914 and German shipyards would soon expand U-boat construction, building 51 during 1915.

Meanwhile, Britain enjoyed some success in disrupting German trade. By November 1914, there would be 221 German merchant ships laid up in German ports, 1,059 more in neutral ports and 245 interned in Allied ports[16]. Britain applied the blockade with caution to avoid offending neutral countries, particularly the United States, and to avoid upsetting the Foreign Office. Imagine the relationship between comfortable civil servants trying to pacify neutral nations and the sailors who had to enforce the blockade through winter storms in old ships. It would soon become clear that storms were just one of the dangers.

On 5th September 1914, the Royal Navy suffered a tragic wake-up call far from blockade duties when U-21 torpedoed scout cruiser HMS *Pathfinder* off St Abbs Head. This was the first ever sinking of any vessel by a motorised torpedo, with the loss of 260 men. Only 16 were saved. The Admiralty was slow to heed this warning and on 22nd September, a U-boat attacked three elderly British armoured cruisers, on patrol together off the Dutch coast and manned mainly by naval reservists. The ships were HMS *Aboukir*, HMS *Cressy* and HMS *Hogue* of the patrol Cruiser Force C. Some senior naval officers had not favoured the use of these older ships that might encounter modern German warships. With typical naval humour, they nicknamed them 'The Live Bait Patrol'. On this day, they were cruising at about 10 knots, without zigzagging, in an area where no one had reported any U-boat activity. They were not to know that Kapitänleutnant Otto Weddigen was nearby in U-9, having sheltered from a storm. When he spotted the cruisers, Weddigen fired a single torpedo at 0625 and struck HMS *Aboukir*. She lost the use of her engines and started to list. Believing that she had struck a mine, her commander, Captain Drummond, requested help and the other two went to her aid, slowing and moving close before they realised their mistake. They were sitting ducks and Weddigen torpedoed both. All three sister ships sank. Rescuers saved over 800 men, but 1,400 men lost their lives. Among them were thirteen boys who had been in training at the Royal Naval College at Dartmouth only a few weeks earlier. The youngest was 14, the oldest, 16[17]. Then, on 15th October 1914, U-9 under Otto Weddigen sank 23-year-old Edgar-class HMS *Hawke*, with the loss of 524 men. The Admiralty finally had to take U-boats seriously.

---

16 Osborne, E W (2004). *Britain's Economic Blockade of Germany, 1914-1919*. p 61. London: Frank Cass
17 Dartmouth's Great War Fallen. The "Unjust Load": Dartmouth Cadets and the First World war

During October 1914, unknown to Germany, the British Grand Fleet had moved to Lough Swilly, County Donegal, while the Scapa Flow base in the Orkneys was undergoing urgent and vital improvements to its anti-submarine defences. Six Super-Dreadnoughts of the Second Battle Squadron sailed out of the lough on 27th October for gunnery exercise. One of them, HMS *Audacious*, commissioned just one year and six days earlier, struck a mine and felt a thud. Her captain thought a U-boat had torpedoed her, so warned the other ships away, having learned from the recent *Aboukir, Hogue, Cressy* disaster. They later discovered she had struck an enemy mine. She sank slowly, fortunately with the loss of only one life. *Audacious* cost a shade over £1.9m in 1912, (perhaps £197m in 2015) and a mine, which might have cost the equivalent of around £400 had destroyed her. The story was hushed up by Britain and only made public by a 'delayed announcement' in *The Times* newspaper on 14th November 1918.

The war at sea had started in earnest and the Royal Navy had quickly and painfully discovered its vulnerability, losing six ships with 2,272 casualties in 56 days. The Admiralty belatedly realised that torpedoes, particularly those carried in U-boats, were a major threat and that mines were another. Once it dawned on the world's most powerful navy that inexpensive U-boats and cheap mines could sink or seriously damage 30,000-ton battleships, things had to change. In the autumn of 1914, the actions of three U-boats, U-19, U-9 and U-27, with a combined surface tonnage of only 1,800, plus a single mine laid by a converted merchant ship, caused Britain to mothball its huge battle fleet. The Admiralty regarded Dreadnoughts as too expensive and vulnerable to take their chances against U-boats and mines.

> *'The real limitation, which no navy was about to admit, was that these ships were designed to perpetuate a naval strategy that was already obsolete.'*[18]

The Royal Navy quickly needed a large, safe anchorage, hence the hastening of work to fortify Scapa Flow, which it had chosen as the Battle Fleet base. With the Royal Navy's Dreadnoughts in hiding, the two-power strategy was obsolete. The Royal Commission on the Supply of Food and Raw Material in Time of War had recorded that *'command of the seas was essential and was Britain's primary aim'*. What now for Britain's imports of food and raw materials?

Early U-boat successes encouraged new thinking in Germany. Hugo von Pohl, High Seas Fleet Chief of Staff, wrote a memorandum to Chancellor

---

18 Angus K Ross, Professor, US Naval War College, Rhode Island

Theobald von Bethmann Hollweg, proposing a U-boat blockade of Britain. If Germany had invested in U-boats pre-war instead of in capital ships, they might have been able to establish and maintain such a blockade. Had they done so the result and duration of World War 1 might have been different.

Britain's first merchant ship loss to a U-boat was not long in coming. U-17 under Johannes Feldkirchner sank the SS *Glitra* on 20th October 1914, west of Stavanger, where she was heading with a cargo of coal, oil and iron. Although she was small (866 gross registered tons) and 33 years old, her story has two important elements. First, it added credence to the potential of commercial warfare as a counter to the Royal Navy's blockade. Second, Feldkirchner conducted his attack in the best seafaring traditions and in compliance with what most understood as international law. After the U-boat party boarded, the *Glitra*'s crew lowered and boarded their lifeboats and then sailors from the boarding party opened valves to flood *Glitra* until she sank. No one fired a shot or a torpedo. The Royal Norwegian Navy torpedo boat HNoMS *Hai* towed *Glitra*'s lifeboats to the Norwegian port of Skudeneshavn[19].

It quickly became clear that the best, perhaps only, way to beat submarines was to lure or force them to the surface and then either ram them or sink them with guns. Ramming had to remain an opportunistic rather than a tactical choice.

In Britain, Lord Fisher repeated his warning on the destructive potential of submarine-launched torpedoes, again to Winston Churchill. As 1914 drifted into 1915 and beyond, many others raised questions that became urgent and serious, verging on desperation. By the end of 1914, U-boats would have sunk only 14 ships, but in the following year, they destroyed almost 750, including the liners *Lusitania*, *Arabic*, *Ancona* and *Persia* with the deaths of almost 1,900 people, including women and children, from just these four attacks.

In this desperate situation, merchant shipping had the very limited choice between two countermeasures, both of which could only work against surfaced U-boats. The first was to arm merchant ships with defensive guns. Although this had already started, it had been a struggle to acquire guns because of demands from the Western Front. The second idea, adopted by both Britain and France in late 1914, was to conceal guns on seemingly innocent and vulnerable-looking merchant ships, intended to tempt U-boats

---

19   Hegland, Jon Rustung & Lilleheim, Johan Henrik (1998). *Norske torpedobåter gjennom 125 år* (in Norwegian). p 43. Hundvåg: Sjømilitære Samfund ved Norsk Tidsskrift for Sjøvesen. ISBN 82-994738-1-0

to the surface for stop-and-search and opening them up to counter-attack. Defensive arming of merchant ships was already happening and Q-ships would not be far behind.

Meanwhile, Britain's early and rigorous blockade caused hardship in Germany, where the authorities gave priority to the needs of soldiers over those of the civilian population. The principle difference between the British and German approaches was that Britain conducted its blockade using surface ships to stop and search, while some of Germany's U-boats shifted from that approach towards submerged ambushes, resulting in growing numbers of civilian deaths. Pressure for a U-boat blockade of Britain eventually succeeded and with its modern battle fleet confined to port, the German government established a war zone in the seas surrounding the British Isles. It made a declaration that from Thursday 18th February 1915, it would sink all shipping in these waters including neutral vessels, without warning. For the first time in history, the world experienced unrestricted submarine warfare under which German warships and U-boats were authorised by their government to sink commercial vessels such as freighters and tankers without warning and in defiance of the cruiser rules. During March 1915, U-boats sank twenty-eight British merchant ships and this was just the beginning. Attacks by U-boats on merchantmen rose to over seven hundred for the year to the end of November and peaked at 124 in June alone[20]. Many took place in the South West Approaches, the Irish Sea, the Bristol Channel, the northern North Sea off the Moray Firth and across the Long Forties. One such sinking, that of the RMS *Lusitania*, would change the nature of warfare at sea for all time. Meanwhile, would arming British merchant ships to defend themselves be a deterrent or a provocation? Would Q-ships be convincing enough to tempt U-boats to surface and face battle?

---

20   https://uboat.net/wwi/ships_hit/losses_year.html

Armed Response

Defensively Equipped Merchant Ships (DEMS)

In the seventeenth to nineteenth centuries, ships known as East Indiamen traded between European countries and India carrying cargo, passengers, their own militia and guns. The arms were notionally for defending themselves against pirates, but also for encouraging uncooperative indigenous people to cooperate. Traders, explorers, and colonialists used armed merchant ships regularly. As early as 1881, Captain Sir John Colomb MP, who had served at sea as an officer in the Royal Marine Artillery, forecast the need for arming all British merchant vessels in a future great war at sea. In a lecture delivered at the Royal United Service Institution on 13th May of that year, he had predicted –

> *'that the exigencies of maritime war will necessitate our arming not merely a careful selection of the best, but every ocean-going British steamer. We must prepare in peace to give them, at home and abroad, armaments and trained instructors and then on the declaration of war bid them follow their avocations and let our enemies know that we mean to carry on our sea trade in spite of their teeth, under the banner, if you like, of "Defence not Defiance"*[21]*'.*

This would not happen for over thirty years, but when it did, would it give commanders of enemy warships a ready-made excuse to attack what they perceived to be a warship?

Although Britain was not at war in 1913, First Lord of the Admiralty Winston Churchill told Parliament on 26th March that he had asked some ship owners to arm their first-class liners to protect themselves against

---

21 Hurd, Archibald (1924). History Of The Great War, The merchant marine Vol. II. London, John Murray

possible attack from an enemy's cruisers. He told them that he expected other nations to regard them only as merchant vessels, provided their armament was available only for defensive purposes. Neither the Hague Convention (1907) nor the Declaration of London (1909) forbade defensive armament, but resistance by a merchant vessel to lawful stopping and searching would mean that the warship could take it and its cargo as a prize, or sink it[22].

Defensively equipped merchant ships (DEMS) were regular cargo and passenger vessels plying their trade while carrying a single defensive gun, usually mounted at the stern. They were distinctly different from armed merchant cruisers, passenger liners that the Admiralty requisitioned and converted into heavily armed, though not armour-plated, warships. The Royal Navy bestowed the prefix 'HMS' and a pennant number and such vessels sailed under the White Ensign.

Many merchant shipping companies armed their ships as the war progressed and suitable guns became available. As in all such matters, there were rules. From the outset, the instructions issued by the Admiralty to masters of defensively equipped vessels contained a clause stating that any gun placed on board for defence was only as an effective help towards the completion of voyages, the main objective. Gun fitters normally mounted the weapons on the sterns of vessels. In some waters, they fitted guns in one port and removed them at another, such as between Gibraltar and Port Said.

So, how might these principles affect ships such as P&O's SS *Persia*, once they fitted a single stern-mounted gun? The Kaiserliche Marine knew about the defensive equipping of British merchant ships and of the existence of British armed merchant cruisers. For example, one former P&O liner became armed merchant cruiser HMS *Mantua*. She carried eight 4.7" (120 mm) guns and was thus distinctly different from SS *Persia*. The *Mantua*, variously identified by pendant numbers M51, MI77 and MI40, flew the Royal Navy White Ensign, while the SS *Persia*, as all the merchant ships, flew the Red Ensign, affectionately known as the 'red duster'. U-boats carried books with pictures and the latest information about British ships to aid recognition when sighted. U-boat captains thus had the means to distinguish between passenger liner SS *Persia* and the former SS *Mantua*, the heavily armed warship.

With the benefit of over 100 years of hindsight, imagine yourself behind the periscope of a U-boat when you spot a British merchant ship. You could

---

22   Tucker, Spencer C (Ed) (2014). World War I: The Definitive Encyclopedia and Document Collection, p 456

sacrifice your secret presence by surfacing and ordering the ship to stop. If she complied, you could follow international law by boarding, searching and then evacuating and sinking her if she was carrying contraband. What if she doesn't comply? What if she turned and attempted to ram you? What if she turned away to escape? Even in those days, accountants influenced submarines. Typically, a U-boat's magazines held 300 rounds for its deck gun, destructive but cheap, while torpedoes were costly. 'Surface, warn, stop, sink with guns' would satisfy both accountants and international lawyers as they sat at their desks on dry land. But what if the ship carried a gun mounted on her stern? Would she open fire? What if your U-boat, unprotected by armour-plating, sustained damage, making her unable to submerge? Would you not take a risk-management approach and stay submerged, valuing your U-boat and crew higher than the cost of a torpedo?

While the speed, firepower and armour of surface warships had advanced, submarines as warships were revolutionary. Their commanders and crew still needed first-rate seamanship skills, gunners needed range-finding equipment and accuracy from a rolling platform, engineers had to adapt to maximise diesel and electric power, keep the air breathable and the ballast tanks balanced between diving, submerged cruising and surfacing. As for the commander, navigation while submerged brought new challenges, as did firing torpedoes accurately. Beyond this, every man who served aboard a submarine in any navy had to overcome any misgivings about claustrophobia, lack of privacy, living in a permanent stench, noise, dripping condensation, unchanged clothes and constant dim artificial light. Mastery of underwater warfare needed exceptional and courageous seamen such as a young man from Schleswig-Holstein named Christian August Max Ahlmann Valentiner – more about him later. But first, we will look at Q-ships, those innocent-looking nautical predators designed to cure the U-boat problem.

Lieutenant Commander Godfrey Herbert

Q-ships were the nautical version of wolves in sheep's clothing, usually tramp steamers converted to carry concealed guns behind fake collapsible cabins and structures. They were secret weapons and the authorities held the Defence of the Realm Act 1914 to ensure it stayed that way. The Royal Navy introduced them as a U-boat countermeasure in the absence of any means of spotting submerged U-boats other than by chance sighting of a periscope. Their designers intended them to look sufficiently like vulnerable cargo ships so that they might tempt U-boats to surface and order them to stop. Once this had happened, Q-ship crews would drop their camouflage structures, hoist White Ensigns of the Royal Navy to replace Red Ensigns of merchantmen and open fire. Sheep would transmute into ferocious wolves. One of these vessels and her commander, Godfrey Herbert, is central to my theory.

Godfrey Herbert was born in Coventry on 28th February 1884[23] and attended Stubbington House School, Hampshire, a preparatory school for boys in readiness for Royal Navy service. He became a naval cadet in HMS *Britannia* in 1898 and in June 1900 enlisted as a midshipman.

Later, as a sub-lieutenant, he volunteered for the new submarine branch and in 1905 undertook specialised training in depot ship HMS *Thames*. The Royal Navy appointed him as second-in-command of HMS A4, an early British submarine. Under skipper Eric Nasmith, the two men and their crew survived when A4 sank in 90 feet (27 metres) of water during trials off Spithead that October. The first day's trial had gone well, but on the second day, A4 had to operate inside a breakwater because of rough seas. Her crew

---

23 Halpern, Paul G (2008). *Herbert, Godfrey (1884–1961)*. Oxford Dictionary of National Biography (online ed.), Oxford University Press. https://www.oxforddnb.com/view/10.1093/ref:odnb/9780198614128.001.0001/odnb-9780198614128-e-98170

had trimmed her for sea water but the change to fresh water reduced her buoyancy and she settled lower than before. Water poured in through an open ventilator and she sank, settling at an angle of forty degrees. Nasmith and Herbert battled against the water, as chlorine gas spread from the batteries. They groped their way to the controls in total darkness and blew air into the ballast tanks, lifting A4 back to the surface. The crew followed their evacuation procedures but an explosion caused her to sink again. Salvage teams recovered and repaired her and put her back into service. *The Times* later commented that:

Lieutenant Commander Godfrey Herbert DSO

> '*Nothing but the admirable steadiness of the men and the splendid presence of mind of Lieutenant Nasmith and Sub-Lieutenant Herbert could have saved the country from another appalling submarine disaster.*'

Two recent submarine accidents had incurred fatalities, the first in March 1904, when SS *Berwick* struck A1 off the Isle of Wight and she sank with the loss of all 11 aboard. The second, in June 1905[24], was in Plymouth Sound, when a suspected battery explosion sank A8 with the loss of 15. Nasmith was the first submarine captain to survive in this series of accidents, so it was no surprise that he faced a court martial and was found guilty of negligence. However, he and Herbert were both praised for their cool-headed recovery. Godfrey Herbert would later take command of submarine A4 but would first see service on the China Station. Before returning to Britain in 1911, he took command of C-class[25] coastal defence submarine C36, and in company with C37 and C38, completed an epic voyage from Portsmouth to Hong Kong, escorted by the armoured cruiser HMS *Monmouth*. Their journey confounded submarine sceptics in Britain's navy. However, a later prank misfired and Herbert's reputation suffered. He dressed in a white sheet, had

---

24 https://www.nmrn.org.uk/research/submarine-losses
25 Described as very good but with too small a radius to be able to truly operate on enemy coasts. *The Technical History and Index*, Vol 3, part 21, p 5

himself fastened to C36's periscope and ordered the submarine to move slowly across Kowloon harbour at periscope depth with him appearing to walk on water. His superior officers were far from amused[26].

In 1913, the Navy appointed Herbert in command of submarine C30 and promoted him to lieutenant commander on 31st December 1913. In 1914 he took command of the powerful ocean-going submarine D5, in which he intercepted the modern German cruiser SMS *Rostock* at close range, with a chance to sink her from only 600 yards (550 m). Determined to ensure a hit, he ignored Admiralty rules against firing two bow torpedoes simultaneously. He fired both, seconds apart and waited for the impact. Silence. Somehow, he had missed this sitting duck, this prestigious target. *Rostock*'s escorts spotted the torpedo wakes and hunted D5 for three hours. Only later did Herbert remember that live torpedoes were forty pounds heavier than training torpedoes, so they ran deeper on the wrong setting and passed beneath *Rostock*'s keel.

On 3rd November, Konteradmiral Hipper's battlecruisers and cruisers bombarded Great Yarmouth. SMS *Stralsund* also laid mines to disrupt British coastal shipping. Herbert's D5 rushed to the scene, struck one of the mines and sank with the loss of 21 lives[27]. He was one of apparently only five survivors. So, what does a submarine commander with no submarine do next? He admitted his dual torpedo discharge against the *Rostock* and escaped sanction, but was becoming known in the navy for all the wrong reasons.

Early in 1915, as the U-boat threat grew, Godfrey Herbert joined an early Q-ship, the Great Eastern steamer SS *Antwerp*, which carried two concealed twelve-pounder guns. Antwerp retained her regular captain and crew, to which the Royal Navy added Herbert, along with seamen and Royal Marines. While the regular captain was still master, he had to follow Herbert's instructions. The ship patrolled between Harwich and the Hook of Holland, with the flamboyant Herbert disguised as a Dutch pilot wearing a blond wig. They cruised around hoping a surfaced U-boat would intercept, but none appeared during the six-week posting, so they were then redeployed to the Western Approaches.

Unknown to Herbert, German U-boat hero Otto Weddigen, who had previously sunk the three warships, HMS *Aboukir*, *Cressy* and *Hogue* in one attack in 1914, was patrolling the same area, now in U-29. On 11th March,

---

26 Coles, Alan (1986). *Slaughter at Sea: The truth behind a naval war crime.* p 39. London, Robert Hale Ltd. ISBN 978-0-7090-2597-9

27 https://www.maritimequest.com/warship_directory/great_britain/submarines/pages/d_class/d_5_roll_of_honour.htm

Weddigen stopped SS *Adenwen* sailing in ballast from Rouen to Barry and, as was his custom, gave the crew time to board lifeboats before attempting to sink their ship, telling them:

'We wish no lives to be lost'.

Later that day he stopped and sank the SS *Auguste Conseil*, apologising to the French captain for what he had to do. He had become known as a strict observer of international law, dubbed 'the polite pirate' by *The Times* and 'this intrepid pirate' by Roger Keyes, Commodore of the British submarine fleet[28]. On 12th March, U-29 sank two more British ships, SS *Indian City* and SS *Headlands*, off the Scilly Isles. Radio messages alerted Herbert who was 60 miles off, and Q-ship *Antwerp* made her best speed to the scene. Meanwhile, Weddigen stopped and sank SS *Andalusian*. Herbert picked up the *Andalusian*'s crew and then turned towards the watching U-29, which submerged and disappeared. Sighting a North Sea ferry 30 miles (45 kilometres) west of Land's End, over 350 miles from her normal route, Weddigen would naturally have been suspicious. Herbert had cruised for weeks looking for a U-boat and as soon as he had found one, he lost it. His frustration must have intensified.

Weddigen headed home around northern Scotland where U-29 inadvertently encountered the British Grand Fleet, all zigzagging in anti-submarine mode. He snatched the opportunity to attack battleship HMS *Neptune* and launched a torpedo, but her zigzag worked and the torpedo passed by harmlessly. As Weddigen continued tracking *Neptune* through his attack periscope he failed to see or hear HMS *Dreadnought* close on his starboard side. Lieutenant Commander Piercy, officer of the watch on the mighty battleship, spotted a periscope one point off the starboard bow and shouted the alarm. Captain Alderson reacted quickly, turning *Dreadnought* like a destroyer at high speed. As her huge bow smashed into the U-boat, U-29's identification number was clearly visible just before she was cut in two. Both halves sank immediately. The polite pirate and his crew, who together had sunk three old cruisers and killed 1,400 British seamen in September 1914, were now themselves lost at sea.

Godfrey Herbert's posting on SS *Antwerp* had been fruitless and he had turned his mind to improving the capabilities and disguises of Q-ships. He inundated Captain Henry Grant, his senior officer, with ideas to make Q-ships more effective. Grant was Assistant Director of Operations in the Admiralty and had the ear of the First Sea Lord, Admiral of the Fleet the

---

28 Grey, Edwyn A (1994). *The U-boat War 1914-1918*. Barnsley: Pen and Sword

Rt Hon Lord Fisher. Fisher listened to Herbert's ideas and gave him permission to explore them further, ordering him to select a suitable ship, oversee its conversion, hand pick his crew and patrol where he thought best. Herbert had already identified a ship he thought perfect for the role and now had a great opportunity to prove his ideas worked. It was not a blank cheque – Fisher needed Q-ship results.

In February 1915, two new Q-ships were authorised which would operate under Herbert's directions. The Navy had earlier requisitioned the 14-year-old SS *Baralong* as a squadron supply ship, pendant number Y9.5, which was refitted and armed with three concealed guns. She joined the Q-ship fleet in April 1915. Her merchant crew remained, including her skipper, George Swiney, who joined the Royal Naval Reserve (RNR) and became the ship's navigating officer. In total there were over 60 men aboard, a mix of Royal Navy, Royal Marines, RNR and merchant seamen. Herbert requisitioned 3,000 empty casks to fill the holds closest to the bow and the stern and loaded coal in the two holds amidships, closest to the furnaces. The buoyant casks would keep *Baralong* afloat even if hit, holed and taking on water.

SS Baralong was launched in 1901 and converted and armed as a Q-ship in Pembroke Dock in the spring of 1915. She carried three concealed guns and an arsenal of small arms

When he briefed his crew, Herbert adopted the pseudonym of William McBride to conceal his real identity. He banned uniforms, insisting on shabby clothes to fit the ship's tramp steamer role and outlawed naval and military terminology and behaviour. The ship took on ammunition in Devonport and embarked on its first patrol from Folkestone to the east and the western tip of the Scillies, accompanied by Q-ships *Princess Ena* and *Lyon*.

In three months, U-boats sank or damaged 24 vessels in his area, but Herbert failed to find any of the perpetrators in that period. By the time he heard of a U-boat attack and made best speed there, the attacker had long since disappeared. Boredom and frustration set in and trouble was never far away. After some of *Baralong*'s crew wrecked a Dartmouth pub, Herbert bailed those arrested but sailed during the night leaving no one to appear in court.

On 7th May 1915, after news of the U-boat attack on RMS *Lusitania*, *Baralong* rushed from near the Jersey coast, as best an ageing freighter could, to try and aid the stricken liner. *Baralong* arrived too late to assist, or to hunt the perpetrator. Herbert and his crew later witnessed the bodies of men, women, children and babies laid out for identification in three locations in Queenstown, experiencing helplessness and all-consuming rage. It seemed that total war had arrived. Mercy and pity had become dated sentiments. The words of First Sea Lord, Admiral of the Fleet Lord Fisher, '*The essence of war is violence. Moderation in war is imbecility*' became a reality for Godfrey Herbert and *Baralong*'s crew.

On 10th May there were 154 funerals, the lengthy cortège consisting of whatever wheeled vehicles they could commandeer, escorted by soldiers from the Connaught Rangers and Royal Dublin Fusiliers. Many of the dead remained unidentified. All were carried in a hurried collection of coffins to the churchyard in Queenstown, County Cork, for burial in a common grave. The effect on the people of the port, town and district must have been deeply traumatic. For many Royal Navy personnel, on whose watch the tragedy had happened, the shock transformed into unforgiving anger and a lust for revenge on U-boats and their crews. What they endured through those days would have bloody and lasting consequences. Sub-lieutenant Gordon Steele of the *Baralong* later remembered the bitterness of the crew:

'It just required the sight of those silent figures of drowned children from the Lusitania, as they were laid out on the front at Queenstown in a temporary mortuary to rouse the deepest hatred in the Baralong's crew, composed as they were of a mixed collection – naval, mercantile and marine ratings – who had never so hated before. At an impromptu meeting, the crew agreed to show no mercy to any U-boat man who fell into their hands.'[29]

---

29   Lake, Deborah (2009). Smoke and Mirrors, Q-Ships against the U-boats in the First World War. p 79. Cheltenham: The History Press

The sinking of the RMS *Lusitania* without any warning angered millions across the world and unleashed vengeful demons in many naval minds, including that of Godfrey Herbert. In E Keble Chatterton's book *Amazing Adventure – A Thrilling Naval Biography* (narrating the Naval Career of Commander Godfrey Herbert), he writes about events of 19th August 1915[30]:

> '*U-24, U-27 and U-38 actually managed to sink eight vessels amounting to over 42,000 tons, including the well-known White Star liner Arabic which lost forty-four lives. Such things, coupled with the loss of the Lusitania in the previous May, stirred British sailordom to white-heat anger, and those aboard the Baralong were wild with desire to destroy an unchivalrous enemy who had sent children, women and men passengers to death unwarned.*'

How would the Royal Navy and its few Q-ships respond?

It still took more than a month for a U-boat to be lured to destruction, but not by a Q-ship. This happened off Aberdeen, on 23rd June 1915, when the trawler *Taranaki* deployed as a decoy with the submerged British submarine C24 beneath on a tow line incorporating a telephone link. When U-40 took the bait and surfaced nearby, C24 received the information by telephone. Attempts to slip her tow line failed but she eventually surfaced, the rope still dangling from her bows, and torpedoed U-40 with the loss of 29 lives. The crew of C24 rescued Kapitänleutnant Gerhardt Furbringer and two of his crew.

On the evening of 24th July, Q-ship *Prince Charles* commanded by Lieutenant William Penrose Mark-Wardlaw finally encountered a U-boat, which turned out to be U-36 under Kapitänleutnant Ernst Graeff, in the uncommon act of capturing a prize ship. His prize was the three-masted American ship *Pass of Balmaha*, propelled by sail and steam, carrying cotton from New York to Archangel in Russia and thus to Germany's enemy. Wardlaw pretended to ignore what was happening which provoked U-36 into firing a warning shot, a clear order to stop, which he did. U-36 left some of her crew aboard the prize ship, approached to about 600 yards range and turned broadside on, as if to sink *Prince Charles*. The intended victim promptly opened fire on the U-boat and sank her with the loss of 18 lives. *Prince Charles*'s crew rescued fifteen survivors including Graeff.

---

30   Amazing Adventure p133

The plan had finally worked; the first genuine Q-ship success. The term *U-Boot-Falle* (U-boat trap) would quickly become part of the language of U-boat crews. Germany continued to accuse Britain of starving German civilians by their unbending blockade and in Britain, outrage spread at Germany's failure to follow the cruiser rules, particularly in the sinking of RMS *Lusitania*. Things were about to get worse.

Captain Herbert Richmond of the Admiralty Special Service Branch apparently sent for Herbert and told him:

'*The Lusitania is a shocking business and our unofficial answer is — take no prisoners from U-boats.*'[31]

When the time came, Godfrey Herbert set himself and his crew to take revenge on any U-boat crew — no misgivings, no scruples. All they needed was to find one. What sort of people commanded the crews of the U-boats that Herbert now reviled? One of them was a courageous and skilled Kaiserliche Marine officer named Max Valentiner.

---

31   Coles, Alan (1986). *Slaughter at Sea?: The truth behind a naval war crime.* p 50. London, Robert Hale Ltd. ISBN 978-0-7090-2597-9

Kapitänleutnant Max Valentiner and U-38

Christian August Max Ahlmann Valentiner was born in Tonder, Schleswig-Holstein, on 15th December 1883, where his father, Deacon Otto Friedrich Valentiner, was pastor of a local church. The town had been in Schleswig-Holstein, the part of Denmark that had become a province of Prussia in 1866. At the age of 18, Valentiner joined the Kaiserliche Marine as a Seekadett in the April 1902 intake, known by month and year, so Crew 4/02. This intake would eventually provide at least thirty-one U-boat commanders in World War 1.

He moved to the Marineschule (Naval College) at Kiel in 1903, enjoying and specialising in diving. After graduating, he showed great courage on two different occasions when he rescued men from drowning. The Kaiserliche Marine promoted him to Oberleutnant zur See in 1908 and he learned gunnery skills in the Marine Artillery Battery at Kiel, before becoming Salvage Officer aboard SMS *Vulkan*, a twin-hulled ship designed to recover sunken U-boats. He would soon get his chance.

In January 1911, training submarine U-3 sank near Kiel, leaving only her bow and periscope visible. The mishap trapped thirty men in an air pocket in the torpedo compartment near the bow and others in the U-boat's tower. Unfortunately, SMS *Vulkan* was undergoing repairs and unavailable to help. A floating crane partly lifted U-3, exposing her bow and torpedo tubes. Valentiner used a hammer to bang a Morse-code message on the hull and someone inside responded, tapping that men were alive but in need of air. Valentiner asked them to open a torpedo tube cover, only possible from inside. He thought it might provide an escape route. It would be tight and claustrophobic, but perhaps their only hope after five hours with no air supply.

After a long delay, the torpedo tube cover edged open, releasing foul fumes. Valentiner decided that this tight gap would have to be enough. His team dropped a rope down the eight-metre (25-feet) tube, instructing those inside to tie on to it so that those outside could pull them out in turn. They rescued two men but the third jammed in the tube. Max pushed him back down the tube with a pole. The situation was desperate.

For the third time in his naval career, Valentiner risked his life. He squeezed down the tube, followed by a volunteer, and found several crewmen apparently unconscious, perhaps dead, with the remainder in a collapsed state. The two rescuers dragged each of the men to the mouth of the tube and tied them onto the rope. They pushed each one as high up the tube as possible, until those above could pull them out. Two exhausting hours later, they had dragged, pushed and heaved the thirty men out. All survived. Meanwhile, three men remained trapped in the submerged tower. Night fell. An attempt to lift the U-boat closer to the surface failed when a cable slipped and U-3 plunged to a depth of 13 metres (40 feet).

Dockyard workers had hurried repairs to SMS *Vulkan* and at last she joined the rescue at 2300, thirteen hours after the first alarm. Two divers tried to attach *Vulkan*'s lifting equipment but were worn out after an hour. Valentiner donned a diving suit, and with another diver went down to U-3 in the cold darkness. They eventually attached *Vulkan*'s cables and she winched the U-boat to the surface between her twin hulls. Men jumped aboard, opened a hatch and entered the tower. They found three warm but lifeless bodies. All resuscitation attempts failed.

On 1st July 1911, Valentiner became commander of the new U-10, one of five U-boats sent on an exercise in the Skagerrak, between north Denmark and Norway. Their mission was to prevent German ships, which were simulating Russian warships, from penetrating the Baltic from the North Sea, an operation that Germany might need one day against that potential enemy. U-10 was the closest U-boat to the Norwegian coast, which turned out to be on the course chosen by the approaching vessels. At 1600 U-10's lookouts spotted approaching smoke. The 'enemy' fleet was steaming in two parallel line-astern formations. Valentiner positioned U-10 between the two lines which would then pass each side of her. He ordered four training torpedoes, two at the bow and two at the stern, to be set to turn ninety degrees after firing. At launch, their path would be parallel to the warships, followed by a right-angle outward turn. As the two leading ships passed each side, Valentiner fired in quick succession. All four torpedoes were hits, two on each ship. Both hoisted flags that indicated that the U-boat had sunk them and they were unable to continue the exercise. Vizeadmiral Lans later praised Valentiner's skill and boldness, but Valentiner expressed dissatisfaction at having used four torpedoes to sink only two ships. He believed that he could and should have 'hit' four ships, one with each torpedo.

The Kaiserliche Marine promoted Valentiner to kapitänleutnant zur see on 22nd March 1914, and nine days later sent him to the Submarine School in Kiel as an instructor. This lasted until 4th August, the day on which Britain declared war on Germany. He took command of U-3, the submarine from which he had saved 30 men. She was gasoline powered and slower than new diesel-powered U-boats.

The Kaiserliche Marine ordered him to patrol the Gulf of Riga where Russian warships were based. U-3 rendezvoused with the ageing German light cruiser SMS *Amazone* which signalled that mines hindered access into the gulf. Valentiner was unable to get within range of any Russian ships and returned to base. Prince Heinrich, Grand Admiral of the Kaiserliche Marine and brother of the Emperor, summoned him to Berlin to account for his failed mission. The prince was hostile and ignored Max's effort to explain, shouting over him:

'I had expected that at least you had sunk two Russian vessels.'

This startled Max but he replied:

'Your Royal Highness, my boat is like an old horse. You can give it as much sugar as you like, but it cannot gallop any more.'

The prince ordered him out, the audience appearing to have gone badly. However, on 5th December 1914, the Imperial Navy appointed Valentiner commander of U-38, Germany's newest ocean-going diesel attack submarine and even invited him to select his own officers from the submarine school. Perhaps he made a better impression on the Prince than he thought, or his success during the Skagerrak exercise had earned him lasting credit.

At some point after joining the Imperial Navy, Valentiner became known simply as 'Max'. Was this a simple preference or perhaps an attempt to discard the name Christian that might burden his conscience in wartime acts of killing? In April 1915, he finally took U-38 to sea and went to work around the British coast, sharpening his skills on Britain's North Sea fishing boats, giving his deck gunners frequent practice after first allowing evacuations. Between 18th April and 23rd August, he made 57 attacks in which he captured three vessels as prizes and sank 52. Two more were failures in which he attacked larger ships. On 20th June he torpedoed armoured cruiser HMS *Roxborough*, damaging but failing to sink her. Three days, fifteen fishing boats, two steamers and one sailing vessel later, U-38 sank the 110-ton trawler *Vine* and then returned to Kiel. From there she embarked on an unusual mission off North Wales that developed to become a major influence on future events.

Great Orme to *Baralong*

At midnight on 13th August 1915, Max Valentiner in U-38 rendezvoused with U-27, commanded by Kapitänleutnant Bernd Wegener, 50 miles off the North Wales coast. Valentiner had selected his friend and cousin to provide backup for a special but unusual U-boat mission and the Imperial Navy had ordered a second U-boat in case Valentiner encountered problems, in which case the backup crew could complete the mission. The task was to locate and rescue some escaping prisoners of war, German naval officers, at Great Orme's Head on the North Wales coast. Valentiner would have been highly motivated as one of the prisoners was Heinrich von Hennig, a friend and colleague from Crew 4/02, their shared cadet intake to the Kaiserliche Marine of April 1902, where strong bonds formed.

Dyffryn Aled was a remote country house near Llansannan in Denbighshire, North Wales, used as a prisoner-of-war camp for about one hundred, mainly German naval officers, plus a small number of interned civilians. Among those held were three officers who regarded it their duty to escape. Korvettenkapitan Hermann Tholens had been second-in-command of the German cruiser *Mainz* when she sank during the Battle of Heligoland Bight on 28th August 1914. Destroyer HMS *Garry* had captured Kapitänleutnant Heinrich von Hennig and most of his crew of U-18 after trawler *Dorothy Gray* rammed the U-boat on 23rd November 1914. Von Hennig had just discovered key weaknesses in the defences of Scapa Flow but was unable to use his radio so was heading back to port carrying the crucial news. Hans von Heldorf was the third escaper about whom nothing is known. The isolated position and inhospitable terrain resulted in only moderate security being in place at the camp, although there were bars on many windows, a legacy of the days when it had served as what was then known as a lunatic asylum.

Tholens had initiated the escape via a verbal message carried by a German civilian interned at Dyffryn Aled but released in an exchange scheme at Christmas 1914. He then wrote and received a series of seemingly innocent family letters until he received one telling him about a marriage on 14th August[32]. The wedding date was the coded date for their rendezvous with a U-boat off Great Orme's Head.

The trio broke out late on the evening of the 13th and walked through the night towards Llandudno, arriving early on the following morning. They bought breakfast in a seaside café then climbed Great Orme, known in the Welsh language as Pen-y-Gogarth, perhaps awed by its size and scale. They searched out a spot where they believed they could scramble down to sea level and then hid through the daylight hours in bramble bushes close to the lighthouse. The U-boat would watch for their electric lamp signal on the following two nights.

Valentiner arrived off the Orme and waited in vain for the agreed torch signal. He instructed his cousin Wegener to return to active patrolling. The escaped prisoners had found it impossible to relocate their intended route down in the darkness, afraid to use their lamp because of coastguard patrols around the mighty headland. The two nights passed without contact after which Valentiner gave up as planned and U-38 returned to her patrol.

The fugitives were arrested while still in Llandudno. A military court sentenced them to 84 days imprisonment which they served in Chelmsford Gaol before being returned to Dyffryn Aled.

After Bernd Wegener left the mission, he made up for the scant success of recent months by sinking four ships on the 18th and one on the 19th August, described by Godfrey Herbert as *'a beautiful calm day'*.

This second attack by U-27 on the 19th would have catastrophic and far-reaching consequences when she intercepted the British freighter SS *Nicosian*, 73 miles off the Old Head of Kinsale, and stopped her, following the cruiser rules. A party of six of the U-boat crew boarded the ship to check and search. They found that she was on passage from New Orleans to Liverpool carrying 250 mules and some munitions for the British Army on the Western Front. A team of American mule-keepers accompanied the mules. Kapitänleutnant Wegener's subsequent decision to sink the *Nicosian* was justifiable under the Declaration of London list of 'absolute contraband'

---

32   Tholens, Hermann (1932) Rendezvous with a Submarine. In: Ackerley, J R, et al (1932) Escapers all : being the personal narratives of fifteen escapers from war-time prison camps 1914-1918. p 282. London: The Bodley Head

which included in Article 22, items 1, 2 & 3: *'arms, projectiles, explosives'* and in item 7: *'Saddle, draft and pack animals suitable for use in war.'*[33] He ordered *Nicosian*'s crew to lower and board her lifeboats along with the mule-keepers so that U-27 could sink the ship by gunfire.

By this time, the wireless operator aboard the SS *Nicosian* had started to send SOS messages, the first stating that she was chased and a second, at 3.10 pm telling:

'Captured by enemy submarine. Crew ready to leave. Lat 50.22N, Long. 8.12W.'

Five minutes later another message told:

'Crew nearly all left. Captured by two (sic) enemy submarines.'

Baralong then picked up a few signals such as:

'Help! Help! For God's sake help!'

Herbert altered course to the south-west and headed towards the *Nicosian* at *Baralong*'s best speed which was only 10 knots (19 km/h; 12 mph)[34]. After 20 minutes, *Baralong* was still about two miles off and Herbert hoisted the international code signal 'To save life only'.

When *Nicosian*'s crew and the U-boat boarding party were clear of the ship, U-27 opened fire, interrupted when they noticed a cargo ship under the ensign of the neutral United States approaching and signalling with flags, requesting permission to pick up[35] those in the lifeboats. Perhaps surprisingly, even naively, Wegener consented, his suspicions not raised by a merchant ship heading towards rather than away from a U-boat conducting a sinking. He ordered U-27 to cease fire and manoeuvred down the port side of SS *Nicosian* to intercept the rescuer. The approaching vessel turned down the starboard side of the *Nicosian*, disappearing momentarily from U-27's sight. Aboard the 'steamer', Q-ship commander Godfrey Herbert could not believe his luck. While still hidden from the U-boat, he ordered the Stars and Stripes lowered and hoisted the White Ensign of the Royal Navy. His gunners cleared and loaded three 12-pounder guns for immediate action. At last, the Q-ship HMS *Baralong* was going to war.

As Herbert steered between SS *Nicosian*'s bow and her lifeboats, U-27, now closer, came back into full view. *Baralong* opened fire with all three of her guns and with rifles at a range of about 600 yards (550 metres). The second shot hit the base of U-27's tower and she began to capsize, only

---

33 Declaration concerning the Laws of Naval War. London, 26th February 1909
34 Chatterton, Edward Keble and Herbert, Godfrey (n. d.) *Amazing Adventure: a Thrilling Naval Biography: Cdr Godfrey Herbert.* p 135
35 International flag signal VIC-QRA 'Save Life'

managing to fire one retaliatory shot against the thirty-four fired that rained on and around her. She *'went down with a terrific escape of air'*. Confusion clouds the events that followed, but according to American muleteers from the *Nicosian*, twelve of U-27's crew, gunners who had been firing on the *Nicosian* and others from the conning tower, jumped into the sea. They joined the six men of the boarding party in trying to clamber up the lifeboat falls to get aboard SS *Nicosian*. Some succeeded, despite Herbert's order to shoot them away. Meanwhile, *Nicosian*'s boats had drawn alongside the *Baralong*. *Nicosian*'s captain told Herbert that *'he had a cargo of 700 or 600 mules for the British Government'* and had also left rifles in *Nicosian*'s chartroom, so Herbert warned Corporal Collins and the twelve Royal Marines he had sent to board the *Nicosian* to watch out for snipers in case the Germans had found the rifles. He advised Corporal Collins that they would *'be desperate men, that he was to take no chances, but shoot first'*. Others claim that he had simply told the Marines to find the remainder of the U-boat crew and to take no prisoners. He does not appear to have told them what action to take if they found unarmed U-boat sailors. The Marines who boarded *Nicosian* found the U-boat men in the engine room and seem to have shot them all and thrown the bodies overboard[36]. Herbert later explained the six deaths as *'six of the enemy had been found but they succumbed to the injuries received from a lyddite shell shortly afterwards and were buried at once.'*[37] Kapitänleutnant Wegener had jumped from *Nicosian* into the sea still wearing his life jacket. He apparently put his arms in the air in surrender but Corporal Collins shot him in the head.

Afterwards, Lieutenant Commander Herbert reported to the Admiralty that he had ordered the shootings to prevent the Germans from scuttling *Nicosian*. An alternative version was that *'they might set the large amount of fodder alight'*[38]. If the Germans had scuttled *Nicosian*, Herbert felt the Navy would blame his negligence in allowing it to happen. How U-boat crewmen could have found and opened any seacocks aboard a large and strange ship to sink it so quickly by scuttling remains unexplained. Censorship in Britain

---

36   Memorandum from the German Government concerning the Murder of the Crew of a German Submarine by the Commander of the British Auxiliary Cruiser "Baralong". 'Before public notaries, Mr E Ansley, county of Hancock, State of Mississippi, and Charles J Denechaud, municipality of Orleans, State of Louisiana, on the 5th and 8th October, 1915, six US citizens made sworn depositions concerning the murder of the crew of a German submarine by the commander of the British auxiliary cruiser "Baralong"' . http://www.Vlib.us/wwi/resources/archives/texts/t050925/Baralong.html
37   Compton-Hall, Richard (1991) *Submarines: And the war at Sea 1914-18*. p 204. London: Macmillan
38   All italicised lines, except footnote 35, from *Amazing Adventure: a Thrilling Naval Biography: Cdr Godfrey Herbert*. pp 138 and 139

curbed the report, but this lasted only until the muleteers returned home to the United States and told their version of the story to newspapers and made statements to Public Notaries. These statements contained broadly similar information with some variations over details. Their accounts appeared in front of both houses of the British Parliament in January 1916 in the form of a memorandum from the German government, delivered by way of the American Ambassadors in Berlin and London.

The Reichstag debated the 'cowardly murder' in January and included an announcement that Germany would take unspecified reprisals. The Prussian Ministry of War added the name of Captain William McBride, the pseudonym used by Lieutenant Commander Herbert, to their '*Black List of Englishmen who are Guilty of Violations of the Laws of War* vis-à-vis *Members of the German Armed Forces*' and demanded his trial as a war criminal. Britain replied by offering an impartial tribunal if this also included the sinking of the SS *Arabic* by U-24 on 19th August 1915 (of which more in the following chapter), the firing on lifeboats of the collier *Ruel* on 21st August 1915 by Max Valentiner in U-38 and an attack on stranded submarine E13 in neutral waters. The Germans dropped their demands but still threatened reprisals. The Admiralty protected Herbert by continuing to name the commander of the *Baralong* as Captain William McBride. He was awarded the Distinguished Service Order (DSO) and the crew of the *Baralong* a prize bounty of £185 (perhaps £19,000 in 2015 value), seemingly for the sinking of U-27.

Elsewhere, Max Valentiner had returned to his mission, sinking ten vessels off the west coast of Wales on 17th August, nine without casualties, but the navy collier SS *Glenby* lost two crew members, killed by shells fired as they evacuated the ship.

The *Arabic* Pledge

SS *Arabic* left Liverpool on 18th August 1915, with 186 passengers including Americans, French, Russians, Belgians and Swiss, and even one German in possession of a Home Office permit[39]. Emergency preparations in case of any need to evacuate had been meticulous. There were 248 crew members under the command of Captain W Finch.

On the following morning, she was outbound from her stop at Queenstown, heading for New York, when U-24 torpedoed her about 50 miles south of the Old Head of Kinsale. *Arabic*'s lookouts had spotted a ship stopped about five miles away and, as they drew closer, saw that she was down by the bow, her lifeboats heading for the Irish coast. She was the SS *Dunsley*. *Arabic* had been zigzagging and her master altered course to keep clear of any submarine that might be in the vicinity. He also ordered the sending of a wireless message reporting the *Dunsley*'s predicament and position.

Passengers and crew were watching the *Dunsley* settle when Second Officer Steele shouted warning of a torpedo trail off *Arabic*'s starboard bow. It was too close to avoid and there was a shuddering explosion and plume of water starboard aft. Steele telegraphed 'Stop' and then 'Full Astern' to the engine room to stop her quickly and enable the safe lowering of her boats Captain William Finch ordered everyone to their lifeboats. No one had seen a U-boat. The emergency preparations made before departure worked well and the crew swung out lifeboats and then filled and lowered them quickly. The *Arabic* sank in only eight minutes with the loss of 21 crew and 18 passengers. It could have been much worse.

---

39 Hurd, Archibald (1924). History Of The Great War, The merchant marine Vol. II. London, John Murray

Captain Finch directed operations, assisted by officers Bowen and Oliver until the last moment when Mr Oliver dived overboard and Mr Bowen slid down the No.1 lifeboat fall. The captain went down with his ship before rising to the surface. He swam to a boat, helped two firemen, a woman and a baby aboard, before taking command of the lifeboats around. On the first sighting of the *Dunsley*, *Arabic* had sent out a distress signal which drew a speedy response from patrol vessels which picked up 390 survivors and landed them at Queenstown.

Kapitänleutnant Rudolf (Rudi) Schneider in U-24 had made the attacks and claimed that the liner was trying to ram his vessel, but as U-24's torpedo struck the *Arabic* aft, and no one aboard ever saw a U-boat, this is not easy to envisage. Yet again, HMS *Baralong* rushed to the aid of a stricken ship, but as SS *Arabic* sank quickly, *Baralong* was once more too late and Lieutenant Commander Godfrey Herbert again infuriated.

On 22nd August, a press aide to President Woodrow Wilson released a statement that the President was considering what action he might take if they found that the attack was deliberate. Many interpreted this as a threat to diplomatic relations between the United States and Germany. After a series of high-level international discussions, the German Ambassador to the United States, Johann Heinrich von Bernstorff, made what became known as the '*Arabic* Pledge':

'Passenger liners will not be sunk without warning and without insuring the safety of the non-combatants aboard providing that the liners do not try to escape or offer resistance.'[40]

Realism rather than humanity probably triggered this statement. The Kaiserliche Marine still did not have enough U-boats to pursue effective unrestricted sea warfare over the long term, so needed to avoid killing United States citizens and causing that country to abandon its neutrality. However, if U-boats always had to surface to stop and search merchantmen according to the cruiser rules, this would increase the risks to crews and U-boats. U-boat commanders were intelligent men and confident that if they sank a ship, theirs would be the last word. They could claim that a ship was an armed cruiser, or had attempted to ram them, or had failed to stop when ordered, or was a troopship. Any harmful evidence would be out of sight and normally out of reach on the seabed. U-boat crews felt that

---

40 History Of The Great War – The Merchant Navy, Volume 2, (Part 1 of 2) by Sir Archibald Hurd

obeying the *Arabic* Pledge would endanger them and seriously hamper their operations. Its concessions angered them.

Max Valentiner had lost his cousin Bernd Wegener in an attack by Lieutenant Commander Godfrey Herbert in command of the Q-ship *Baralong* that had seemingly descended into murder. He next learned of the death of his close friend Klaus Hansen on U-41, killed in another Q-ship attack by the same vessel, recently renamed *Wyandra,* but under a different captain. He wrote:

'I received the terrible news about the death of my dear friend Klaus', commander of the U-41, and how Klaus was the victim of a U-boot Falle (U-boat Trap), a Q-ship attack. He mentioned the 'infamous *Baralong*' as the ship that 'did away with my friend' and then wrote that only one officer and two enlisted men survived. In fact, one officer (Crompton) and only one enlisted man (Godeau) survived the U-41 sinking. Valentiner also seemed to think that someone shot Klaus 'perhaps whilst swimming to rescue others', but a direct hit killed him while he was still on U-41's tower, so Valentiner was seemingly confusing his friend Hansen's death with that of his cousin Bernd Wegener. Actions involving the same Q-ship killed both men; Wegener seemingly murdered and Hansen failing to spot a U-boat trap. Both may have been naive. In the swirling fog of wartime communications, Valentiner may have received distorted or exaggerated accounts or simply misunderstood or confused their fates, but the result was identical – both men, cousin and friend, were killed by guns of one British Q-ship. The mutual respect that had existed between men of both navies before the war was breaking down in more bitterness and reprisals.

Shortly after Valentiner heard of Hansen's death, he took U-38 into harbour for repairs and went on leave. He visited his parents in Sønderborg and was in despair at finding that they were starving. He witnessed similar widespread suffering went he went on to Berlin, referring several times to the German population suffering from the lack of food and supplies caused by the British blockade. This seems to have filled him with a merciless urge to starve the British by a continuation and escalation of a U-boat blockade, while Kaiserliche Marine surface warships remained in port. On arrival in Berlin he asked a colleague:

'Why does our main fleet not do anything? Why do they never go out?'

His colleague told him; *'The fleet has to be saved for peace'*.

British armed merchant cruisers continued to enforce the blockade of Germany very successfully. The German battle fleet lay in Wilhelmshaven, neither willing nor permitted to venture out because the Royal Navy lay in wait in Scapa Flow for just such an attempt, hoping to force a major sea battle, but reluctant to embark themselves because of U-boats. Stalemate prevailed. German civilians starved while the authorities directed limited food supplies to soldiers in their trenches. However, during June, July and August 1915, U-boats hit 353 ships, the majority British, in a highly successful and damaging counter-blockade. Britain's loss of so many ships, men and vital supplies ultimately threatened chances of victory, but transport of essential supplies had to continue. The U-boat pressure was immense and the government, Admiralty and navy had no solutions in sight. Could Britain survive the growing crisis?

U-boats – The Unwilling Exodus

Instead of allowing U-boats the freedom to build on their mounting successes, politicians in Berlin made a momentous decision. Germany abandoned the U-boat blockade of Britain and on Monday 20th September 1915, it ordered U-boats out of British waters. Berlin directed some of them to the Adriatic and Mediterranean, close to busy shipping routes, but with presumed lower risk of killing United States citizens. U-boat commanders who had enjoyed remarkable success around the British Isles were convinced that, if able to have continued, they could sink ships faster than Britain could build them and thus change the outcome of the war. They might have been right. The order to leave British waters was an attempt to appease the American government. Already embittered by what they saw as Q-ship murders, this angered the commanders even more. Along with many others, Max Valentiner had enjoyed good hunting in British waters. Between 15th April and 23rd August 1915, he had made fifty-two sinkings, taken three prizes and damaged two other vessels[41]. Only two of these attacks had cost lives.

The Mediterranean provided a vital waterway for troops from Australia, New Zealand, and India and for supplies from the east. These would now come under a new threat. Entente warships remained ill-equipped for any form of U-boat warfare. Once in the Mediterranean, U-boats would be able to operate year-round, far from the extreme winter storms that hampered operations in the Atlantic and the North Sea. Between August and November 1915, German U-boats reached the Adriatic base at Cattaro (now Kotor, Montenegro), south of Dubrovnik, with access to Mediterranean shipping routes. Their arrival had three positives for Germany – reducing the risk of the USA joining the war as their enemy; supporting Germany's Austrian

---

41   https://uboat.net/wwi/ships_hit/losses_year.html

and Turkish allies; and disrupting shipping through the Mediterranean. However, during October, November and December 1915, overall U-boat successes were more than halved by the piecemeal migration. Attacks fell from 353 in the previous three months to only 167.

Kapitänleutnant Claus Rücker was the first to herald U-boat presence in the Mediterranean when his U-34 stopped, shelled and sank the 4,107-ton British steamer SS *Natal Transport* south of Crete on 4th September. There were no casualties. Walther Forstmann followed Rücker in U-39 and during his voyage from Germany to Cattaro, Forstmann sank 11 vessels and damaged another. U-33 transferred next under Konrad Gansser, with twelve previous 'kills' in northern waters. He quickly became more successful on his voyage to the Adriatic. In one week in the Mediterranean, he sank 12 vessels, equal to his previous total, and his spree only ended because he arrived in Cattaro.

Waldemar Kophamel made his first Mediterranean sinking on 3rd November but only remained in command of U-35 until 12th November, when the Imperial Navy promoted him to Korvettenkapitän and appointed him commander of the Submarine Flotilla operating out of Cattaro. His last sinking before taking up his command was the SS *Californian*, previously damaged by U-34 and criticised in 1912 for failing to assist the sinking RMS *Titanic*.

U-38's final activity around the British coast lasted for only nineteen days in August 1915, during which time she sank 30 ships and damaged one. Max Valentiner's last northern success came on 23rd August with the sinking of the 4,572-ton SS *Trafalgar* off Fastnet. There were no casualties. Valentiner returned to Kiel to prepare for the transfer and while there was involved in a conversation with Admiral Henning von Holtzendorff, who had assumed the post of the Kaiserliche Marine's Chief of the Admiral Staff on 3rd September 1915. Max boasted:

'Excellency, I guarantee that I will sink fifty thousand tons on the journey to the Mediterranean.'
'You cannot give such a guarantee, Valentiner.'
'I do give it, your Excellency!'[42]

He would not sink another ship until early November, after passing through the straits of Gibraltar.

---

42 Valentiner, Max (1934). *U38. Wikingerfahrten eines deutschen U-Bootes*. p 80. Berlin: Ullstein

In the wake of the *Lusitania* and *Arabic* sinkings, the Kaiser's government had adopted a conciliatory position, subordinating naval considerations to political concerns to reduce American antagonism. Holtzendorff's appointment seems to have been intended to preserve the fiction of imperial control over naval policy, which had largely passed to hawkish Grand Admiral Alfred von Tirpitz. He quickly converted von Holtzendorff to his views and gained an ardent supporter[43]. Tirpitz fervently believed that the only way for Germany to win the war was through unrestricted submarine warfare, blockading and starving the British Isles with U-boats unhampered by international law. He would eventually resign in protest, but his stance had probably influenced Max Valentiner and fellow U-boat commanders, many of whom already felt that this was the only way to win a war bogged down in a muddy and murderous stalemate on land.

'Unrestricted' in the U-boat warfare context is a simple word with a deadly meaning. It would mean no warnings, no stopping, no searching and no allowing those aboard into lifeboats. It would be a merciless 'sink on sight' campaign. Valentiner wrote later:

'The kind of war I was fighting there was quite simple, only very time-consuming. I could not, according to the rules of the German government, fight an annihilating combat war, as we had suggested. If it had been for us submarine captains, we would have laid with our boats around England and sunk everything that came our way. We could have continued our business at night with torpedoes and England would certainly not have felt comfortable in our sights. It would have forced peace.'[44]

He blamed his government for failing to commit to the potential victory formula that U-boat commanders had already demonstrated – turn the tables on Britain, repay her blockade, sink her vital merchant ships, strangle her into negotiations. A few more months might have been enough.

When U-38 left on her long voyage to the Mediterranean, Valentiner already believed that many at the very highest levels in the Kaiserliche Marine shared and supported his bellicose beliefs, but despaired at politicians who believed it safer to avoid alienating the United States, like poker players who had folded a royal flush. He was now confident that Tirpitz and Holtzendorf

---

43 Notes on the memorandum by Admiral von Holtzendorff of 22nd December 1916 regarding unrestricted U-boat warfare. Translated by Dirk Steffen. http://www.gwpda.org/naval/holtzendorffmemo.htm

44 Valentiner, Max (1934). *U38. Wikingerfahrten eines deutschen U-Bootes.* p 81. Berlin: Ullstein

were fervent believers in unrestricted submarine warfare and agreed with fellow U-boat commanders that in any attack, the safety of the U-boat and crew were paramount. The only way to make this possible was to remain submerged, making warnings to merchant ships impossible. The pastor's son seems to have evolved into a passionate believer in this form of attack with its opportunities for more success and perhaps some vengeance and retribution. Now he had to seek satisfaction elsewhere.

U-38 was quickly back in action on 3rd November, when she sank the 3,500-ton British registered SS *Woodfield* only 20 miles inside the Straits of Gibraltar, an event sadly marked by the deaths of eight of *Woodfield*'s crew. Next, U-38 intercepted a converted Liverpool fruit ship north of Oran, HMT *Mercian*, requisitioned and used as a troopship. *Mercian* was carrying 400 infantrymen and horses of the Lincolnshire Yeomanry from Southampton to Salonica. U-38 was seemingly unable to use torpedoes, so bombarded *Mercian* with her deck gun. *Mercian* zigzagged so that U-38's gunners had to change range and aim constantly, but she still took heavy damage and casualties. After shelling for over an hour, U-38 stopped firing and *Mercian* escaped. The attack had killed 23 men and wounded 78. She made harbour in Oran, where the troops marched in a funeral cortège for those who had lost their lives. Valentiner sank the 5,000-ton Japanese SS *Yasukuni Maru* on the same day with no further casualties.

Having sunk two ships on 4th November, the French vessel *Dahra* and the Italian *Ionia*, Valentiner went on to attack the 1,650-ton French steamer *Le Calvados*, carrying Senegalese troops from Marseilles to Oran. Torpedoed and shelled, she sank with the loss of 740 lives, mostly soldiers. Only 55 survived[45]. The lifeboats on SS *Calvados* could have carried 250 while there were 800 aboard. By the time she arrived in Cattaro, U-38 would have damaged one ship and sunk 14 others, all of which enabled Max Valentiner to exceed his boast to Admiral von Holtzendorff that he would sink 50,000 tons on his voyage. Lamentably, he would also kill 1,053 people in pursuit of this ambition and probably to avenge the deaths of his cousin and best friend and vent his anger at what he saw as his government's appeasement.

All through this period, Austria was at war with Italy, but Germany was not. The Kaiserliche Marine had to treat Italian vessels as neutrals and had ordered her warships not to attack Italian ships in the eastern Mediterranean. However, west of Cape Matapan at the southern tip of mainland Greece, German U-boats took to flying Austrian flags while sinking large merchant

---

45 Anon (1915). German submarines in the Gibraltar Straits. *The Times* (41006). London. 8th November. Col A, p 8

ships, claiming they were troopships or armed auxiliary cruisers, thus bypassing the cruiser rules. Recently, under the Arabic Pledge, Berlin had ordered U-boats to follow these rules with merchant ships – stop, search and evacuate before any further action. Would these rules and orders protect Italian passenger liners such as the SS *Ancona*, departing Naples on 5th November?

SS *Ancona*

The SS *Ancona*, an 8,200-ton liner, left Naples on Friday 5th November 1915, calling on the next day in Messina before departing for New York with 322 passengers, 174 crew and about 2,500 tons of general cargo. On Sunday, 7th November, *Ancona*'s wireless operator heard a signal from what he thought to be the four-funnel liner SS *France*, renamed *France IV* for war service[46]:

'We are being shelled and torpedoed by German submarine.'

It gave no position. But it was the SS *France IV*, an elegant 4,000-ton vessel, which had transmitted the message while U-38 shelled and eventually sank her, hence the absence of any further transmissions. There were no casualties.

The following morning, Monday 8th November, roughly midway between the coasts of Sardinia and Tunisia (between Capo Carbonara and Bizerte), *Ancona* encountered patchy fog but continued at full speed with lookouts posted, blowing long blasts on her whistle to warn other ships in the poor visibility. The lookouts could barely see but strained to listen for the whistles of other ships. Half an hour later, still in the fog, they heard a whistle and thought it to be a ship they had sighted earlier. About noon, *Ancona*'s deck officers took advantage of a gap in the fog to take sun sightings and fix their position. They saw another vessel in the haze; not the steamer they expected, but a submarine. A gun boomed and a shell landed ahead of *Ancona*'s bow. Was this a warning shot ordering *Ancona* to stop, or an attacking shot that had missed? *Ancona*'s Capitano Massardo, thinking the latter, reacted promptly and ordered the hoisting of the Italian ensign, the closing of all watertight bulkheads and a rapid change of course. He turned

---

46 'Le paquebot France'. Compagnie générale transatlantique (French Line)

Ancona's stern to the U-boat, set both engines to 'full ahead' and zigzagged away. The U-boat, Valentiner's U-38, fired again and set off in pursuit.

Ancona was capable of sixteen knots, as was U-38, but with *Ancona* zigzagging and U-38 on a straight course, the gap closed quickly and the shots became more accurate, causing serious damage and injury. *Ancona*'s wireless operator sent out a signal: '*Ancona bombarded and torpedoed* (sic)' giving her position, but because wireless equipment had been damaged, he did not know whether anyone would receive his signal. Terrified passengers and crew hurried to the lifeboats.

Ancona's Capitano Massardo eventually abandoned the attempted escape, stopped engines and ordered his helmsman to come around to starboard. Scared and desperate people were boarding lifeboats even though *Ancona* was still making about ten knots. Before she stopped completely, the crew lowered seven boats, boarded by crew and passengers. The submarine approached, still firing at intervals, the ship shuddering and people screaming as she took more damage and casualties. U-38 then hoisted an apparently new Austrian flag and stopped some 250 metres away. Some passengers, including women and children, were still aboard the liner. Aware of the imminent danger and that there was nothing more they could do, the captain and his officers put on life jackets, joined others jumping into the sea and boarded a nearby boat.

The gunfire stopped as the submarine came closer to *Ancona*'s starboard bow. Moments later an explosion threw up a column of water at her bow. She reared up before her bow fell under the waves and she sank with about 30 people still aboard. Everyone in the lifeboats was at the mercy of the U-boat crew. Those in the captain's boat pulled others from the sea. He was desperate to rescue everyone until his officers reminded him that their boat was already seriously overloaded and that saving more might mean the loss of all. The submarine had probably fired between 60 and 80 shells.

Shells were striking people in the boats close to the ship, but they pulled away and clear. The submarine continued firing on the ship for a further 20 minutes and Dr Cecile Greil, a New York physician and passenger, estimated that the bombardment had lasted about 45 minutes. After the shelling stopped, she saw a 'comet-like form' rushing through the water, followed by an explosion throwing up a huge plume of water. It was a torpedo. *Ancona* turned on her side and sank at 1.32 pm by Dr Greil's watch.

Captain Massardo was in a lifeboat with 12 other crew and 15 passengers; men, women and two children. He knew that they were 60 miles north of the Tunisian coast. It was by then 3. 00 pm, so he raised the lifeboat's sail and headed south. They could see the distant sails of five other lifeboats and managed to stay in contact almost until dawn as the weather deteriorated. At first light, the captain's boat sighted land so continued under sail and at 10 am landed on what they found to be Zembra Island, where members of a small military outpost looked after them and telegraphed news of their landing to Tunis.

A small steamer, the *Eugenie Besal*, arrived the next day with third officer Salvemini and 25 further survivors, who had landed on the Tunisian mainland. The French minelayer *Pluton* picked up the occupants of six other lifeboats and disembarked at the French naval harbour in Bizerte at about 11. 00 pm. Dr Greil boarded *Pluton* and looked after the wounded. *Pluton* had picked up 100 survivors and *Torpedo Ship 329* had rescued a further 26. With the 88 who had come ashore from lifeboats at Zembra, Sidi Baoud and Rades, the number rescued reached 214, so of the 496 aboard when *Ancona* left Messines, they had lost 282.

On 9th November, U-38 attacked and sank another Italian passenger steamer, the 3,960-ton *Firenze*, off Syracuse on the east coast of Sicily. The *Washington Evening Star* reported on 14th November:

> 'The submarine, showing the Austrian flag, came close to the steamer and destroyed the ship's steering gear by a shot. The commander of the submarine ordered that everyone take to the boats as the vessel was about to be sunk. Six boats were launched and in these, every person found a place. Upon the first boat arriving in Syracuse, an Italian destroyer was sent in search of the others. All the boats have now been found except one with six passengers, one of whom is a woman and fourteen of the crew.'

Note the mention of a false flag again[47], deflecting blame away from a German U-boat and onto the Austro-Hungarian U-boat fleet that operated from Pola in the Adriatic. Rome newspaper *Il Messaggero* reported that U-38 had fired 28 shells into the *Firenze* before she sank. Had Valentiner taken a liking to attacking passenger ships? The U-boat commanders' league table kept totals of tonnage sunk and on just two days Valentiner added 12,000 tons to his score, but with no mention of 302 innocent passengers. Washington's

---

47 According to *World War 1 at Sea – Austro-Hungarian Navy* (https://www.naval-history.net/WW1NavyAustrian. htm), the initially small Austrian submarine force was unable to play a role outside the Adriatic and by early 1915 the Germans were sending U-boats into the Mediterranean, in part to attack the Allied fleet off the Dardanelles. As Italy had declared war on Austro-Hungary but not Germany, the German boats operated under the Austrian ensign and were temporarily commissioned into the Austrian Navy.

Sunday Star of 14th November reported that a lifeboat with six passengers and fourteen crew was missing. News from the Mediterranean continued to arrive. On Friday 26th November, the *Daily Mirror*'s headline read:

'The Ancona Crime: Survivors From The Sunken Liner Reach Port After Their Terrible Experience' with a full front page of photographs, and other newspapers covered the story. Recently arrived U-boats sank eighteen vessels in the Mediterranean in October 1915 and forty-four in November. It is unlikely that anyone planning to sail through the Mediterranean that December could have been ignorant of the risk. One of these sailings was to be that of the SS *Persia*, due to leave Tilbury on 18th December on her scheduled mail run to Bombay and Karachi, with calls at Gibraltar, Marseilles and Valletta.

On 9th December, Max Valentiner's U-38 sailed on a bizarre and unwanted venture, doubling as a cargo vessel and tugboat. It had to tow UC-12 (Kapitänleutnant Karl Palis), both U-boats being loaded with weapons and money destined for Bardiyah on the Libyan coast to arm and persuade Senussi tribesmen to attack and harass the British and Indian armies on the Suez Canal. UC-12 was a small coastal mine-laying submarine with a maximum surface range of 750 nautical miles at 5 knots. Kotor to Bardiyah without diversions and dives could take her five and a half days. U-38 could complete that voyage in under two days, hence the towing role and the frustration. However, light Italian warships and armed fishing boats patrolled the Strait of Otranto where the Adriatic joins the Mediterranean. During their approach, U-38 and UC-12 cast off the tow line and submerged, planning to rendezvous once through the strait. They failed to meet. U-38 continued alone and U-39 later interrupted her attack role to find and tow UC-12 towards Bardiyah. Meanwhile U-34 loaded more weapons and headed south with an order to tow UC-12 back to Cattaro. These two U-boats met, but could not risk towing in the heavily patrolled Ionian Sea, so UC-12 struggled home alone. The Imperial Admiralty Staff (Admiralstab) regarded the time and effort their top U-boats had expended in delivering a modest quantity of weapons as a costly diversion. Imagine also how the commanders of the three torpedo attack U-boats must have felt, acting as freighters and tugs instead of fighting to alter the course of the war by sinking enemy cargo vessels. They were already angry at their recent orders sending them away from the British coast.

The December Departure of SS *Persia*

In early December 1915, London was wet, windy and relatively mild, with less sunshine than average. Those bound for Egypt and India might have been looking forward to leaving London's gloom, even though the news about U-boat successes on that route had become intimidating. Since the sinking of the RMS *Lusitania* back in May, the mantra that Britain ruled the waves had carried less conviction. Through the summer and autumn of 1915, over 500 U-boat attacks had taken place in waters around the British Isles, but newspaper reports were starting to suggest that the threat might recently have moved to the Mediterranean. While there had only been two U-boat attacks there in September, this had risen to 40 during November, 12 of which had been against passenger liners.

Shipping companies pressed on regardless. Britain relied on uninterrupted supplies of food and war materials, all carried by sea. The recently merged British India and Peninsular and Oriental (P&O) lines continued to advertise services, including ten sailings leaving London in December 1915 for various ports in Australia, China and India, all passing through the Mediterranean.

Captain and Crew

The SS *Persia* had a crew of over 300 men and women for her December departure, of which 226 were Indian and Goan out of Bombay and the balance joined in London. India supplied mainly seamen, trimmers and firemen, while Goa provided the purser's team of cooks, waiters and some stewards. The London-based crew consisted of officers and engineers, more seamen and skilled trades, plus cabin stewards and six stewardesses. A passenger list indicates that 166 passengers boarded the SS *Persia* in Tilbury on 18th December.

The master of the SS *Persia* for this voyage was William Henry Selby Hall, born in 1858 in Greenhithe, just across the Thames from Tilbury Docks, from where he now sailed regularly for P&O. William became an orphan at the age of six on the death of his father, Walter Hall, a civilian chief coastguard officer, in February 1865. His uncle, Thomas Hall, became guardian for William, his brother Percy and sisters Frances and Jane. William attended the Royal Navy College, Greenwich, and the Incorporated Thames Nautical Training College, on HMS *Worcester*. He became a deck apprentice at the age of 17 and served aboard the 1873, three-masted iron ship *MacCallum More* between 1876 and 1880 to learn the skills of his chosen trade. The normal next step would have been to qualify as a second mate by examination, but for the next two years, he worked as an able seaman on the Falkland Islands route, failed his navigation examination in January 1882 and then qualified in May of that year. He later joined P&O as a junior officer and worked through the officer ranks before being given commands in the eastern Mediterranean and on the Bombay-to-Japan service[48]. It was with over 30 years' experience as a deck officer, including 22 as the holder of a master's certificate, that this seasoned mariner would take SS *Persia* to sea on 18th December 1915.

In his personal life, William had married Mary Johnson in Streatham in July 1883. They had a daughter, Amy Aileen Mary Selby Hall, born in 1888, and a son, Charles Otley Hall, born in 1890. In 1907, one William Henry Selby Hall, a 'widower', married Helen Monica Maude Mary Hargrave in Clapham. She was the widow of Eric E Kershaw who had been a Royal Navy surgeon who died in 1901. She had two children, Ronald Hargrave Kershaw, born 1894, and Lorna Hargrave Kershaw, born 1901. The first Mrs Hall and a daughter Amy, by then 22 or 23, appear on the 1911 census as living in Portslade and it

William Henry Selby Hall, master of P&O liner SS Persia

---

48 *The Ballarat Courier*, 4th January 1916

describes Mary as having been married for 27 years. William and Mary's son died in 1912, aged 21, and both their names are on his headstone. If William was married to two women, how had he managed to keep this secret since 1907? Where did his second wife live? On 21st August 1915 there might be a clue. A Mrs Helen Maud Selby Hall and Miss Lorna Hargrave Kershaw arrived together in London on the P&O ship SS *Karmala*, having travelled as first-class passengers. They gave their last places of residence as 'Egypt and Malta' both places where the *Karmala* had picked up passengers.

For the SS *Persia*'s voyage to Bombay departing on 18th December, Captain Hall commanded a capable crew in all deck department duties covering cargo, crew and watch-keeping. His chief officer was Gerald Clark, thirty-nine-year-old son of a Norfolk farmer, who joined P&O in June 1896 and who had earned the South Africa Transport Medal for services carrying troops and supplies during the Boer War. He became a chief officer in October 1909 and served in this role on both the SS *Namur* and SS *Nore* before joining *Persia* as chief officer in May 1915. Second Officer Harold Wood, aged 33, joined Shaw, Savill & Company in 1908, indentured as a deck apprentice, and after gaining his certificate of competency, usually called a 'second mate's ticket', joined P&O in March 1913. He had served aboard *Persia* since June 1914. Third Officer Stuart W Boyd was originally from Ontario before his parents moved to New Zealand. He worked for New Zealand Shipping Company and P&O, qualifying as a second mate in March 1906. Fourth Officer Harold Ranger Parton was born in Blackheath, the son of a Professor of Modern Languages. This was his first voyage after gaining his second mate's ticket, so he was a relative novice. The boatswain (bosun), C W Anderson, supervised the team of eight able seamen who carried out all the routine, emergency and maintenance duties required, including steering as directed by the officer on watch. Forty-eight Indian seamen completed the deck team, supervised by their Tindals and Serangs.

Communications between ship and shore, plus weather and position reports, were in the hands of 22-year-old George Dewey who, despite his relative youth, had previously served as Marconi operator in five ships before joining the SS *Persia*.

Chief Engineer Ernest Jeffery was responsible for the operation and maintenance of the machinery on board the ship. He was the son of a Southampton builder and had qualified as a marine engineer working for the Union Steamship Company before moving to P&O in about 1886.

Second Engineer Henry Edwin Eves, born in Plumstead in May 1875, son of James Eves, an engine fitter, provided experienced support. Henry didn't have a traditional seafaring career. After leaving school he became an apprentice fitter and turner at the Royal Arsenal at Woolwich before moving to Glasgow in 1896 where he worked as a plant fitter at J & J Boyd's Shettleston Ironworks. His next move was across that city to work as a fitter at the Acme Gas Engine Company. In 1897 he joined P&O as an assistant engineer, but left in 1899 and returned to the Royal Arsenal to work as a turner in the laboratory. In 1901 he set up in business as a motor engineer, but this did not last and in August 1902 he returned to the sea with P&O, perhaps to support his growing family. He trained in Victoria Docks and earned his certificate of competency as a second-class engineer on 10th September 1906, while living in East Ham, and his first-class certificate on 29th September 1908. All the ships on which he served sailed from Tilbury, close to his home. In 1915, he was living in Gravesend and had served on several P&O ships for fifteen years, before joining the SS *Persia*. Henry and his wife Mary Ann had three children.

One of the third engineers, Walter Hickingbotham, aged 39, was the son of a joiner. He was a Freeman of Lincoln, educated at St Martin's School and Christ's Hospital Terrace, Lincoln, before joining Messrs Robey & Co as an apprentice fitter. After he completed his apprenticeship, he joined the Royal Navy as an artificer at the age of 21, but after an accident he left the Navy as an invalid two years later. He signed up in the merchant marine with P&O in about 1906. He joined the SS *Persia* from HMS *Macedonia* in March 1915. The Royal Navy had requisitioned her in August 1914 and converted *Macedonia* into an armed merchant cruiser, pendant number M59[49]. Walter served as a lieutenant engineer, taking part in convoy escorts and at the Battle of the Falklands on 8th December 1914. He went home on sick leave before joining the SS *Persia*. Another third engineer, Wesley Hazlewood, aged 21, was the son of house-builder Thomas Hazlewood of Brixham. Before going to sea, Wesley was an apprentice at the Noss Engineering Works, Dartmouth, for Simpson, Strickland & Co Ltd, manufacturers of steam engines and boilers. A note on his previous ship's crew list in October 1915 stated that, although he was the fourth engineer, they rated him as a third engineer, so he seems to have been very competent. Assistant engineers Victor Berry and Harold Matthew were both aged 22. Berry was the son of wine cooper James Berry of East Ham and Matthew the son of Scottish marine engineer William Matthew of Leytonstone, Essex. This was Harold's first voyage on the SS *Persia* after he joined P&O in June 1914.

---

49   https://naval-history.net/OWShips-WW1-08-HMS_Macedonia.htm

Several of *Persia*'s other officers were supernumerary, those over and above the normal number or not part of the regular staff. *Persia* regularly sailed with several supernumerary crew members, as did other ships. Second Engineer (Supernumerary) Harold Turner, aged 43, was the son of linen draper William Turner of West Ham. He had worked for P&O for over 10 years, but this appears to have been his first voyage on the SS *Persia*. Third Engineer (Supernumerary) James Ireland, aged 30, was the son of a stonemason from Forfar. He had served his apprenticeship as a mechanic in a local factory in Forfar before moving to a large engineering works in Newcastle. He joined P&O in 1907 and had served on the *Persia* for two years. Assistant Engineer (Supernumerary) William Mollon, aged 24, was the son of Joseph Mollon, a shipwright of Hartlepool. He served an apprenticeship as a marine engineer in Hartlepool, then worked for several companies before joining P&O in 1915. December 1915 appears to have been his first voyage aboard *Persia*. In the crew of engineers, there was also an electrician, a winchman, a refrigeration mechanic, a boilermaker, plus a large team of Indian coal-trimmers and firemen under their tindals and serangs, Indian equivalents of bosun's mates and bosuns.

On this voyage, the SS *Persia* carried the usual members in its Purser's Department, but without an actual purser. Key members of this department included Daniel Coughlan, head steward; William Henry Dowling, head saloon waiter; A J Butler, chef; George Walton, second chef; Antonio Gabriel Baretto, baker, plus a full team of stewards, cooks, servants, barmen, waiters and scullions. We know a little more of some others:

Frederick Fairchild, born in 1892 in Thurlby, near Bourne, Lincolnshire, son of Joseph, a publican and dray maker of the Blue Bell Inn, and his wife, Sarah Ann. According to the Reverend J S Pettifor, vicar of St Firmin's Church, Fred was a 'highly respected parishioner, a Sunday School scholar and a valuable member of the church choir'. By 1901 his father was farming at Ivy House and in 1911 Fred worked as a milkman on the farm. He joined P&O in October 1913 as a general servant and baggage steward on the SS *Mantua*, before he transferred to the SS *Persia* in August 1914. Fred was busiest on embarkation and arrival days and at sea when passengers would request luggage be brought to them so that they could replace clothes as the climate became hotter or cooler. He had to turn his hand to whatever duties instructed when passengers did not need baggage assistance.

Mary Anne Pennington (née Turner) was born in 1883, probably in Gosberton, Lincolnshire, and in the first decade of the 1900s became a lady's maid in the household of Lord Lister, of antiseptic fame. She was a housemaid in that household in the 1901 census and probably became a lady's maid to one of Lord Lister's sisters. She gave up this job to marry Francis Laudicino, whose father had emigrated from Naples, but he left her to bring up two small children alone. One life-changing evening, she was having a fish and chip supper, as always in those days wrapped in newspaper, when she spotted a P&O advertisement seeking stewardesses. She applied successfully, handed her children to her sister, known as 'Scary Aunty Madge' and went to sea. With her background as a lady's maid, she soon gained a position in first class, where she became known as 'the Duchess', because of her immaculate dress and impeccable manners. She served on the SS *Novara* before transferring to SS *Persia* in 1914.

George Walton, second saloon chef, was born in 1879, youngest son of Thomas John Walton and his wife Elizabeth. Thomas was the beer house keeper of the *Sportsman* pub in Plumstead and he kept pigs in a nearby field. A local football club, Dial Square, first played on the Isle of Dogs, but changed its name to Royal Arsenal and moved to Plumstead Common and then to the pub's field in Griffin Manor Way, which became known as Piggy Walton's Field. Despite its impoverished and itinerant start, the club would eventually prosper and become the legendary Arsenal Football Club. George's mother paid for him to train as a chef at Romano's Restaurant in the Strand, but despite his high-class training, he was working as a factory cook when the twentieth century dawned. He married Elizabeth Ruth Fox from Kent in 1910 and worked as a tobacconist and a railway restaurant-car cook before joining the New Zealand Shipping Company as a chief cook. Late in 1915, he was due to return home on leave, but generously took the place of another chef whose wife was about to give birth. Instead of going home for Christmas, George travelled to Tilbury, where he signed on as second saloon chef aboard the SS *Persia*.

The SS *Persia* carried a defensive gun and trained gunners who counted as passengers rather than crew, although it was clear that if ever needed, they would act only under the captain's orders. There were two known gunners aboard the SS *Persia*: Lawrence Arthur Wellington who enlisted in the Royal Marine Artillery in 1898 and in 1901 served on HMS *Jupiter*, a Majestic-class battleship in the Royal Navy. He left in 1910 after 12 years' service and went to work on the Great Eastern Railway. Following the outbreak of World War 1, he took up gunnery duties on defensively equipped merchant ships, moving from one ship to another as required. He served on the ships *Maloja*, *Nyanza*, *Arabia* and *Caledonia*. He was supposed to join the SS *Medina* on 1st December 1915 but apparently failed to appear and came back to London just in time to join the SS *Persia* for her voyage on 18th December. Also aboard was a Bombardier Curtis, understood to be another ship's gunner.

Persia carried people from all levels of society, supported by men and women with a wide variety of both experience and skills to ease their passage. She and her sister ships could each carry up to 550 passengers. They were served with three meals each day through the voyage and had to be entertained, warmed, cooled and supplied with baggage as they changed clothes for warmer climates. They had to have a complete laundry service, beds changed, cabins cleaned, fresh food, water and fuel loaded in ports along the route and all of this carried out by the visible crew. In her unseen depths, trimmers moved large quantities of coal to firemen to keep furnaces stoked and maintained, optimising the output of steam from six boilers to her engines that produced 11,000 horsepower, enough to push her 8,000 tons through the water at up to 18 knots. They hauled and shovelled coal, swept, cleared and removed furnace ashes that they tipped overboard, most of the time in the intense heat of furnaces and boilers which worsened with southerly progress.

In order to keep passengers and crew in good health, the ship also carried its own doctor, Surgeon Officer William Everett, the son of a wine and spirit merchant and hotel keeper. William attended Kettering Grammar School before qualifying with an MB Mast Surg in 1889 and MD in 1893 at University College, Edinburgh. From 1895 until 1907 he worked for the Kent County Asylum, Chartham, before joining P&O as a surgeon officer.

As Captain Hall and his officers prepared for the voyage, discussions and plans were likely to have focused on the U-boat threat. The sinking of RMS *Lusitania* back in May had created shock and anger across much of the world. Since then, attacks on passenger vessels included those on the SS *Arabic*, when 40 died, and on the SS *Hesperian*, with 32 dead, both on transatlantic routes. Attacks on *France IV* and the Italian liner *Ancona* then cost 282 lives with more from the Italian *Firenze*, when 20 were missing and presumed drowned[50]. All these ships carried passengers who could and should have escaped. There were increasing demands for more rigorous checks on safety equipment, signs, the conduct of lifeboat drills, wireless procedures, crew briefings, lookout procedures and route selection.

Before Captain Hall departed, he arranged for his apparent wife, the former Mrs Kershaw, and her daughter Lorna Hargrave Kershaw, to return home to Malta. P&O rules would have forbidden them from travelling on

---

50   *Evening Star*, Washington DC, 14th November 1915, p 16

his ship, even though she would be carrying fewer than half her passenger complement. Instead, they booked to travel aboard the SS *Medina*, departing on Christmas Eve for Australia and China, just as Captain Hall's ship should be arriving in Marseilles.

Many passengers whose duties called them to Egypt and India would have had little or no choice about travelling on SS *Persia*. However, including those disembarking in Gibraltar and those boarding in Marseilles and Valletta, there would be 182 bookings on a ship that could carry up to 530. Of course, the approach of Christmas could have dissuaded potential travellers too. Passengers came from a wide cross-section of post-Edwardian society including missionaries, clergymen, salesmen, a rice-dealer, YMCA volunteers, engineers, jute-millers and traders, a newspaper owner, students, a United States consul designate, two brides-to-be, two doctors, a King's messenger, a lord and a modest number of military officers including some returning to duty after recovering from wounds.

Passengers came from a wide cross-section of post-Edwardian society from a postcard by Cyril Mordaunt Richard
© P&O Heritage Collection www.poheritage.com

On Saturday 18th December 1915 loading of cargo, coal, water, food and baggage aboard *Persia* was complete. Her modest holds carried a mixed cargo of no military significance, such as cement, railway fixtures, paint, iron bars, books, medicines, draperies and over 1,500 tons of Christmas and other mail. Personal baggage arrived with passengers, some who had said their farewells days or hours ago and miles away from Tilbury, while others arrived with the loved ones they were leaving behind, lingering over precious moments.

Calls of 'All aboard' echoed along the wharf. Tardy passengers hurried up the gangplank, arms stretched behind for desperate final fingertip touches. Dockers and seamen released lines and cast off springs. Water churned as tugs took up the slack and moved *Persia* slowly off her berth. The feelings of each person looking down from her decks and of those weeping and waving on the quay, must have covered a wide range of human emotions, shaded by sadness and anxiety. She moved serenely down to the lock and finally out into the tidewater of the Thames. For over two hundred Indian and Goan members of *Persia*'s crew, these were contrasting moments, marking the beginning of their homeward voyage. Other crew members, those out of Tilbury, were leaving homes and families exactly one week before Christmas Day, sailing into uncertainty, perhaps peril. For most, these moments were probably agonising, parting from loved ones after a year of a war that had gone better for Britain's enemies on land and at sea.

SS Persia leaving the Thames
© *P&O Heritage Collection www.poheritage.com*

Later, *Persia* made her way carefully past minefields at the eastern end of the English Channel then headed west towards the U-boat danger zone in the Western Approaches, south-west past Ushant, across Biscay and down the Portuguese coast towards Gibraltar, her first port of call.

After U-38 had discharged her cargo in Bardiyah, she sailed east, returning to commercial warfare (*Handelskrieg*) by torpedoing the 11,000-ton SS *Yasaka Maru* without warning off Alexandria on 21st December.

U-38 at ease – photographed from a friendly vessel, perhaps another U-boat or a supply ship.

Marseilles and Malta

The SS *Persia* enjoyed an uneventful voyage to Gibraltar, where she delivered and collected mail. Thirty-eight passengers disembarked and five boarded. After a brief stop, she departed for Marseilles and sailed north-east for almost two days, 690 miles past the Balearic Islands, waters under the responsibility of the Marine Nationale (French Navy) based in Toulouse. She arrived in Marseilles in time to enjoy Christmas Day, take on more passengers and load more mail. Head Saloon Waiter William Dowling tells how chef Albert Butler came to the Saloon to carve a boar's head. Baker Antonio Gabriel Baretto made an iced cake, and Dowling ensured that everyone had the wines they needed[51], while the children enjoyed a Christmas party.

No one appears to have disembarked from SS *Persia* in Marseilles simply because it would have been much easier, quicker and potentially safer to use the cross-Channel ferry and the French railways for such a journey. Sixty-three passengers boarded, many having used the Bombay Express from Boulogne to Marseilles, by way of the Folkestone cross-Channel ferry. The French railway had reintroduced the service in November 1915 and most of its users seem to have been those better able to afford this option and enjoy a few more Advent days at home. Others, such as Thomas and Cecilia Clark, reasoned that by not sailing through the Western Approaches and across Biscay they might bypass any U-boat threat.

There was a similar mix of passengers boarding in Marseilles as London, with the addition of more businessmen, missionaries, army officers and jute managers; a real cross-section of Edwardian society together aboard the SS *Persia* for better or worse.

---

51   William Dowling's typewritten memoir: A True Story – An account of the sinking of the *Persia*, December 1915, circa 1965

Everyone has a story, some made public, but most kept private. Those aboard were no different, with families, loves, children, friends, jobs, problems, hopes and aspirations. A few of their stories follow.

Four Sisters of the Congregation of Daughters of the Cross had joined the SS *Persia* in London for their return to the Order's convent in Karachi, having reached the end of a stay at the Convent of Carshalton House, Surrey. The Sisters were also to act as chaperones for Miss Maisie Markwick who had attended finishing school in England and was returning to her family in India. The four nuns came from distinctly different backgrounds.

Sister François Xavier (Clara Adins) aged 27, had joined the Order ten years earlier. She had taught the skills of Valenciennes lace-making and embroidery at the convent-run Institut Marie-Thérèse in Liège, Belgium.

Sister Gerard Majella (Susanne Scholer), who had served for 15 years, had lived in India for eight years as an important contributor to the school, convent and orphanage in which she worked. She returned to Europe in 1913 for health reasons but as she recovered, she went to Belgium to nurse badly wounded soldiers at the Mother House of the Order in Liège. These included amputees and men burnt in an artillery attack on Fort Chaudfontaine. The blast damage, fire and toxic fumes killed at least 58 and the surviving defenders surrendered when it became impossible for them to breathe properly.

Sister Julie Anna (Marguerite A T Raulin), aged 25, had been a member for three years and Sister Xavier Marie (Marie-Josephine Molhaut), aged 28, for four years.

The Young Men's Christian Association (YMCA) had already done good work in support of servicemen in World War 1, particularly when Lord Kitchener's appeal brought thousands of volunteers into the British army in towns across the country that simply could not cope with the influx. The YMCA set up around 250 centres in Britain, providing refreshments, books, magazines and papers, even space for men to write letters home. In November 1914, the YMCA crossed into France and through 1915 expanded up to the Western Front and to Egypt and the Dardanelles. A YMCA party joined the SS *Persia* to support troops in Egypt, including Indian soldiers who were defending the Suez Canal, seen by the German government as Britain's jugular vein because of the large volumes of cargo and troops passing through. Mr Arthur Johnson led the party, accompanied by Leonard Gascoigne, Reg Heams and Harry Hopkins[52], heading to Cairo

---
52 Information from conversation with Jeremy Kidd, grandson of Reg Heams

and Alexandria. Reginald Heams was the elder son of Mr and Mrs Heams of Kettering Road, Northampton. Twenty-four years of age, he was a clerk at Sears and Company at the outbreak of war. Reg had already given valuable help to the YMCA for some time and eventually left his employment to join the organisation permanently at the divisional office in Tring. In his little spare time, he was captain of Princess Street Cricket Club and secretary of Mount Pleasant Football Club[53]. The party boarded in Tilbury and Leonard Gascoigne's nineteenth birthday would fall on Boxing Day somewhere between Marseilles and Valletta.

Miss Adelaide Helen (Ellen) Rebecca Bull, born in 1859, was previously an elementary school teacher in Frensham, Surrey. She joined the Church Missionary Society at the Bhil Mission, Biladia, Gujarat, India, and returned to England in May 1915 for a holiday. She joined the SS *Persia* for the return voyage, along with Agnes Lees, a recruit to their mission.

Agnes Lees was the daughter of draper William Lingham Lees and his wife Mary Ann of King's Norton, Worcestershire. Born in 1882, she was ninth of 11 children and a pupil at the King Edward's High School for Girls, Birmingham. Agnes became well known in religious circles in the Birmingham area, where she worked as a clerk in the Cadbury's chocolate works at Bournville, then for a jeweller's merchant. In the summer of 1914, she entered the Church of England Missionary Home in South Kensington for training. Eighteen months later, at the age of 32 and accompanied by her mentor, Miss Bull, she set out on her voyage to a new life at the Bhil Mission.

The Reverend Homer Russell Salisbury was a pastor, professor, administrator, editor and missionary with the Seventh-day Adventist Church. From Battle Creek, Michigan, he later became secretary to the President of Battle Creek College. He then taught in Claremont Union College, South Africa, studied Hebrew in London, taught Hebrew and Church History in Battle Creek, then went to England and established the church's college at Duncombe Hall. He was its principal for five years, ordained in 1904 and appointed South England Conference President in 1905. In 1913 he became President of the Indian Union Mission and sailed from New York to join the SS *Persia* in Marseilles, bound for India. He had received warnings against sailing on a British ship and had intended to board a Dutch steamer but changed his plans.

Elizabeth Stephens Impey was born 1877 in Northfield, Birmingham, the second of the seven children of Quakers Frederick and Eleanor Impey.

---

53   *Northampton Daily Chronicle*, Monday 3rd January 1916

Known to her family as Elsie, she went to school at Weston-super-Mare and moved to The Mount School, York, before attending a physical training college. She spent six years teaching physical exercises to school children and families, enjoyed and taught swimming and gymnastics, was a good horsewoman and a great shot. She became captain of Worcestershire's Ladies' Hockey Club and played for Midland Counties. When 27, she began to study medicine at the University of Birmingham, flourishing under the assistance of her aunt, Dr Annie Elizabeth Clark, a pioneer woman in medicine, and went on to become one of the earliest female medical students at Edinburgh University. After completing her degree, she served as a surgeon at Birmingham Maternity, London Temperance and Swansea General Hospitals and, on the outbreak of war, joined a group of doctors and nurses to look after sick and injured civilians in France[54]. Part of Elizabeth's motivation when she set out to practice medicine was a great interest in India and her concern for the urgent need for women's medical services there. It came as no surprise to her family when she applied for and received a post at the Dufferin Hospital for Women, Lahore, in November 1915. Dr Impey accepted immediately and her father and other family members saw her off from Tilbury. All were aware of the U-boat risks, but Elsie was undeterred and embarked full of hope.

Christian (Chrissie) Maitland was born in Aberdeen in 1886, daughter of Adam Maitland, a future Lord Provost of 'the Granite City'. She gained a BSc at Aberdeen University and went on to gain an MB ChB[55] from Edinburgh University in 1911. Dr Maitland travelled to Ajmer, Rajputana, India, in 1912 as the first medical missionary from the Presbytery of Aberdeen. There she met her husband-to-be, the Reverend Alexander (Alec) Colquhoun Grant, whose father was superintendent engineer of the Clan shipping line. Alec graduated in Classics from Glasgow University in 1906 and became travelling secretary of the General College Department of the Student Movement until the United Free Church of Scotland ordained him in 1911 and offered him the opportunity of becoming a missionary for the Presbytery of Aberdeen in Ajmer. Late in 1914, Dr Maitland contracted enteric (typhoid) fever and returned home to recuperate. Alexander then travelled home on special leave and the couple were married on 18th November 1915 at her home, Rubislaw Den House in Aberdeen, when she became Dr Christian Maitland Grant. Exactly one month later they joined the SS *Persia* for their return to India, he aged 31 and she 29.

---

54 *Daily Express*, 3rd January 1916
55 Bachelor of Medicine, Bachelor of Surgery

There were several wives travelling to rejoin their husbands in India, accompanied by eighteen children and infants.

Rose Mooney was born in Pimlico, London, in 1887 and endured an impoverished childhood. Her father died in 1893 when she was only five and her penniless mother raised her. Rose met Edward Burcombe from Battersea and later married him, by then a sergeant, in Colaba near Bombay, in October 1911. On 12th June 1914, Rose wrote a postcard to her mother at Carey Place, Vauxhall Bridge Road, posted in Pachmari Bazaar, a hill station in the Madhya Pradesh State. The postcard reads:

'Dear Mother, hope you are quite well. Shall write next week. You can find baby and I in this group. She has five teeth at present. Love etc. Rose.'

This baby, Rose's daughter Helen, had been born in 1913 in Shwebo, Burma, and travelled to London with her mother for the birth of a second child, Edward. Rose visited her mother with both children before boarding SS *Persia* for their return to her husband, by then a sergeant major. One of Rose's cousins, Edith Smith, accompanied Rose on the voyage to help care for Helen, aged two years two months, and ten-week-old baby Edward. While Rose had become a seasoned traveller, it could have been daunting for her cousin.

Mary Elizabeth Everitt, known to her family as Cissie, was the sixth of thirteen children of Harry, a nursery foreman, and his wife Mary. It seems likely that she was the Miss M Everitt who joined the SS *Caledonia* in second class on 9th October 1913, bound for India. She was employed on this voyage by a Mrs Bliss as a nurse for her 11-month-old daughter. While aboard, 26-year-old Mary met first class passenger William George McGinn, a jute merchant. Cheap jute had replaced flax in Dundee's textile industry and, by 1900, Dundee was home to over 100 jute mills. Many men travelled regularly between Dundee and Bengal as pioneers in that region's impressive growth in the industry and William was one of them. He and Mary were married in Calcutta in October 1914. In 1915, the new Mrs McGinn travelled back to England for the birth of her first baby, normal practice for expectant mothers of British employees. She gave birth to a son, Quintilla Gustave McGinn, on 5th August 1915 in Shirley, Solihull. After the birth, she stayed with her sister Ethel in Acocks Green before joining SS *Persia* to return to India with her tiny son for a happy reunion, accompanied by an ayah, nameless on the passenger list.

Marcel and Hilda Conran-Smith had taken their only child, six-year-old Louis, to school in England before travelling back to India, missing Christmas together as a family: perhaps difficult for them but heart-breaking for a young boy. Marcel was Superintendent of the Indian Telegraph Service and Hilda was the daughter of Louis Crossley, the well-known Halifax carpet manufacturer.

Mrs Helen Maude de Burgh Codrington was the daughter of Richard Vaughan, a Bengal Army officer. She had married Harry de Burgh Codrington, Assistant Director of Transport Commands (Southern Army) 4th Quetta Division. In 1914, their daughter Marjorie Doris Codrington married Major Percy Penn Gaskell at Rawalpindi and in December 1915 visited her family in Surrey. She was six months pregnant with her first child and was accompanied by her mother, Helen Maude. Both the Codrington and Vaughan families were partly Irish and had been in India for several generations. India was home to all of them. She could stay to give birth in Esher with her in-laws as her husband wished, or return to Quetta on the Afghan border. Mother and daughter decided that home at Quetta was best. They bought first class tickets at the last minute, spent a day shopping in the Army and Navy Store to buy outfits for themselves and for Marjorie's expected baby, then travelled to Marseilles by train to join SS *Persia*.

Mrs Helen Maude de Burgh Codrington with her son Kenneth and daughter Marjorie, Simla c. 1906. Marjorie, by then Mrs Penn Gaskell and 6 months pregnant, was aboard the SS Persia with her mother.
By kind permission of James Crowden

Joyce (or Julia) Minnitt (née Galloway) was born in April 1879 in Bengal, the daughter of John and Mary Galloway. In June 1909 she married John Anson Minnitt in Bangalore. John, from Derbyshire, ran an engineering business in Bombay and Joyce did what many expectant mothers chose, returning to England to have her second baby. Her daughter Christine was born in March 1915 at Chapel-en-le-Frith, Derbyshire, where she also visited her mother[56]. She was returning to her family in Bombay with Christine and boarded the SS *Persia* in Marseilles.

Arthur Freer Spreckley was one of four sons of Herbert W Spreckley and his wife Florence Lesingham Spreckley. The Britannia Brewery at Barbourne, built in 1850, was the first major brewery in Worcester, taken over by Spreckley Brothers Ltd, who were brewers as well as wine merchants. Arthur became a lieutenant in the Royal Gurkhas and then a captain in the Indian Army. He married Ada Blanche Selina McMinn in Bengal in September 1912 and they had a daughter, Pamela, in 1914 and a son in 1915, both born in India. The family came to England and were due to return to India in November 1915, but their infant son David, too ill to travel, stayed behind when the family sailed[57].

Mary Fernandez had apparently travelled to Britain as a Mrs Bird's ayah but Mrs Bird's identity remains a mystery. A good ayah was a highly regarded asset by any family with children in India, having '*this capacity to completely identify with the children they looked after and it seemed as if they could switch on love in an extraordinary way*'[58]. Many children spent their earliest years in India before returning to Britain to boarding schools for the remainder of their childhood. Ayahs often accompanied children on voyages from India to Britain, when arriving in Britain would often be a sad parting for both child and ayah after four or five years together. Mary had had to wait patiently for a return voyage to her home in India and until *Persia*'s departure had lived in Ayah's House, Hackney, a temporary home for those who had arrived in England with no return voyage engagement. After what might have been several lonely months in Hackney, she was finally able to travel home, although there is no record of any hiring or of who paid for her return trip. Without a child to care for and fill her time, she may have embarked on a lonely voyage.

---

56   Information narrated by Kit Wright, grandson of Mrs Galloway
57   http://www.flintshirewarmemorials.com/memorials/hawarden-memorial/hawarden-sodliers-2/guy-lesingham-spreckley/
58   Allen, Charles (Ed) (1975). *Plain Tales from the Raj*, p 9. Century Publishing Co

Kathleen Hudson was the daughter of Reginald Hudson and his wife Ellen, of Stratford-upon-Avon. Her father ran the family firm of Birmingham printers, Hudson and Son. Kathleen married Charles Felix Stoehr in 1914. Charles, educated at Repton and the Royal Military Academy, Woolwich, gained a commission in the Corps of Royal Engineers and served in India in the Military Works Services, followed by the 3rd Bombay Sappers and Miners. The couple returned from their honeymoon in Norway when war broke out and travelled together to his post in Aden. She then returned to England in the summer of 1915 and spent some of her time raising funds at sales-of-work to help prisoners of war. At the end of her stay, Kathleen joined SS *Persia* on her way to a reunion in Aden.

Dr Lilian Cook was born in Inverness in 1887, the daughter of timber merchant Robert Cook and his wife Mary. She graduated from Edinburgh University as a doctor in 1911 and became a medical missionary in India for the United Free Church. She was returning to India to marry the Reverend John Warnshuis of the American Missionary Society in Bombay and to continue her work.

Mlle Marie Renée Rosalie Derogez, 29, had ignored the U-boat threat to follow her heart. She was travelling from Paris to Bombay on her way to her wedding in Calcutta. Her fiancé, William Augustus Bonnaud, was a 30-year-old barrister and Clerk of the Crown, Calcutta High Court.

Gladys Enid MacDonald was the daughter of James Middleton MacDonald, an Australian chaplain at Oxford University. Her brother Donald, a Royal Navy lieutenant, died on 15th October 1914 when U-9 (Otto Weddigen) sank HMS *Hawke*, a 23-year-old veteran ship used mainly for training, with the loss of 524 men. Enid left her home in Kensington and joined the SS *Persia* on her way to India to marry fiancé Rowland Hatt-Cook who worked for the Public Works Department of the Indian Civil Service. They planned to marry in Bombay in January 1916[59].

As *Persia* left Marseilles, there were three brides-to-be and a recent bride aboard. Elsewhere there would have been three bridegrooms-to-be and a recent husband, all waiting happily but anxiously.

There was also a sad prospective bridegroom on the ship, Robert Ney McNeely, born in 1883 on a farm in Jackson Township, North Carolina. He worked as a teacher from 1900 to 1902 and as a mail carrier for the next two years. The bar at Monroe, North Carolina, admitted him and he served as Monroe's City Clerk in 1907 and its Treasurer in 1908. He received his

---

59   https://greatwarlondon.wordpress.com/2015/12/30/the-loss-of-the-persia/

Bachelor of Laws degree from the University of North Carolina in May 1910 and in 1914 gained election to the North Carolina State Senate. Early in 1915, McNeely passed the competitive examination for appointment to the Consular Service and became engaged to Wilma Whitacre of West Union, Iowa. The year was full of promise. Wilma was a singer who he had met when she performed in North Carolina. Her university described her as:

> 'First contralto of the Beulah Buck Quartet, a graduate of the Iowa State University, also Northwestern University, her voice is of the purest quality with a two-octave range. Blessed with good looks and a gracious cultured manner, she wins her audience the minute she steps upon the platform.'[60]

With his professional and personal life full of optimism and happiness, Robert and Wilma planned to marry in May 1916 and Robert had started to build a bungalow for them in Monroe. In October 1915 he unexpectedly received the offer of the post of American Consul in Aden. He telegraphed Wilma asking her to marry him immediately so that they could travel to Aden as husband and wife. Wilma agreed happily, but her parents did not. They persuaded her to wait and marry Robert in 1916. Robert sailed alone from New York to Liverpool on 27th November aboard the Holland America Line's SS *Rinjdam*, then waited in London for an onward voyage to Aden. Someone apparently suggested that he should not make the voyage on a British ship, but by then he had booked with P&O on the SS *Persia*.

Dundee was home to many of the world's jute mills. Ships sailed regularly between that port and ports of western Bengal, primarily Calcutta. Dundee mills had previously worked with flax, but after they updated their machinery to process jute, over half of Dundee's working population worked in that trade. Many Dundee men and their families lived and worked in the trade in India and eventually transferred manufacture to mills on the Hooghly (Ganga) River, making one billion empty sandbags for trenches on the Western Front. P&O regularly carried jute engineers, managers and their families to and from their work.

Thomas Burns was born in 1866 in Aberdeen, the second son of a very poor family. His family moved to Dundee and at the age of 15, after his father died, he worked in a mill to support his family. His mother Rachel was a washerwoman. Thomas learned quickly and, despite his humble

---

60 University of Iowa Libraries: http://digital.Lib.Uiowa.Edu/cdm/compoundobject/collection/tc/id/15774/rec/7

beginnings, was a mechanical engineer by 1895 and a machine fitter the following year. His wife-to-be, Cecilia, was born in Perth in 1866, the fifth of nine children. Her family also moved to Dundee where she became a weaver in a jute factory. In July 1895 she married Thomas and they had two sons. Thomas went to India in the jute trade and she followed. The gamble paid off and they became prosperous. They left their children behind in Dundee, first in the care of their maternal grandmother and later that of Cecilia's sister Violet Clark, wife of Alexander Clark. Alexander also went to India and by 1899 had become the manager of a jute mill.

Thomas retired from India just before World War 1, a moderately wealthy man with a large house in a select part of Dundee. When war broke out, many young Indian men left the jute industry in India to join the army. Thomas agreed to come out of retirement and return to India to oversee jute production. Thomas and Cecilia booked on the Bombay Express to join SS *Persia* in Marseilles to avoid sailing through the U-boat dangers in the Western Approaches. They travelled with brother-in-law Alexander Clark, heading to his jute mill in Calcutta. He had intended to travel to India on an earlier ship, but his daughter, aged three, fell ill with meningitis and died just before he was due to leave. He cancelled that voyage to bury his child and stay with his family for a while longer. Then he had to return and booked aboard the SS *Persia* with Thomas and Cecilia.

Frank Morris Coleman from Beckenham was a proprietor of the *Times of India* from 1892 when he and Thomas Bennett acquired the newspaper. Frank was a regular traveller to Bombay and since 1901 had held a commission with the British government to reduce expenditure on printing. Although he retired in 1905, he still made business trips to India and on this voyage, his sixteen-year-old son, Arthur, a pupil of Charterhouse, accompanied him to spend his Christmas holidays in India with his father.

George Hoggan, the son of Mr and Mrs H E Hoggan of Rockdale, New South Wales, was well known in commercial circles in Australia and New Zealand, and for many years worked on the staff of Messrs Scott Henderson & Company of Sydney. He resigned in June 1915 to go into business on his own and left Sydney in July on a business tour through Canada, America, England and the Continent. He joined the SS *Persia* at Marseilles to sail to Port Said where he planned to board the SS *Medina* six days later to continue to Sydney.

Signor Benvenuto Mafessanti was travelling on SS *Persia* from Marseilles to Bombay and then on to Mysore, as a contractor for J Taylor & Son, Queen Street Place, London, a company described as 'the very life and soul of the goldfields'[61]. The company sounded prosperous, but Signor Mafessanti had to make this journey in *Persia*'s second class.

Orr families had lived around Lochwinnoch, Renfrewshire, for over 700 years[62]. William Orr Orr*, fourteenth in a line of William Orrs, was born into farming at The Kaim, Lochwinnoch, where his family had farmed since around 1570. William senior had died in 1868 and William junior, his only son, inherited and expanded into business ventures that went far beyond farming. He became a partner in Abbott Engineering of Paisley, an early motor car parts manufacturer, and was also an agent for Bulloch Bros, a large import firm trading extensively in rice from the Far East, particularly Burma. William sailed on SS *Persia* in late December 1915 on his way to India on rice-import business along with his nephew, James Bulloch Dickie[63].

Arthur Russell Smijth-Windham*, 41, was a railway and civil engineer working for the Sudan Civil Service and returning to his post at Atbara in north-east Sudan. He was employed on railway construction, became a divisional engineer stationed at Atbara and gained The Order of the Medjidie, awarded for distinguished services to the Ottoman Empire. Following a period of sick leave in England, he had planned to sail from Marseilles on 19th December but had been unable to get a military permit for Port Said in time, so had to join the SS *Persia* on Christmas Day. His wife of 14 years, Brenda, son William and daughter, Diana[64], remained at the family home in Rogate, Hampshire.

Robert Vane Russell, 42, won the modern languages prize while a pupil at Winchester College before going up to Trinity College, Cambridge, and then joining the Indian Civil Service in 1893. He served in the Central Provinces as an assistant commissioner and then as Superintendent of Census Operations, overseeing the 1901 Census of India. He became Superintendent of Ethnography in 1902. In 1914 he went on sick leave to England where he worked on *The Tribes and Castes of the Central Provinces*[65], a 2,500-page, four-volume work, readying it for publication by MacMillan and Company in 1916, after which he joined SS *Persia* to return to India.

---

*   This unusual-looking name is correct

61 Playne, Somerset and Bond, J W. Wright, Arnold (Ed) (1914–15). *Southern India, its history, people, commerce and industrial resources.* p 351. London: The Foreign and Colonial Compiling & Publishing Co
62 http://www.lochwinnoch.Info/history/local-people/the-last-william-orr-of-kaim
63 Reproduced by kind permission of David Williams, Ottawa, Ontario, Canada
64 http://www.thepeerage.com/p5387.htm#i53863
65 Russell, Robert Vane, assisted by Lal, Rai Bahadur Hira (1916). *Tribes and Castes of the Central Provinces of India.* London: Macmillan & Co

Mr Gustadji Muncherji Cooper had travelled to London after appearing as a defendant in the legal case in Bombay in 1915 of Haji Umar Abdul Rahiman, a furniture dealer and money lender, versus Gustadji Muncherji Cooper, a bookmaker on the turf and owner of a fibre factory. This had gone to appeal at the Privy Council in London and he was returning home after Justice Viscount Haldane had found for Mr Rahiman and ruled that Mr Cooper should pay the costs of this appeal and of a previous High Court hearing[66].

Although there seem to be many accounts of military personnel among the passengers, there were only 35 of them among the 184 passengers aboard, too few for an infantry platoon. *Persia* was no troopship. More information about soldiers was available simply because the military made and kept detailed records, while civilian records varied between those few who kept detailed diaries and wrote long letters and the majority who wrote little of their daily lives. Many of these soldiers had become detached from their units after injuries sustained in battles and were rejoining them after hospitalisation and convalescence. One or two knew each other but they were from a wide range of units of the British and Indian Armies.

Edward Waters Harbin Marsh was born in 1880, the son of a Yeovil solicitor. As a young man, he enlisted in the army and by the turn of the century was a lieutenant in the Mounted Infantry of the 60th Rifles (the King's Royal Rifle Corps). After serving in the second Boer War he transferred to the South Lancashire Regiment and went to India before joining the 13th Rajputs Regiment, later known as The Shekhawati Regiment, deployed to defend the North-West Frontier. Edward was on home leave when Britain declared war and received orders to return to his regiment in India. The regiment then countermanded the order and sent him to an attachment to the 6th (Service) Battalion, South Lancashire Regiment, as Adjutant. In May 1915 he had a brief posting on the Western Front with other Indian Army officers to replace losses from the Indian contingent, before rejoining his regiment. As part of 13th Division, he landed at Cape Helles (Gallipoli) in August 1915 to take part in the Suvla Bay Expedition and sustained serious wounds. After recovering in England, Edward, by then Captain Marsh, again received orders to rejoin his unit in India, sailing to Bombay on SS *Persia*[67].

Born in 1895, John Lionel (Lion) Miller-Hallett attended Rugby School and the Royal Military College, Sandhurst. He was commission as second

---

66 Casemine: https://www.casemine.com/judgement/in/56b49612607dba348f016739
67 Bob Osborn of Yeovil's History website: http://www.yeovilhistory.info/

lieutenant in the Indian Army in August 1914, attached to the 7th Battalion of The Royal Fusiliers in Finsbury. In February 1915, he served with the 3rd Battalion The Royal Fusiliers in Belgium and France where he suffered a wound in May 1915 during the Second Battle of Ypres[68], and again in August at Messines Ridge, this time more seriously with a bullet through his abdomen. After more treatment and recovery, he received orders to join the 1st Battalion, 2nd King Edward's Own Gurkha Rifles (The Sirmoor Rifles) in Dehra Dun, Uttarakhand, in the foothills of the Himalayas.

Robert Dunham Tibbs, born in 1893, was the son of Frederick and Georgiana Tibbs of Chigwell, Essex. The family came from London and had long been international merchants. Robert was the third of four brothers and had two sisters. All the boys attended Bancroft's School, Woodford Wells. Robert remained at Bancroft's until 1911 when, following his brother William, he joined Thomas Cook in Bombay. On the outbreak of war, he applied for a commission in the Indian Army. He trained with the Somerset Light Infantry and served with the 97th Deccan Infantry in India before returning to Britain and being attached to the 39th Gauhati Rifles on the Western Front. He became Battalion Machine Gun Officer before wounds saw him sent to Britain for treatment. In late summer 1915, he had recovered sufficiently to rejoin his regiment[69] and boarded the SS *Persia*.

John Alexander Tower Robertson (Jack), born 1886, was the only son of Alexander Tower Robertson, JP, and Ada Jane Robertson of Tweedmouth House, Berwick-on-Tweed. He had worked in his father's business at Tweedmouth Foundry before travelling to Calcutta in 1907, where he became a solicitor in his uncle's practice. He obtained a commission in the Indian Army Reserve of Officers in 1915 and served with the 3rd Queen Alexandra's Own Gurkha Rifles in France before being invalided home to Berwick. He was returning to India in preparation for redeployment on operations in Mesopotamia[70].

John Thornton Lodwick, was born in Sutton, Surrey, in 1882, son of Robert William Lodwick, formerly of the Indian Civil Service, and Florence, his wife. John served through the Boer War as a subaltern in the Royal Lancaster Regiment and received the King's and Queen's Medals. He accompanied his regiment to Calcutta, where he became a military

---

68 Information from Regimental Records, Sirmoor Rifles by letter from C N Fraser, Lt Col (retd) to Richard Lander, Grandson of J L Miller-Hallett
69 Information provided by kind permission of Old Bancroftians Association from Bancroft's School Woodford
70 http://www.newmp.org.uk/article.php?categoryid=99&articleid=1476&displayorder=49

instructor at Palhmalie, Central Provinces, for the 3rd Gurkhas. Later, he held the same position at Istaria, where his grandfather, General Lodwick, had formerly served as British Resident at the Rajah's Court. When the European War broke out, the Gurkhas formed part of the Indian Force. Captain Lodwick went to Europe as Brigade Machine Gun Officer, in which capacity he served at the Battle of Neuve Chapelle. He received the award of Companion of the Distinguished Service Order[71] for conspicuous ability and gallantry in that battle[72]. Captain Lodwick was married at Cheltenham Roman Catholic Church in 1915, to Kathleen, third daughter of the Hon H Crump, CSI. He had applied for permission to rejoin his regiment and was travelling to India for that purpose.

Alfred Ralph Nethersole was born in Deal, Kent, in 1867 where his father John was a farmer and wine merchant according to the 1871 census. Like his father, Alfred attended Cambridge University without an attachment to any college. The Royal Scots Fusiliers commissioned him as a second lieutenant in 1888, then he joined the Indian Army later that year as a lieutenant in the Indian Staff Corps. He progressed to captain in 1899, was adjutant in the Indian Volunteers, 1895–1900, a recruiting staff-officer for India in 1902–5 and a major in 1906, having made his career in the Indian Army. He was travelling to India to join the 83rd Wallajahbad Light Infantry.

Charles Myles O'Reilly, aged 46, received his commission in 1890 and reached the rank of major in 1908. He served in the Tirah Expedition on the Indian Frontier War of 1897–8 and in China in 1900. He was travelling to India with his wife Sybil to rejoin his regiment, the 63rd Palamcottah Light Infantry.

Edward (Ted) Rolleston Palmer Berryman was born in Hartley Wintney, Hampshire, in July 1883, the third son and one of thirteen children of the Reverend Charles and Gertrude (née Palmer) Berryman. He won a scholarship to King's School, Canterbury, before entering the Royal Military College (now Academy), Sandhurst, as a cadet. Later he gained a commission in the 39th Garhwal Rifles, Indian Army. In November 1913, his sister Benedicta (Ben) visited India to see her brother Dick, a doctor in Assam, next visiting Ted at the Garhwal Rifles depot at Lansdowne. The Berryman family were great letter writers and it was Ben who sent news home that the 39th Garhwal Rifles were being mobilised for active service, writing shortly afterwards that Ted had left Lansdowne in high spirits.

---

71 London Gazette, May 1915
72 http://lib. Militaryarchive.Co.Uk/library/Biographical/library/The-VC-and-DSO-Volume-II/files/assets/basic-html/page390.html

Lieutenant Berryman docked in Marseilles on 12th October 1914 and the 39th Garwhal Rifles were in the trenches on the Western Front by the end of that month. They fought through the winter in weather conditions that caused misery for the Indian soldiers, who were then holding one-third of the British line. Poor logistics meant that they spent the harsh winter of 1914–15 in tropical uniforms, deployed for 20 days at a time in trenches where the water came above their knees. In 1915 they went into action at Neuve Chapelle where two Indian soldiers each won the Victoria Cross. On 9th May, Ted sent a postcard home:

'Just a line to say I have been very slightly wounded by a shell, the calf and wrist, absolutely nothing, but shall be out of hospital in two days.'

A telegram to his mother on 11th May from the Military Secretary, India Office told a somewhat different story:

'Regret to inform you that your son Captain E R P Berryman 39 Garwhal Rifles officially reported admitted No 3 General Hospital Wandsworth Common 10 May suffering from gunshot wound left leg.'

When discharged, he went home on sick leave then served in Gloucester on light duties training Territorials with the 3/5th Gloucesters.

Captain ERP Berryman 39 Garwhal Rifles
Reproduced by kind permission of Benedicta Makin on behalf of the family of Colonel Edward Rolleston Palmer Berryman, DSO

Officers and local families exchanged invitations and in early September Ted met 17-year-old Nell (Pauline) Fielding at one such event. After what must have been a whirlwind romance, they went on a family walk in the beech woods near their house in the autumn sunshine on 29th October 1915 which was also the first anniversary of Ted's arrival in the trenches on the Western Front. Ted and Nell later visited her aunt nearby and on their homeward walk, they decided to become engaged. Her family were surprised because of their fifteen-year age difference, but they liked Ted so did not forbid it but told the couple that it could not be public knowledge for six months. The six-month ruling survived for one week as Ted met Nell every lunchtime from her typing school and took her to lunch at the Gloucester Club. Nell's father John Fielding also ate his lunch at the club and he realised that everyone knew the family 'secret' so bowed to the inevitable.

On Sunday 28th November, Ted wrote to his mother to tell her that another inevitability had arrived. He had reported to the India Office and then received further orders to sail to India on the SS *Persia* to rejoin his regiment. He took the boat train to Marseilles and boarded on Christmas Day. His formal engagement would have to wait, but for how long? Once aboard he would soon be aware that his commandant, Lieutenant Colonel Ernest Swiney of the 1st Battalion, 39th Garhwal Rifles, was also aboard. Swiney had persuaded his senior officers to change strategy during the battle of Neuve Chapelle in order to recapture a portion of the trench using bombs and bayonets in the early hours of 24th November.

William Orford Charles Dawson, MRCVS, qualified as a Member of the Royal College of Veterinary Surgeons from the Royal (Dick) Veterinary College in Edinburgh* in 1894. He was serving as a major in the Indian Civil Veterinary Department and returning to this post. Captain Edward Berryman believed that, having seen Major Dawson on the train to Marseilles wrapped in a large greatcoat, he might be suffering from malaria, symptoms of which can include shaking chills.

Owen Gough, the son of Colonel B Gough attended Haileybury School and the Royal Military College. He served with the East Lancashire Regiment in 1907 and with the 12th Indian Cavalry from 1911 as a lieutenant. He was Mentioned in Despatches and awarded the Military Cross in 1915. Lieutenant Gough had returned home from France just before Christmas, but declined to apply for leave so the army ordered him to join *Persia* for her passage to India.

---

* Incorporated by Act of Parliament in 1906, named in honour of its founder Professor William Dick

Humphrey Richard Locke Lawrence was born in March 1888 in London, son of Major General William Alexander Lawrence and his wife Adelaide. He attended The Grange School in Folkestone and Christ Church College, Oxford, gained a commission as a lieutenant on 9th December 1910 before taking a temporary captaincy in the 34th Sikh Pioneers, gazetted on 30th December 1915. In 1913 he married Mary Claudine Wrey. He took a wound in France in June 1915, just before the Indian Corps left for Mesopotamia following the Battle of Loos in September. He completed treatment and convalescence before setting out to rejoin them by way of Port Said.

Engineer Lieutenant Arthur Twining Roch, RN, was the son of John and Martha Elizabeth Roch, of Brownslade, Castlemartin, Pembrokeshire. He married Catherine Wood in Cairo in 1901 and the couple had two children. Arthur became an engineer in the Royal Navy and served aboard HMS *Proserpine* in Gibraltar and then the Suez Canal. In 1915 he received orders to support the British action in Mesopotamia, but had home leave first and was returning aboard the SS *Persia*.

Horace Hayman Wilson was born in August 1874 in Halifax, Nova Scotia, and served as a captain in the Lancashire Fusiliers and, from 25th June 1912, as a major in the 4th Battalion the King's Own (Royal Lancaster Regiment). He was heading for Egypt where he was to serve as staff officer (second grade) on the HQ Staff as gazetted on Christmas Eve 1915. He was married to Isabel Veronica who remained at home.

Colonel Lord Montagu and Eleanor Thornton

A person of significance to the story then and in its retelling now boarded the SS *Persia* in Marseilles on Christmas Day. He was John Douglas-Scott-Montagu, 2nd Baron Montagu of Beaulieu, on his way back to India to complete a crucial mission for the Viceroy, Lord Hardinge. John Montagu was born on 10th June 1866, the eldest son of Henry, 1st Baron Montagu of Beaulieu, and the Hon Cecily Susan Stuart-Wortley, who became known as Baroness Montagu of Beaulieu.

Young Montagu went to Eton and New College, Oxford, representing both at rowing. He chose an unusual line of work in the sheds of the London and South Western Railway (LSWR) working as a mechanic and learning to drive railway engines as part of what would become a life-long interest in mechanical engineering. In 1889 he married Lady Cecil Kerr, daughter of the 9th Marquis of Lothian, with whom he had three children. He represented the New Forest as its Member of Parliament from 1892 to 1905 when, on the death of his father, he entered the House of Lords. His interest in motor cars, still then in their infancy, led him to campaign in parliament for the passing of the 1903 Motor Car Act, the foundation of British motoring law. Pursuing his interest in motoring, he founded *The Car Illustrated, A Journal of Travel by Land, Sea and Air*. Beneath the banner, it stated 'Edited by the Hon John Scott Montagu, MP'. In addition to motoring and motoring fashions it also included articles about speedboats, flying and railways.

During the time that he edited the magazine, Montagu met Nelly Thornton, fourteen years his junior. Nelly was born in 1880 in Stockwell, the fashionable middle-class suburb for entrepreneurs who desired easy access to their London businesses. Her father was an Australian engineer and her mother was Sarah Rooke from London. Nelly had previously worked as secretary to Claude Johnson, the first secretary of the Automobile Club, later the RAC. Just before Johnson left the club to join Charles Rolls at

C S Rolls and Company, later Rolls-Royce, Nelly joined Montagu as his personal assistant on the magazine. At some stage, she changed her forenames, discarding Nelly to become known as Eleanor Velasco Thornton[73], which probably suited the social circles into which she merged with Lord Montagu. The mutual attraction grew and love blossomed. Eleanor gave birth to a daughter Joan, born on 5th April 1903, who went into foster care nearby, where John could keep a discreet eye on her progress to ensure that she wanted for nothing. While a handful of those closest must have known out of necessity, this situation was not for wider public consumption, particularly as Montagu already had a daughter with his wife, Lady Cecil. Eleanor continued her work with John. At some stage she modelled for sculptor Charles Sykes and may have been the inspiration for Sykes's Spirit of Ecstasy, the graceful bonnet ornament adopted by Rolls-Royce to adorn their cars.

Eleanor Velasco Thornton, private secretary to Colonel Lord Montagu
By kind permission of Ralph, 4th Lord Montagu of Beaulieu

When Britain declared war on Germany in August 1914, huge numbers of soldiers were mobilised and battle fleets readied. For Lord Montagu, by then with thirty years' experience as a militia officer, duty called. Many of London's called-up reservists were Metropolitan Police officers and their rapid departure to the Western Front left the force seriously under strength. The Commissioner, Sir Edward Henry, needed to recruit special constables to fill the gaps. Lord Montagu, known for his exceptional organisational skills and a wide range of influential contacts, had retired from the Territorial Army as a colonel in 1912, so seemed a good choice for such a role. He started work at Scotland Yard on 6th August 1914 as Director of Organisation, Special Constabulary.

---

73 Velasco is a medieval Iberian family name which roughly translates as 'little raven' and may have been a subtle reflection of her mother's surname 'Rook'

The first enrolments occurred within four days and the force quickly recovered its establishment strength of 20,000. Each recruit needed training, basic equipment and one of the legendary armbands to show that they were on police duty. Once ready, they guarded places of strategic importance such as London's power stations, reservoirs and water supplies. Lord Montagu went further by organising help from car and motorcycle owners to speed up the movement of special constables and he also persuaded motor-boat-owning friends to patrol the Thames. Seven weeks later and by then reinforced, the Commissioner hoped and expected that he would stay but the army recalled him to the Hampshire Regiment Reserve Battalion.

Lord Montagu's 7th Battalion, along with the 4th, 5th and 6th Battalions of the Hampshire Territorial Force, were part-time soldiers, primarily intended for home defence although the government felt that the Royal Navy's power made an invasion of the British Isles unlikely. Elsewhere, a military vacuum was developing in India as 290,000 Indian and British soldiers transferred from there to the Western Front and the Empire's lifeline, the Suez Canal.

Hampshire reservists were 'invited to volunteer' for overseas duty and a large majority did so. Each battalion was then subdivided and in September a reserve battalion, the 2/7th came into existence with Lord Montagu in command. He had initial responsibility for guarding England's south coast between Hurst Castle, west of Lymington, to Poole. He deployed his junior officers to recruit across the New Forest and quickly built his battalion from 300 to the full strength of 800 men which meant readiness for deployment.

John Montagu's efforts over the autumn of 1914 left him exhausted and ill, but despite this, he and his 2/7th Battalion, The Hampshire Regiment, boarded the old, overcrowded and slow troopship, HMT *Dunera* in Southampton on

Colonel Lord Montagu, 2/7th Hampshire Territorial Brigade
By kind permission of Ralph, 4th Lord Montagu of Beaulieu

12th December and sailed the next day. On 7th January 1915, the *Dunera* arrived off Bombay, where the troops transferred to the railway system. They then endured a forty-two-hour journey to cover only 197 miles to Secunderabad. After hundreds of men had left families and friends a few days before Christmas, reality quickly dawned when they found their role was to protect the local ruler, the Nizam of Hyderabad, seemingly from his own people. They were to remain there for fourteen months.

Lord Montagu soon discovered his battalion was far from any combat action and although he was proud of his men and his post, his natural tendency and skills were more useful when leading his battalion or implementing significant change and innovation. He welcomed opportunities to go on two expeditions, the first to the Khyber Pass and the second to the Malakand Pass. Moving through these regions, he quickly realised that the Indian Army was acutely short of motor vehicles, including lorries and armoured cars. Carrying supplies on horses and mules to troops guarding the Khyber Pass was a logistical nightmare.

Britain's motoring pioneer realised that troops defending India needed to be mechanised, far beyond their forty assorted armoured cars scattered across the whole subcontinent. On 7th April 1915, Lord Montagu joined the Army general staff as Inspector of Mechanical Transport to the Government of India, an enormous challenge for which he was both well-fitted and highly motivated. During visits to garrisons where armoured cars were based, he found that though they were few, they were of many different types, complicating maintenance, armament, supplies and training. He promptly recommended standardisation, unified training and properly equipped stores and garages, before moving on to look at supplying divisions in the field.

He found that were only a dozen army lorries in the whole of India and that supply convoys typically consisted of over 600 mules and almost 300 handlers. Such a straggling mass, over a mile long, could take a day to cover 10 miles and, on arrival, would deliver one day's supplies to a division. Lord Montagu calculated that 20 lorries with 40 men could transport the same stores over 60 miles in one day. He reported that mechanisation was urgent and vital and confirmed that the vast and primitive road system needed rapid and major improvements to handle motorised traffic across India. He identified the lack of aircraft and airfields and made recommendations to resolve this serious weakness in India's intelligence and defences. The Viceroy of India, Lord Hardinge, a close friend, understood the situation fully and asked Montagu to return to Britain to persuade the government to meet India's needs, despite supplies of motor vehicles and aircraft to the

Western Front having the highest priority. Colonel Lord Montagu oversaw the setting up of India's first AMUs (Armoured Motor Units) using vehicles donated by wealthy Indians and Europeans, including No.1 AMU which had three Rolls-Royce cars armour-plated in an Indian Railway's workshop[74].

Lord Montagu was uniquely qualified for the difficult negotiations that lay ahead. He had served in both the House of Commons and the House of Lords, developed mechanical engineering skills, been a pioneer in the development of motorised transport and a military leader and had a wide range of influential friends and acquaintances. He left India on 22nd July 1915 on a journey to the heart of government in Britain. On arrival, he lobbied quickly for aeroplanes for the North-West Frontier and eventually received an offer of a mix of eight Avros and Royal Aircraft Factory BEs from David Henderson, Head of Military Aeronautics at the War Office, for delivery in the autumn[75]. Armoured cars were in short supply and much in demand in the Middle East, but Montagu organised despatch of some to India. Next, he turned his attention to studying the use of motorised communications on the Western Front and to planning for use of the aircraft in India.

He was what we would now know as a workaholic, often lacking patience with some around him. Unhappily, this sometimes included his wife, Lady Cecil. She also worried about her husband's health and was concerned that he had to return to India when already tired by his strenuous efforts. Lady Cecil also learned that Eleanor Thornton would be travelling part of the way with him.

Eleanor wrote to Lady Cecil before she and John departed, touching on her worries about his compulsive work habits:

> *'He still continues to do too many things, to be in three places at once. He will never rest…'*
>
> *'I have spent my life since schooldays trying to save him in little ways but it doesn't seem that I can do much.'*

She then mentioned the forthcoming voyage to India and though she downplayed the U-boat threat in the Mediterranean, she knew it was real. She wrote:

---

74 Families In British India Society: https://wiki.fibis.org/w/Royal_Tank_Corps
75 Tritton, Paul (1985). *John Montagu of Beaulieu*. p176

'It is awfully kind of you to give your sanction to my going as far as Port Said. I hate to spend the money but you have the satisfaction of knowing that as far as human help can avail, he will be looked after. I do not think for one moment that there will be trouble in the Med. But supposing…well, then the lord will have an extra chance, for there will be my place in the boat for him, even if he has to be stunned to take it.'[76]

Before leaving, Lord Montagu had a chance meeting with his cousin Lord Mark Kerr who advised him to buy a Gieve waistcoat. This looked like a naval officer's waistcoat but contained an elaborate system of tubing and an inflatable bladder to work as a buoyancy aid without the cumbersome appearance of a conventional lifebelt[77]. Lord Montagu took his cousin's advice, buying one for him and one for Eleanor, although it was not the stylish sort of accessory that she would normally choose to wear.

Lord Montagu and Miss Thornton travelled to Folkestone, crossed the Channel to Boulogne and then boarded the Bombay Express to join the SS *Persia* in Marseilles. Eleanor had booked as far as Aden, seemingly to complete the report being prepared for Lord Hardinge. She would then disembark and return home through the dangerous Mediterranean, while John continued to India and the Viceroy.

---

76 Tritton, Paul (1985). *John Montagu of Beaulieu*. p179
77 http://www.thevintageshowroom.com/life-saving-waistcoat/

The Maharaja Enigma

Passengers already aboard and those joining in Marseilles might have been concerned if they had learned that a wealthy Indian ticket holder, a Maharaja, had arrived in Marseilles with his large retinue in order to board SS *Persia* but had then changed his mind. It seems that he claimed to have heard from a secret source that the ship faced the risk of attack. His source remains unclear, but he decided that most of his party would not travel on the ship. His wife, the Maharani, later disputed his version.

Maharaja Sir Jagatjit Singh Bahadur, GCSI[78], ruler of Kapurthala, a princely state in Punjab, had been on a tour of Europe and the United States since the spring of 1915 with his wife the Maharani Prem Kaur. The 43-year-old Maharaja had married five times, his most recent wedding having been at a civil ceremony in Paris in 1907 and in Kapurthala in 1908 to Anita Delgado Briones, from Andalusia, former member of a dance group that performed in small theatrical productions and who was now the Maharani. Their son, Prince Ajit Singh[79] stayed in Paris with his grandparents, Anita's parents, while the Maharaja and Maharani travelled in the United States and Canada. The Maharaja had stopped off to pay a visit to the thousands of Indian troops protecting the Suez Canal on his outward voyage, visited Canada and the United States and met King George V and Queen Mary in London. The King thanked him for his 'ungrudging assistance' with war matters. The Maharaja was particularly at home in France and went to Paris in October, where he also visited Indian soldiers on the Western Front. On his travels, he may have spent a million pounds on gemstones, jewellery, watches and gold bullion to take back to India, with some for his wife.

---

78 Knight Grand Commander of the Order of the Star of India, 1911
79 Correspondence in September 2015 with Elisa Vásquez de Gey, Biographer of Maharani Prem Kaur

The Maharaja arrived in Marseilles to join SS *Persia* on Christmas Day, along with his retinue and over 200 chests. At some point he claimed to have received information from 'a secret source' that the Germans were planning to attack the SS *Persia* and discussed what it was best to do with his friend, adviser and constant companion, Inder Singh. They concluded that the Maharaja, his wife, their son and some of his retinue should not sail on the *Persia* but should board a later ship. Did the SS *Persia* have the bulk of the Maharaja's belongings, jewellery and bullion aboard when she left Marseilles, a treasure that might have been worth the equivalent of £103m a hundred years later[80]? If there was to be an attack against the SS *Persia*, would any passenger choose to preserve his own life while letting fate safeguard such a fortune? To this day this remains one of the great mysteries surrounding the loss of SS *Persia*.

However, a different explanation for their not sailing on the SS *Persia* appeared in a letter written by the Maharaja's wife, Maharani Prem Kaur, on 18th February 1916, to Narciso Díaz de Escobar who, among many distinguished roles, was for a time Civil Governor of Malaga[81]. One line translates as:

> 'we have to give thanks to Providence that we were saved because I had a feeling that I did not want to travel on that ship although we had purchased tickets and (I) took my child with me on a Dutch ship'.

The entourage of the Maharaja which remained aboard SS *Persia* included his principle trusted adviser Inder Singh with servant Mlle Guyot, a maid, B Mangal Singh, B Partab Singh, J N Sahai and Kathleen Read, the Prince's governess. J N Sahai was the first Indian graduate from Queen's University, Belfast, and was training to be a lawyer. He had gone with the Indian Volunteer Ambulance Corps to the Front, but continued his studies and had passed the final bar examination. He then received orders to go to Egypt, so joined the *Persia*. Kathleen Read was the daughter of a Grimsby timber merchant who had worked in Spain since 1899. In the summer of 1915, the British Ambassador in Madrid introduced her to the Maharani who asked her to become a governess for her eight-year-old son. Kathleen had agreed to marry an English businessman based in Chile in 1917, so felt able to join the Maharaja's entourage until then.

---

80 Historical UK inflation rates and calculator: http://inflation.iamkate.com/
81 In author's collection

Did the Maharaja receive international intelligence about a threatened seaborne attack on SS *Persia*, or did the Maharani tell him that for whatever reason, she had no intention of sailing aboard the ship? If the latter, his advisers might have suggested that he should claim the threatened attack to avoid losing face over a domestic issue.

A second mystery concerns the source and method of communication of any information about an intention to attack the SS *Persia*. Who could the information have come from and in what form? Telephones and the telegraph were available but insecure. It was only eleven months since the first transcontinental telephone call on 25th January 1915[82]. Wireless was still largely inaccessible to most and portability was not a typical characteristic. The Royal Navy had a string of naval wireless stations along the British coast and across the Mediterranean and had also come into possession of three codebooks with which they deciphered coded German naval communications[83]. Germany had a powerful wireless transmitter at Norddeich that could reach from the eastern coast of Greenland to the Red Sea. If a ship or U-boat had sent or received any such message within this vast arc, the Royal Navy may have been able to intercept and decode it. What prevented the Maharaja from taking the humanitarian high-ground and sharing his knowledge with more than 500 on the ship including over 200 of his own countrymen in the crew? Perhaps the Maharani had grown anxious about recent U-boat attacks in the Mediterranean and this had prompted her to ask him not to take them aboard. We are unlikely ever to know the whole story.

Unconnected with the Maharaja's departure, three of *Persia*'s crew are on record as having left the ship in Marseilles. They were Able Seamen A White and A Scrivener and General Servant and Writer F J Clark. It became clear afterwards that Scrivener stayed aboard and Clark may have done so also – all part of the ongoing confusion about the precise numbers on the ship. She probably carried 199 passengers when departing for Valletta, Malta, 635 miles and just over one-and-a-half days away. The voyage should have been through relatively safe waters as France had 14 battleships, 6 armoured cruisers, destroyers and submarines in Valletta and, in May 1915, had moved ships to Brindisi on the Italian Adriatic coast and to Corfu[84]. The Royal

---

82   *New York Times*, 26th January 1915
83   Wyllie, James and McKinley, Michael (2015). *The Codebreakers*. p 9 and p 19. London: Ebury Press. ISBN 978-0-09-195772-8
84   Smith, Gordon. World War 1 at Sea: French Navy. https://www.naval-history.net/WW1NavyFrench.htm

Navy also operated out of both Gibraltar and Alexandria, but although they possessed many vessels and considerable firepower, neither navy seemed to have much appetite for exposing ships to ambush by submerged enemies. When the ship arrived in Valletta, twenty-two passengers disembarked including five of the Negus family who had joined in Tilbury. SS *Persia* then boarded a further seven diverse passengers, making the final count one hundred and eighty-four.

Lieutenant Colonel Henry Backhouse[85], 7th Battalion, Cheshire Regiment, was born in 1873 in Wardleworth near Rochdale, son of a 'cardboard, pasteboard and blanket manufacturer'. He attended Macclesfield Grammar School before joining his father's 'paper staining' business. In August 1914, he was mobilised with the Territorials and trained with the 1/7th Cheshires in various locations. Whilst at Baldock in April 1915, he succeeded Colonel E W Greg on his retirement from command and took the battalion to Gallipoli in July. He assumed temporary command of the 159th Infantry Brigade on 14th August after the wounding of Brigadier General Cowans. In November 1915, he was suffering from disabling sciatica and rheumatism and the Brigade evacuated him from Gallipoli to hospital in Malta. He left hospital on 12th December for a rest camp but, with no army transport available, boarded *Persia* on 28th December at Valletta to rejoin his regiment, now in Egypt.

Also leaving Malta were Charles Bigham, son of Viscount Mersey, Military Attaché to Egypt; Vishindas Gepaldas of the business of Dhanumai Chelleram, Jewellers of Bombay, and Joseph Jacamo, a Malta resident. Lieutenant Colonel Edward Stuart St Aubyn, the second son of John St Aubyn, 1st Baron St Levan of St Michael's Mount, also boarded the SS *Persia*. He was at one time Chief of Staff in the General Staff Branch, responsible for training, intelligence, planning operations and directing battles and had been invested as a Knight of Grace in the Order of St John of Jerusalem; a royal order of chivalry first constituted in 1888[86]. On this voyage, he was serving George V in the role of King's Messenger, hand-carrying secret and important documents to British Embassies, High Commissions and Consulates wherever needed, a personal service reputedly first used by

---

85 http://macclesfieldreflects.org.uk/1915/12/30/backhouse-henry-td/. Information supplied by Macclesfield Reflects, the Macclesfield Great War Commemoration Group

86 Mosley, Charles (Ed) (2003). *Burke's Peerage, Baronetage & Knightage*, 107th edition, 3 volumes. Stokesley: Burke's Peerage & Gentry. http://thepeerage.com/p47943.htm#i479422 http://www.unofficialroyalty.com/december-1915-royalty-and-world-war-i/

Richard III in 1495[87]. Mr Neramal Parmanand and Mr S Dolumal also boarded. Unknowingly, these seven people had become *Persia*'s last ever passengers to board while twenty-two had been the last to disembark peacefully.

Comparing lists of those boarding and leaving suggests that there were 184 passengers aboard when *Persia* slipped out of Malta into the Mediterranean night. Many of them must have feared the danger they still might face, while some preferred not to think about it and others would never have allowed it to prevent them from doing what they had to do. However, even if German or Austrian U-boats prowled somewhere between Valletta and Port Said, *Persia* would still be unfortunate to meet one at close quarters in the short winter daylight.

Aboard by Chance

Spare a thought for some people who never intended to join the SS *Persia* until circumstances conspired otherwise. These included Alexander Clark who had stayed at home when he lost his daughter to meningitis; the Reverend Homer Russell who planned to take a Dutch ship but changed his mind; Arthur Russell Smijth-Windham unable to get an earlier travel permit; Lieutenant Colonel Henry Backhouse who could not find a berth on a troopship; Mary Fernandez who had waited months for a voyage without luck; Robert Ney McNeely, the newly appointed United States Consul to Aden who had been warned against travel on a British ship but only after he had booked passage aboard the SS *Persia*; George Walton, second chef, who had been going home for Christmas until he learned that a colleague's wife was expecting a baby imminently and had volunteered to replace him on *Persia*'s departure from London.

---

87 https://history. blog. gov. uk/2014/03/25/the-silver-greyhound-the-messenger-service/

Last Days, Hours and Minutes

Chief Officer Gerald Clark would write later:

(SS Persia) *'Left Malta on Tuesday 10 pm, 27th (sic) December, bound for Bombay, taking the course from that Port suggested by the Naval Authorities.'*[88]

It is important to note that in December 1915 the last Tuesday was the 28th, not the 27th. Postcards and letters written aboard *Persia* before she sailed show postmarks dated 28th and the Hon Charles Bingham wrote in his autobiography that *'on the night of 28th December I went on board the SS Persia.'*[89] The SS *Persia* made what would be her last-ever departure, less than half-full of passengers, but well-loaded with mail and a modest amount of mixed cargo, none of which had any military significance.

The SS *Persia* had received naval 'suggestions' that included route guidance and orders to 'destroy confidential papers if stopped by an enemy ship'. However, the decision to depart Valletta at 10. 00 pm on the 28th was Captain Hall's, so that *Persia* could pass through the narrower parts of the Mediterranean in darkness. U-boats could spot ships' smoke out to the horizon in daylight, while 14 hours of winter darkness enabled faster ships to exceed 200 nautical miles under its safer cover. Yet beyond the potentially dangerous narrows, U-boats might also lurk where routes converged and diverged around Port Said and Alexandria – they might be anywhere and the risk was clear. On 24th December at 10.10 am, U-34 had torpedoed the French liner *Ville de la Ciotat* without warning[90] 150 miles south-west

---

88   Inclusion with letter from W Taylor, Secretary, Peninsular & Oriental Steam Navigation Company to the Director of Naval Intelligence dated 20th January 1916.
89   Mersey, Charles Clive Bigham, Viscount (1941). *A Picture of Life 1872-1940*. London: John Murray
90   U-34, Kapitänleutnant Claus Rücker

of Cape Matapan, the central of the three finger-like promontories at the southern tip of Greece, not far north of the direct route between Valletta and Port Said. The human cost was eighty-one lives. The daily political journal *Le Petit Marseillais* cabled this news to London from Valletta on 27th December so the Royal Navy and Marine Nationale in the port must have known, as must the officers aboard the SS *Persia*[91]. The safety of the Suez Canal lay about 935 direct nautical miles away[92] (1,076 miles, 1,732 km), about 2 days and 14 hours at 15 knots[93] with an arrival in the canal's convoy assembly zone off Port Said about breakfast time on New Year's Day. This estimate would not allow for any precautionary anti-submarine zigzags or wider detours.

On their first day at sea after leaving Valletta, Captain Hall ordered a lifeboat drill. Some passengers regarded it as a harmless diversion that added the spice of adventure to a quiet day[94]. The 10.30 am drill demonstrated the ship's emergency whistle signal of five blasts that would instruct all passengers and crew to go immediately to their appointed lifeboat stations wearing lifebelts. Deck officers instructed them that, if needed, they must follow the drill as practised, assembling promptly on the promenade deck, also known as the hurricane deck. Crewmen would lower lifeboats from the boat deck to that deck, where everyone would be able to step straight into them. After the drill, the crew left the boats swung out from the davits ready for quick use. Engine-room orders were that in the event of a mine or torpedo strike they must stop engines immediately to enable the lowering of loaded lifeboats[95]. Safe evacuation needed *Persia* to stop and avoid dragging her boats alongside at dangerous speed.

Colonel Lord Montagu was one of those who understood the U-boat risk fully and sometime after leaving Valletta expressed it in conversation with his friend Colonel the Honourable Edward Stuart St Aubyn, travelling as a King's Messenger, who responded:

'John, you seem depressed'.

Montagu replied:

'I am afraid I shall be until we get to Port Said,' words which would turn out to be far-sighted.

---

91 *Le Petit Marseillais*, 1st January 1916
92 The P&O Pocketbook Table of Distances, p 25
93 http://www.sea-distances.org/
94 Hurd, Archibald (1924). *History Of The Great War, The merchant marine Vol. II*. Chapter VIII: The Sinking of The '*Persia*'. London, John Murray
95 Hurd, Archibald (1924). *History Of The Great War, The merchant marine Vol. II*. Chapter VIII: Summer 1915 to early 1917 (Part 1 of 2). London, John Murray

Away to the east, it seems likely that after sinking the *Yasaka Maru*, U-38 called into Beirut for supplies and meandered north to Turkey, possibly the port of Iskenderun. A photograph in Valentiner's book about his service in U-38 shows her flying a Turkish flag close to rocky cliffs, with goat carcasses suspended on a rope and captioned *'The Captain's Birthday'*. His birthday had been on 15th December, in or around Bardiyah, so perhaps he had merged this birthday with a Christmas break for his men in friendly Turkish waters. Later, U-38 skirted the Turkish coast north of Cyprus and sailed west-south-west past the south of Crete.

As the last Wednesday of 1915 ticked over into Thursday 30th, U-38's log[96] recorded the local weather conditions:

'30th December 1915, Eastern Mediterranean south of Crete, wind westerly (force) 3, clear skies, waves west 4.'

Wind force 3 is a gentle breeze creating wavelets beginning to break; sea state 4 is a moderate sea with average wave length, and fairly frequent white wave crests unlikely to have troubled U-38 but which would hamper sea-level visibility for daytime lookouts aboard surface ships looking for periscopes. The next entry was routine:

'0h 30 (Half-past midnight) Surfaced, charged battery'.

Regular and frequent battery charging aboard submarines was essential. Batteries fed electric motors to power the submarine and all its systems whenever submerged. This procedure required a submarine to be on the surface and clear of any potential dangers when diesel motors propelled her while generating and storing the required electricity. This sometimes continued through the night and into the following morning if the horizons were clear.

Submariners cherished time on the surface to get out onto the deck and breathe fresh air, a brief escape from the foul and wet conditions inside. Condensation was the bane of their lives. It dripped on them as they slept and continuously wet their clothes, towels and bedding. Odours from upward of 30 unwashed men in cramped conditions and with primitive toilets made their rush into fresh air understandable. It seems odd that the first thing many submariners did when first on deck was to light a cigarette or a pipe, both strictly forbidden below deck. Lookouts manned the tower, essential in darkness to avoid any accidental collision and in daylight to

---

96   From the archive of The Maritime Museum, Buckler's Hard

spot and react to threats and opportunities, ordinarily faraway smudges of smoke: friend or foe? When this happened, submarines tended to dive and rely on periscopes to monitor events on the surface, but there was a catch once the range shortened. If submarines were moving, their periscopes could leave noticeable wakes, known as 'feathers', clearly visible in calm water. However, as sunrise approached, restless waters would mask feathers, favouring submerged hunters rather than surface prey.

At about 7.30 am on 30th December, the SS *Persia* emerged from the protection of night and into the possible dangers heralded by sunrise. Extra lookouts took up their posts, binoculars ready, aware that straining constantly to spot a periscope in the surrounds of restless water would be arduous and knowing that a tired blink might be fatal. Her route appears to have passed about 70 miles south of Crete, perhaps 140 nautical miles (160 miles, 257 km) north of a direct route[97]. On this day, the twelfth of her so far uneventful voyage, she passed into that part of the Mediterranean known as the Levantine Sea, close to the Pliny Trench, almost two-and-a-half miles deep. Her public saloons remained cheerfully decorated with trees, streamers, bunting and patriotic flags. Staff in the Purser's Department continued to organise games, charades and parties to keep passengers entertained as they continued to work behind the scenes to prepare New Year celebrations.

After breakfast, many passengers enjoyed the air and stretched their legs. The British credo in India, where most were heading, was to keep fit and avoid catching *'some dreadful disease or other'*[98]. As the day warmed, some played deck cricket behind nets, a little light practice on their way to India where men of all ages played in their leisure hours. Others sauntered gently under the shade of upper decks or awnings, chatting or simply thinking as the sea slid by. Gerald Fisher played quoits with a young woman and a 'Canadian gentleman'. Lord Montagu had chatted with one of the gunners, Lawrence Wellington, on the poop by the ship's gun. Some of the men probably engaged in 'spot the U-boat' wagers and challenges and no doubt those who could afford binoculars would be happy to share their lack of success with others who made polite or anxious enquiries. Those minded to recline took to the deckchairs, some with rugs over their laps, writing letters or diaries, people-watching, reading quietly, telling stories to a child, snoozing, or simply sheltering from draughts and air currents confused by the ship's easterly progress in a westerly breeze. Given the small number of passengers aboard, there was copious space. The newly married Grants

---

97   Calculations show the direct route as 935 miles and the great circle as 934 miles.
98   Allen, Charles (Ed) (1975). *Plain Tales from the Raj*, p 107. Century Publishing Co

were returning to their missionary work and spent the morning talking with new missionary Agnes Lees and arranging to have lunch with Dr Lilian Cook, a medical missionary with the United Free Church. Dr Cook and Dr Grant may not have met previously but they had both earned their medical qualifications at Edinburgh University and become pioneers for women in the medical profession. The Reverend Grant may have become more widely known among some of the passengers after officiating at a service in the saloon on Boxing Day when the congregation had sung *Eternal Father Strong to Save* – for those in peril on the sea. Smoke from *Persia*'s funnels heralded her progress, but her peril was invisible. Aboard U-38 at 11.50 am according to U-38's clock, the following translated entry appears in her log:

> *'Cruiser with course for Alexandria in sight. Dived, cleared 2nd tube for bow attack. Set depth to 3m. I can see Cruiser with two masts and two funnels of around 9,000 t (tons) that I assume to be a troop transporter. I assume his speed is 13 sm (seemeilen/knots). The cruiser has a 7cm gun at the rear of the ship.'*

Valentiner had lingered here in the hope of ambush opportunities while Hall had hoped to avoid this risk by following his admiralty advised route. Partly by planning and partly by mischance SS *Persia* was now in deadly danger, like an insect near a spider's web.

This long-range assumption seems to have provided Valentiner with justification to sink the approaching ship rather than to make a time-consuming and potentially risky rise to the surface to stop her and make a search. He was now committed to attacking a peaceful passenger liner without warning, ignoring international law, his own government's orders and the *Arabic* Pledge. If *Persia* had been a troopship, she would have been a legitimate war target, but the timing of entries in U-38's log shows that Valentiner seems to have decided she was to be sunk before he could have identified her properly. Could he really have seen past her out-swung lifeboats to identify a gun on her poop from so far off? His assumption was dubious at best. As she approached, he would not have seen hundreds of soldiers jammed over every possible space on deck. The smell of copious horse dung, unwashed human bodies, crude and overcrowded toilets drove most to stay day and night in the fresh air above decks, competing for space also needed for training and physical exercise. It seems unlikely that any U-boat commander could mistake a troopship for a lightly loaded passenger ship. Less than two months earlier, Max Valentiner had attacked a genuine troopship, the French vessel SS *Calvados*. He could not have forgotten the 740 killed or how tightly packed they were on deck.

Tiffin Torpedo

Right on cue, Head Saloon Waiter William Dowling sounded the gong for lunch, 'tiffin' as it was known by regulars on the Empire Run. He ushered his guests to their tables where waiters stood ready. Children had already eaten their routine earlier meal after which nurses, maids or ayahs took them to their cabins for a mid-day nap or story. Adults were able to relax knowing that they could enjoy their meal undisturbed. Passengers continued to filter in beneath the decorations and sat to view the menu. In this First Saloon, on the main deck forward of the leading funnel, a lady asked Head Saloon Waiter Dowling,

"Cannot we have some ports open, head waiter?" These larger ports were normally kept closed when weather or war zones dictated, but no other form of ventilation or fans would be available until they sailed into warmer regions south of the canal.

"Without instructions I dare not open any ports," he replied.

"Can you get permission?" she persisted and others joined in to support the request. William Dowling passed on the request to the steward in charge, who in turn passed it up to the bridge. Somewhat to their surprise, permission was granted and the saloon staff opened the ports as requested, directly over the sea, not far above the waterline. There were fifteen ports on each side of the saloon but no record remains of how many they opened on one or both sides.

The Second Saloon on the spar deck aft lay directly beneath the poop and *Persia*'s defensive gun. Agnes Lees described the atmosphere there as happy, with Port Said only twenty hours or so away. She ordered soup followed by Cornish pie. Her colleague and mentor, Adelaide Bull, who had been slightly delayed, arrived and ordered soup. Whoever allocated passengers to their tables may have had a mischievous sense of humour, seating two

William Dowling, head saloon waiter
By kind permission of Richard Dowling

missionaries with two of the ship's gunners, who had to eat close to their gun station on the poop above. One quipped to Agnes that he had sailed the same waters for nine months and had never seen a U-boat. He added that there were always three men on duty by the gun and plenty of lookouts during daylight hours, just in case.

Second Officer Harold Wood had taken the watch on *Persia*'s bridge at noon, where he found that Captain Hall had remained in charge of navigation and was close-by on the lower bridge[99]. There was a lookout high in the crow's nest, one watching ahead from the forecastle and two seamen on the lower bridge each looking out to his side, plus another seaman at the wheel on the bridge. Aft, the gun crew consisted of two seamen and a marine gunner. All were on alert for any signs of periscopes, but the breeze continued to ruffle the sea, a serious hindrance. They struggled to maintain concentration; watering eyes straining for any glimpse of U-boat presence. Their challenge was akin to spotting a needle in a haystack but with the needle and the haystack both stirring, right out to the horizon. Kapitänleutnant Max Valentiner, somewhere up ahead in U-38, would have welcomed these ideal sea conditions, while Captain Hall aboard SS *Persia* was likely to have been ill at ease.

Valentiner may have used a 'torpedo director', an innocent looking geometric instrument to determine the angle between the moving SS *Persia* and the point at which he should fire so that the torpedo would meet her and cause the most damage[100], ideally between her funnels. An explosion there could strike boilers and furnaces. His preparations followed mathematical

---

99 Letter from W Taylor, Secretary, Peninsular & Oriental Steam Navigation Company to the Director of Naval Intelligence dated 20th January 1916, enclosing crew statements
100 Torpedo Vorhaltrechner Project: http://www.tvre.org/en/home-page

procedures, step-by-step, conscious decisions and calculations, ignoring or refuting the visual evidence that *Persia* did not look like a troopship. Whether to delude Chancellor Theobald von Bethmann Hollweg, his crew or himself, he wrote that she was a 'transporter'. The Chancellor had issued his order on 28th August not to sink passenger ships without warning but to allow provisions for the safety of passengers and crew[101] if they decided to sink any vessels. This was the *Arabic* Pledge, but it did not apply to troopships. Valentiner manoeuvred U-38 into optimum position and range, having calculated angles and distances and waited for *Persia* to arrive at his aiming point. At that instant, he fired. Compressed air thrust the torpedo out of its tube in a surge of bubbles. It gathered speed, driven and stabilised by its contra-rotating propellers. Blades on the torpedo's nose spun through the water unscrewing the detonator lock, arming the warhead so that it would explode on impact. Air driving the torpedo propellers reached the surface well behind it, leaving a milky wake of bubbles as it closed rapidly on the liner, unseen. Valentiner's stopwatch ticked down towards the 42 seconds he had calculated between launch and impact. Tension rose in the cramped U-boat.

Aboard the liner, routine prevailed. Lookouts looked, firemen shovelled and sweated, chefs catered and stokers stoked. In the First Saloon, the moderate rumble of *Persia*'s engines muffled the sounds of food orders, clinks of cutlery, china, bottles and glasses and the soft whooshes of doors to and from the galley. Luncheon, tiffin, was served.

In forty-two seconds, SS *Persia* might have travelled about 1,130 feet (350 m), perhaps twice her length while U-38's torpedo covered about 2,350 feet (720 m). It slammed into *Persia*'s port side slightly forward of her leading funnel and three metres below the waterline, where 160 kg (350 lb) of TNT and hexanite blasted through her plates. Seawater engulfed the cavernous space containing boilers, furnaces, coal supplies and the entire watch of trimmers and firemen. It was a textbook shot into the heart of the ship. The SS *Persia* juddered from end to end as the U-boat crew felt and heard the blast, no doubt cheering the shock wave confirmation of a successful attack.

Second Officer Harold Wood had been on the port wing of the bridge when he spotted the unmistakeable white-feathered wake of a torpedo rushing towards SS *Persia*'s track, initially 4 points (45°) off the port bow. He had perhaps one second to react as the trail of bubbles and *Persia* converged.

---

101 Brune, Lester H and Burns, Richard Dean (2003). *Chronological History of US Foreign Relations: Volume 1: 1607–1932*. London: Routledge. ISBN 978-0-415-93914-0

The torpedo exploded just aft of his position. A second blast fractured the upper deck close to where he stood, releasing a volcanic eruption of smoke, steam and ashes. He must have recognised *Persia*'s deadly peril immediately and rushed to blow the five short whistle blasts practised at yesterday's lifeboat drill. Nothing happened – the explosions had destroyed the steam supply to the whistle and he could not give the alarm he had demonstrated the day before. It was ten minutes past one by SS *Persia*'s bridge clock and her passengers' watches. This differed from U-38's clock that seemed to be about 37 minutes slower.

The next entry in U-38's log, brief and detached, was timed at 12.33 pm.

'Fired. Detonation after 42 seconds'.

It continued –

'Cruiser goes on one side quickly. Dived to 20m and looked around. Cruiser sinks after ten minutes. One boat is put out. U-boat was not spotted by Cruiser. Continued at 20m.'

Valentiner's judgement and aim had been perfect. U-38 had scored a crippling hit, reported afterwards by Chief Officer Clark as *'abaft No.3 hatch opposite the boiler room'*[102]. Almost instantly SS *Persia* suffered further damage from a second explosion, not unlike that reported in the May sinking of the RMS *Lusitania*. Such an explosion could have had one of two distinctly different causes. Some later described the second blast as 'a boiler explosion' and it may have been if the torpedo had destroyed *Persia*'s forward port boiler and its furnaces. This was the judgement of Second Engineer Henry Eves. Cold water, white-hot coal and a ruptured boiler can be destructive in combination, blasting out superheated high-pressure steam and metal debris, potentially fracturing all the decks above.

It is also possible that after breaching *Persia*'s hull, the torpedo exploded into her coal bunkers outboard of the furnaces and boilers. This could have pulverised the coal, instantly filling the large engine room space with fine coal dust. Suspended in a confined space, this haze can be violently explosive, like that in the mine at Universal Colliery, Senghenydd in South Wales, where 439 miners died in a blast of coal dust and methane in October 1913, Britain's worst coal mine disaster. Inside the ship, the explosive dust

---

102 From a statement made to the British Consul General in Alexandria. Cutting from an unknown British newspaper supplied by Benedicta Makin

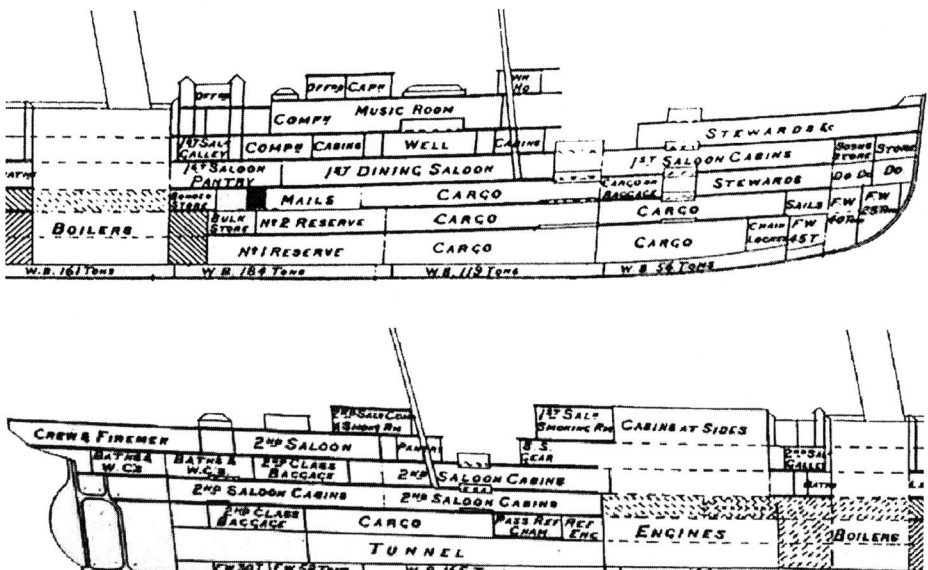

Layout of SS Persia from the starboard side. She was struck by a torpedo on her port side between her bridge and forward funnel. Her forward port boiler is believed to have exploded, destroying any hopes of her staying afloat and she sank stern-first in about 5 minutes. The dark shaded compartment is her strong room where a Maharaja's fortune was thought to have been stored.

needed ignition and there were numerous sources – detonating hexanite, hot shrapnel, burning coals and ruptured furnaces, any one of which could have triggered *Persia*'s doom. Everyone in the stokehold and engine room probably perished instantly in the double blast and the overwhelming flood that rushed into the void, so there was no one to stop or even slow the ship as directed during the previous day's lifeboat practice and the SS *Persia* continued at speed.

Wood hurried down to Captain Hall on the lower bridge, who ordered him to help people to their boats. The captain remained behind to deal with secret documents, such as Admiralty instructions to all ships' masters on what actions to take if threatened with attack or attacked, one of which was never to let those documents fall into enemy hands. The sinking was inescapable, but how long remained? How many could survive?

Second Engineer Henry Edwin Eves
By kind permission of Martin Eves

Whether people lived or died in those desperate minutes must have been a lottery. Those with the lowest chances were the duty firemen, trimmers and engineers who worked around the furnaces and boilers. They would have had no time to think, their deaths coming almost instantly. Second Engineer Henry Eves later told of their plight. He had kept watch in the engine room between 4.00 and 8.00 am, then caught up on paperwork before turning-in about noon to rest before his next watch at 4.00 pm. Two explosions awakened him about 1.00 pm. He dressed quickly, put on his lifebelt and hurried towards the engine room, where he saw the Chief Engineer Jeffery directing the closing of the watertight doors of the tunnel. Eves presumed that the third engineer had been in the stokehold and killed. A process of elimination suggests that that unfortunate man was Assistant Engineer Victor Berry, aged 22. Any attempts to bring *Persia* to a stop from her cruising speed of about 16 knots failed because of the explosions, the torrent of water engulfing the engine room and a '*great quantity of sulphurous gas*'. Second Engineer Henry Eves later judged that the explosions had been in the forward port boiler, leaving a two-foot-wide steam-filled fracture across the deck. Seeing that there was little else that he could do, he went to help people board their lifeboats[103].

Imagine the helpless panic of parents who had fed their children and taken or sent them to their cabins for post-lunch slumbers, and of the children themselves. In the saloon, the elderly and infirm might have been unable to rise out of their chairs or stay on their feet across the sloping deck. The off-duty crew, asleep in their bunks, awoke to find themselves engulfed by seawater. For others trapped in cabins or tangled in ropes, hope would

---

103 The National Archives: PRO ADM 137/1139 – Mediterranean – Merchant Vessels attacked by Submarines, 1915, December. p 378–9

have turned rapidly to despair as the sea closed over the ship and filled air pockets. Hopefully, the end came quickly for all those for whom there was no escape. Once the ship started her stern-first descent, the light would fade as eyes, mouths, throats and lungs filled with choking water, as they heard the ship's metallic death throes. Then silence. Death for most came long before SS *Persia* touched the seabed 10,000 feet down. Miraculously, of those tangled, trapped and dragged under, some broke free and regained the surface either by luck, huge effort, or both. Some of them would find space in the pitifully few usable lifeboats while for others, their good fortune would not last.

Sound travels through water four to five times faster than air, though its direction is harder to perceive. *Persia*'s dying agonies would sound unmistakeably to the crew of U-38, perhaps subduing their celebrations. After the explosions, the underwater sounds confirming her destruction changed, as her hull twisted and her bulkheads ruptured. Thousands of tons of cargo and coal shifted, sliding and crashing inside her. The banging, rumbling, wrenching and groaning spread underwater around her, punctuated by the bursting of rivets. The U-boat men would hear all this but not the agony of broken bodies, the distress of children screaming for parents or the despairing cries of separated families and friends.

Valentiner's interest in the SS *Persia* was over and his tonnage on the U-boat commanders' league table had received a weighty boost. Even although he had written her up as a troopship, he must have known better. New orders went out to the U-38 crew. At 1.12 pm Valentiner recorded:

'Course 296 in the opposite direction to the cruiser'. At 1.50 pm his log shows *'Plume of smoke in sight'* as preparations started for another victim.

Battles for Survival

Only those who cheated death on that day can tell us what happened and the heroism and self-sacrifice of some who died lives on because some survivors later made it their business to share what they saw. The accounts that follow come mainly from letters to families and friends and, in one case, from a small book published in India. Similar information comes from different perspectives, sometimes additional, sometimes contradictory. There were later extracts from newspaper accounts, press statements and reports, but nothing official – the SS *Persia* and all her lost souls would never merit a Board of Trade enquiry.

Lord Montagu recalled that at about 1.10 pm, as they were sitting down to tiffin, there was a terrific explosion abaft the main saloon. He knew from the whiff of explosives that a torpedo had struck the ship. Passengers who had left their lifebelts behind went at once to fetch them from their cabins and all headed for their stations. The port side of *Persia*'s main deck was already submerging while she was still travelling at cruising speed. Montagu and Eleanor made their way together to the No.6 boat station on the port side, but the force of water tore their hands apart and she was swept away out of sight. He stopped, shocked, bereft and isolated, near his boat station where he quickly realised that it would be impossible to escape from that side of the ship, so climbed towards the starboard side, hauling a stranded lady passenger with him. Only a few minutes after the explosions, the ship was on her port side and going down stern first. Seawater swept him overboard. There was an uprush of steam and smoke from the engine room and as she sank, the vortex created by the sinking ship dragged him deep, striking his head and body against pieces of wreckage. It seemed a long time before he escaped the downward pull and then rose quickly and resurfaced. He found the mouthpiece of his Gieve waistcoat and blew air in to keep himself afloat. He thought that no more than four minutes had elapsed from the torpedo strike until *Persia*'s disappearance.

Charles Grant, an American business passenger, was sitting in the dining saloon and had just finished his soup. The steward had just asked what he would like for his second course when there was an explosion, filling the saloon with broken glass, smoke and steam. He recalled that everyone got up and went towards the deck as if it was yesterday's boat drill and he reported to his lifeboat on the starboard side. The vessel was listing to port and he clung to the rail. *Persia* listed further and it quickly became impossible to launch any of the starboard boats jammed in against the ship. He climbed over the starboard rail and slid across *Persia*'s hull into the rushing sea. He went under, tangled in ropes, but managed to free himself, regain the surface and clamber onto some floating wreckage. The last he saw of the *Persia* was her bow pointing high in the air only five minutes after the explosion.

Dr Lilian Cook later wrote:

'It was lunchtime and most people had sat down to lunch and had just begun when it happened. No warning, nothing but a terrific crash and immediately almost the saloon was empty.

The Grants (the Rev. Grant and Mrs Grant of Aberdeen), another lady and I waited for a few seconds as there was no use adding to the panic, and when we thought the others would have had time to get their belts and come again, we began to descend. By this time the water was splashing through the porthole and the steps were slippery, but we got down and I am glad to remember that beyond being pale we were quite composed.

I went into my cabin and got two belts, tied mine on, and I even remember looking to see it was the right way round. The ascent to the deck was much more difficult for the water was coming in everywhere, but we got up. The Grants were very good but seemed overcome, and I had to shout to Mr Grant to put on his belt which he had in his hand. There was no use attempting to get into the boats, for the ship was listing, and I decided it was best to jump, so we jumped from the rail.

This seems to take a long time to tell, but the boat sank in 4 1/2 minutes from the crash. When the first shock was over, I came up, surrounded by wreckage, and I was about to wonder what I would hold of when I felt myself being pulled down by a native steward. That was horrid, but as we each had on a life-belt I shook him off and swam towards a half-empty boat. I am very grateful now to Dr Ida Scudder for her swimming lessons, for I got along well, and as I neared the boat, I heard a man say "Come along, you are swimming like a fish". So I went and was helped into the boat full of 10 very wet people.

There was an awful scene around us – drowning people, upturned boats and so on, and we could only take in a certain number. We pushed off and soon joined up with three other life-boats, and very soon we were drifting away from the scene of the disaster. There were four ladies in the boat, a few military men, and a lot of Lascars. All that afternoon we watched for smoke and saw several boats on the horizon – one we think was fired on for we saw the explosion – but they all passed on the other side. We lay huddled together all night to keep each other warm, and when dawn broke, we got the boats together and took counsel. We had a biscuit each, and the promise of a thimbleful of water later, for we had only half a keg, and then we began to watch again. We were all that day and towards evening we were getting a little down for the sea was getting up, and in little boats, it was no joke, but I felt sure we were going to be picked up, and at the end of 30 hours we were. There were 16 ladies saved, and they were all very brave. I think they behaved awfully well. It was nothing for me to have to be calm for I've faced a good number of horrors in my day, but they hadn't. There was no time to see much of other people, but people helped each other all they could. I only wished I could do more. One girl tells me I tied on her life-belt, but I don't remember doing it, but we kept quite cheery, which was something.'[104]

Coincidentally, Lilian found her friends Mrs Eulalie Hutchison and Mrs Agnes Shanks in the same lifeboat.

Captain Edward (Ted) Berryman described the torpedo strike as a muffled bang at which people rose from their seats and began to file out of the saloon with no panic or rush, described later by someone else as *'just like going out of church'*. He and others went to their cabins for lifebelts and then to their lifeboat stations. He was to be in boat seven on the starboard side, but as the ship was already listing to port, that boat lay jammed on the ship's side. As the list passed 45 degrees, he held onto the rail then eventually climbed over it and walked across the ship's side, by then almost level, to where his lifeboat had jammed and caught hold of its ropes in case it came loose. *Persia* lurched and her keel came out of the water. A rush of water carried him away. He saw *Persia* right herself and then sink rapidly, stern first, momentarily leaving her bows towering thirty feet straight up before sliding under, suddenly and silently disturbing the water but causing little suction. He described the sea as having a nasty swell and being covered in debris with many people groaning and crying and he reckoned that the sinking had taken a little over five minutes from the torpedo strike.

---

104 Cablegram published in *The Daily Record*, 26th January 1916

Walter Smith, assistant engineer of a condenser plant in Port Said, was returning to his work. He was travelling second class, sharing his cabin with a friend, Ernest Knight. Walter was in the cabin washing his hands for lunch when he heard and felt the explosion. He immediately got his lifebelt and started up to the deck. On his way, he saw a lady and asked why she did not have her lifebelt. She seemed confused so he gave her his belt and went back to his cabin for another. When he left his cabin for the second time, he noticed some distressed and crying women and children. One was a French woman leaning up against the rail in the corridor outside the cabins seemingly unable to help herself. He pushed her along, which roused her, and when they got on deck someone took the lifebelt from her, fastened it around her and pushed her overboard. On the boat deck, he found his travelling companion, Knight, and another man in one end of their boat and the carpenter and a sailor in the other end. They were struggling to get the boat free and had removed three of the pins that secured it but the fourth had stuck. Knight shouted for an axe but without luck. Smith found a broken oar and Knight hit the jammed pin until it gave way. *Persia* was over at a steep angle, so the boat swung out beyond the side of the vessel and then smashed back into it. They all lost their balance and one man pitched over the side into the sea. Knight fell from the boat and Smith could only see his fingertips clinging on to its side before he managed to scramble back on board again. *Persia* was settling, stern first. While Smith was helping in their boat, he saw another boat being lowered, full of people. Suddenly, one of the ropes broke, the end of the boat dropped and everyone plummeted into the sea. The other davit rope then gave way and the boat landed in the water the right way up and quite dry, but empty. People who had fallen or jumped off *Persia* further forward began to climb into the empty boat until there were twenty to thirty people aboard. She remained fastened to the *Persia* by a rope, being towed along, when Smith then saw another empty boat crash down on top of her, crushing most of those aboard between the hulls. Knight and Smith had failed to get their davit ropes loose and *Persia*'s stern was going down, but they finally unhooked. Knight yelled for a knife to cut the painter that still attached them to *Persia*, which would drag them under when she sank. Smith passed Knight his pocketknife and he sawed through the painter. Suction dragged their boat across the stern of the sinking ship but once free of the rope, they stayed afloat with only six aboard – three passengers and three crew.

Agnes Lees[105] and her missionary guide and mentor Adelaide Bull, hurried to reach their boat station by passing beneath a canvas awning normally there to protect them from the sun. *Persia* was on the point of sinking and the awning dragged them both beneath the churning water. Agnes lost contact with Adelaide and groped blindly to find the edge of the canvas. She found it, dragged herself around its edge and shot to the surface, gasping for breath, but there was no sign of Adelaide.

Steward Charles Leonard Martin[106], still two months short of his nineteenth birthday, had been serving lunch when the torpedo hit the ship. He rushed to get his lifebelt and then to his station, No.5 on the starboard side. The chief engineer was also at that boat station but it was impossible to lower the boat. Martin grasped the davit but suction dragged him underwater as *Persia* sank. He surfaced, dazed and confused, and floated for a while, finally managing to scramble onto a capsized boat with maybe 20 others.

Major Charles O'Reilly and his wife Sybil made their way towards their boat station, clinging together along the steeply sloping deck. Mrs O'Reilly tangled her foot in the cricket net left in place after that morning's game. The Major struggled to free her but waves washed him off his feet. He recovered to see her extreme peril and tried to tear and enlarge the mesh, to drag her free. The cord was too strong, the knots too tight, the mesh too small. Rushing waves submerged the deck, dragging her down and washing him away.

Second Lieutenant John Lionel Miller-Hallett, Lion to his family and friends, saw that as the crew attempted to lower lifeboats on the starboard side, they became stranded on the ship's side. Captain Hall saw the difficulty when he came along the deck and called out:

'All women and children down to the port side.'

They went quietly but owing to the list of the ship, all the port-side boats were hanging about two yards (2 m) from the side of the ship and out of their reach. Lionel went down to the port side and with Captain John (Jack) Thornton Lodwick threw chairs and anything else that might float to the women and men struggling in the water. He then feared that the cabins behind him and the deck above would trap him on the promenade deck, so walked up to the rail and jumped over the starboard side. He spotted a boat in which he saw the second mate, but though he could reach it, still

---

105 Agnes Lees wrote a booklet published anonymously in India entitled The Thrilling Experience of a Passenger by (sic) The SS *Persia* on the 30th & 31st December 1915 in her own words (Henceforth cited as *The Thrilling Experience*)
106 Charles Martin made an affidavit to the American Consul in Malta, Wilbur Keblinger.

weakened after his serious battle wound in August, he did not have the strength to haul himself aboard. He hung on until someone spotted him and pulled him in.

Persia carried ten lifeboats, one steam launch and four Berthon folding boats constructed of wood and a double canvas skin[107]. With the number of passengers on board, these lifeboats were more than adequate[108], but only if she could have stopped and stayed on an even keel long enough for the crew to load and lower the boats. Some of the boats had smashed against cabins or struck flailing davits. The practice lifeboat drill of the previous day was held in calm conditions. Now they had experienced the shock and confusion of a torpedo attack. Their floating palace was capsizing at unchecked speed, letting water in at an overwhelming rate. People clung to their loved ones, or searched for them frantically, ignoring the lifeboats. Those travelling alone and crew members may have whispered messages of love to those at home, mixed with some strong curses. Prayers, short and frantic, in different languages to different gods, all meant one thing – 'Help us!'

With a long, loud sigh, air rushed from *Persia* through every opening, forced out by the water rising inside her as she sank. A cloud of soot and ash ejected from her funnels as the waves claimed her. Known and feared by seamen, this was *Persia*'s 'black soul', the final soot-polluted breath exhaled by many doomed steamships. It had taken only five minutes for the once-proud liner to surrender to the sea, leaving a mess of flotsam on the inky, soot-and-ash-covered water. In this turbid swell, bodies floated, survivors struggled and pitifully few lifeboats wallowed, all coated in slimy soot.

The last sight of Captain Hall was of him on board, tying his lifebelt around a lady, almost certainly his last ever duty. In only ten minutes his peaceful liner had become an iron coffin for a mass burial at sea.

---

107 In 1877, the Rev E L Berthon started his company in Romsey, Hampshire, building folding boats: http://www.berthon.co.uk/about-berthon/berthon-history
108 Chapter VI of SOLAS (Safety of Life at Sea) 1914 Article 40 "At no moment of its voyage may a ship have on board a total number of persons than that for whom accommodation is provided in lifeboats (and the pontoon lifeboats) on board".

Four-and-a-Half Lifeboats

Life is a shipwreck, but we must not forget to sing in the lifeboats.
Voltaire

SS *Persia*, all five-hundred feet, eight-thousand tons and her cargo of thousands of Christmas parcels, cards and letters, had vanished in moments. Only four of *Persia*'s fourteen lifeboats drifted amongst the scattered wreckage, plus one other upturned in the far distance with a few people clinging on. Bobbing heads and waving arms identified those still afloat and alive. Those beyond help just floated or had already vanished inside *Persia* or the swirl that followed her. Chief Officer Clark shouted orders for the few floating boats to keep together. To improve balance, he transferred some people out of his overloaded small 'accident boat', one normally used only in the recovery of a 'man overboard'. Now, almost 500 people were overboard or trapped on board, with pitifully few in the lifeboats.

Passenger Agnes Lees had clung to a piece of floating wreckage alongside a man who could not speak English[109]. They had both caught hold of flotsam and struggled towards a nearby boat. She grasped the prow while he scrambled aboard, and waited in vain for him to help her aboard too. Swallowing sea water and disappointment, she gazed around, noticing the lovely blues of the sea and sky and the surprising warmth of the seawater[110]. It then dawned on her that the bow of the boat hid her from view. She yelled. Two men peered over, reached down and took her arms They suggested she reach her leg up into the lifelines along the side of the boat to help them help her. Agnes struggled to hook her foot through the rope, but could not reach. Another man then reached over and grabbed her leg and

---

109   The Thrilling Experience
110   17° C – the average sea water temperature off Crete in December 1915

the three men hauled her into the relative safety of the lifeboat. She flopped over a seat, exhausted but alive.

After some recovery time, Agnes started to take notice of fellow survivors and was astonished to see most of them coated in black. She later found out that as *Persia* sank, her funnels ejected that dense cloud of steam, soot, smoke and ash which had rained down just as the awning had dragged her underwater. Then she saw the familiar face of a young French girl who had suffered a bad head wound, leaving congealed blood down one side of her face. Agnes realised her own good fortune but that others needed help, so joined in the efforts to assist those still in the water. She recognised one of the army officers she had come to know, Captain Berryman, swimming towards the boat pushing a young woman she recognised, helpless and cruciform on a collection of planks. Berryman caught hold of the boat and instructed those aboard to help her aboard. Only after she was safely in the lifeboat did he save himself.

Ted Berryman had tried to use several different pieces of wreckage for support but found too many people clinging to each and so decided to try and swim to where he could see four lifeboats, though this was difficult through the pitching wreckage and while wearing a lifebelt. He noticed a lady on her back groaning and crying, exhausted and drifting, so took her in tow, though her skirt kept tangling his legs. Berryman finally caught the attention of some in a boat who hauled them both aboard. The boat was that containing Agnes Lees and the rescued lady was Mlle Derogez who was on her way to her wedding in India.

Some aboard this boat tried to use the oars but lacked the basic skills. They scouted around for more survivors without success. All their watches had stopped at 1.15 pm or 1.20 pm and by then it must have been about 2 o'clock. They tried to keep their boats headed the way *Persia* had been going, hoping to meet passing ships, but it was difficult in the choppy sea.

Agnes noted that in their boat were about twelve lascars and Goanese (sic), a few foreign passengers, about ten Englishmen, both crew and passengers, nine ladies and two children'[111]. The boat was shipping water, so they moved around to improve the balance. Other lifeboats pitched nearby and the fifth was distant. *Persia*'s Second Officer Wood had taken charge of their lifeboat and Chief Officer Clark was in command of their small flotilla. She looked around nearby boats for her mentor, Adelaide Bull, and realised that her companion had probably gone down with the ship. Seeking other

---

111   *The Thrilling Experience*

familiar faces, Agnes spotted Mrs Eulalie Hutchison whom she had helped with her children the evening before. Mrs Hutchinson was clinging to her three-year-old son David, but there was no sign of her eighteen-month-old daughter, Margaret. Agnes later learned that falling debris had struck Margaret and waves swept her away and she realised that Mrs Hutchinson must have been maintaining a brave face for the sake of her infant son.

Another military officer Agnes had come to know, Major Charles O'Reilly, sat in the bow of their boat without his wife Sybil, normally his constant companion. The cricket nets left in place on *Persia*'s deck had become a death trap and she learned that the major had had to watch helplessly, as the net pulled Sybil under. He now sat shocked and grief-stricken, alone in a crowded boat. Agnes continued to scan around, recognising two other recent friends, Alfred Gabour and his niece Clairette, soon discovering that Clairette's mother and brother were also missing.

Waves that had earlier looked small from the decks of SS *Persia* now looked and felt bigger and stronger. The boats lifted, rolled, tipped and dropped on each wave, drenching the survivors repeatedly. Passengers and crew who had never experienced seasickness began to suffer. All the boats were shipping water and needed constant bailing. There were too many people in the chief officer's boat. It was overloaded so badly that it was taking in too much water and risked sinking and some of the passengers needed to move to a more lightly loaded boat. He ordered four Indian crewmen to cross into Second Officer Wood's boat, but Wood protested so eventually three Indians and the baggage steward John (Jack) Pinner transferred. Crew and passengers knew Pinner for being cheerfully noisy. He told everyone that his face had become black after he had been down inside one of the funnels before it spat him out again, but was proud to have hung onto his hat, giving them a moment of light relief. The ship's officers were probably the only ones who knew that they were over seventy miles from the nearest land, far from safety.

At about 4 o'clock that afternoon, they saw a distant steamer and waved clothing tied to oars to attract attention. The ship seemed to stop and shortly afterwards they saw a fountain of water and a pillar of black smoke followed by what sounded like a distant gun. She remained visible for a short while and then vanished. All believed they had just witnessed another sinking victim and history tells that the SS *Clan MacFarlane* sank only five miles from where *Persia* had foundered, the second victim of the day for Kapitänleutnant Max Valentiner and U-38. Fifty-two of her crew perished. He recorded in his log that both ships were troopships – translated as

> 'There on 30th December the armed British steamer *Persia*, 7974 tons, and *Clan Macfarlane*, 4823 tons, held to be transports, due to this dived, torpedo shots dispatched.'[112]

Coincidentally, the Reverend Alexander Grant, a passenger travelling with his new wife aboard the SS *Persia* was the son of Mr CF Grant, superintendent engineer of the Clan Line, owners of the 16-year-old *Clan MacFarlane*.

All four lifeboats tied together to see the night through as the wind freshened and the waves rose. They deployed sea anchors to try and keep their boats from turning broadside across the waves and taking on more water, soaking and chilling them all. In the chief officer's boat, they improvised a shelter with a sail and two piano covers that they had found in the boat. Survivors huddled together for warmth while others kept watch. The women were very thinly clad but some men gave them coats and sail covers and a thin blanket stored on board. They made the girl with the head wound as comfortable as possible. One each of the passengers and crew took ten-minute turns bailing the water, but what they cleared, the waves soon refilled. Everyone had one ship's biscuit from the boat's supplies. Agnes, on her way to India to become a missionary, suggested that they sang hymns and they joined her in saying the Lord's Prayer and singing *O God our Help in Ages Past*[113], *Jesu Lover of my Soul*, *Abide with Me* and *Sun of my Soul*. Agnes proposed that they sang *Eternal Father Strong to Save,* but the sailors told everyone that although it was known as the seamen's hymn, it was unlucky to sing it at sea, something the Reverend Grant had not known during his service on Boxing Day.

In the failing light, they saw the lights of yet another ship quite near. Second Officer Wood balanced on the rolling bow and waved a flare over his head, but the ship's lights faded and disappeared. Prospects looked grim as they faced a cramped, wet, cold night in total darkness. Despite the sea anchors, the boats persisted in turning side-on to the waves, taking on more water and throwing everyone about on the hard thwarts. Captain Berryman lay in the bow, cold and wet, looking after the troublesome rope fastening them to the next boat. There were two children in the boat and one, Mlle Gabour, aged about 6, who Berryman tried to keep warm, kept asking:

> '*Where is that big boat that was coming to help us?*'

---

112 Spindler, Arno (1934). *Der Krieg zur See – Der Handelskrieg mit U-Booten*, Bande III. p 35. (The War at the Sea-The Trade War With Submarines, Volume 3). Berlin: Mittler & Sohn, 1934
113 The Thrilling Experience

Each time she asked she heard the same reply.

'It will be coming soon.'

Perhaps this was as much for the reassurance of adults as for this small child. The other child, David Hutchison, was only three years old. No one realised then that of the 18 children aboard, these two were the only survivors.

The dawn of New Year's Eve brought little comfort except for another biscuit and a sip of water. Though they had two kegs of water, it had turned out that only one was drinkable, a significant failure of the lifeboat preparations. The other boats seemed to be short of fresh water too. After dawn, the chief officer hoisted the sail and tried to tow the other three boats but made little progress. About two hours later they sighted a ship on the horizon and decided that with the help of their sail they should go after it alone and try to attract its attention. They cast off the other boats and tried to intercept her but she sheared off and disappeared and the sailing lifeboat returned.

Things became somewhat fractious. Heated discussions took place as to what was best to do. Some were in favour of each boat going its own way, trusting that one might be picked up and would tell the rescuing ship the location of the others. Others wanted to stay together, mainly because only two of boats had seamen in them, while the other two had only passengers and stewards. By noon the boats tied together again with sail lowered and everyone rested, exhausted. As the boats drifted, Agnes noticed the weather as lovely – blue sky and blue water. She even tried to tidy her salt-matted hair with side combs she had been wearing before the attack. Her attempts to cheer up her companions even included encouraging the others to imagine that they were on a yacht cruise in the Mediterranean, adding a reminder that if they had been at Margate, this pleasure would have cost them a shilling (5p) an hour.

Meanwhile, smokers in the boats had grown increasingly desperate to satisfy their craving. Cigarettes, cigars and tobacco were hopelessly saturated. Agnes allowed one of the men to spread his tobacco on her dress to dry in the sun, but he and others also needed dry paper. He had some sodden five pound notes in his wallet (each equivalent to £515 in the early twenty-first century) and said he would use them 'for swank'. In the end, Agnes dried someone's five-franc notes for cheaper smokes. Agnes described the smokers as having persuaded themselves that they were living in luxury[114].

---

114 Five pounds at 1915 values would be worth over five hundred pounds in the values of a century later. The conversion rate for French francs in 1915 was 25 to one pound, making 5 francs equal to about four shillings and tuppence (4/2d), but more than £20 one-hundred years later.

Time passed without seeing another ship. Chief Officer Clark gathered the boats closer again and told everyone of a new plan as their biscuits and water might not last the long haul to the African coast. His boat, the smallest and easiest to row if the breeze failed, would leave the others and try to find a steamer. If they succeeded, they would send it to pick them all up. Thirty-nine-year-old Gerald Clark had navigated these waters for almost twenty years. If anyone could find a way out of the crisis it would be him. All agreed. Clark's boat headed away, carrying the hopes and wishes of those left behind. The remaining boats tethered and drifted until twilight. The evening brought another biscuit and preparations for a second night adrift. Jack, the baggage steward, asked who had led the hymns on the previous night and asked Agnes to lead them in *O God our Help in Ages Past* as larger waves threatened to capsize them.

HMS *Mallow*

Chief Officer Clark lowered the sail during the night and then hoisted it again in the morning when all on board had a biscuit and a drink of water from the boat's basic supplies. They spotted one or two distant ships but could not attract attention and continued straining their eyes in hope. William Dowling remembered it as a hot morning that cooled into the afternoon and that as the light faded again, they lowered the sail and used it for shelter against the encroaching cold. Clark and Dowling chatted in the stern of the boat and then the chief officer said he would try to sleep for a while and asked the head saloon waiter to awaken him if needed and to keep the head of the boat into the wind if possible. Dowling had never enjoyed good eyesight but kept straining into the darkness for any signs of passing ships. He eventually spotted a faint light and awoke the chief officer. He decided to see how the situation evolved to avoid attracting enemy attention. Everyone wanted to shout and eventually they all called out. Suddenly they were blinded by light, picked out by a searchlight. They started rowing towards whatever vessel was hidden behind the light and soon a ship's bow loomed over them. William Dowling guided the boat close to the companionway then bumped against it and clambered up. He was grabbed by a man who turned out to be a Royal Navy petty officer who told him that it was as well they had shouted as the ship's forward gun had been trained in their direction just in case they were part of an enemy ruse.

They had been rescued by HMS *Mallow* and the crew fed them and gave out tots of navy rum. The women were given officers' cabins and the wardroom. The captain, Lieutenant-Commander Ralph W H Roberts, knew that the other three lifeboats could not be too far away. He already had some survivors aboard and carried the first news that the P&O liner SS *Persia* had been torpedoed by a U-boat and that the loss of life would be heavy.

Away in the dark distance, Second Officer Harold Wood, now the senior officer in the remaining three lifeboats, arranged lookouts for potential rescuers and to keep the boats together. Some attempted sleep. Even when using sea anchors, the boats occasionally turned beam-on, shipping more water. Effort spent on bailing and keeping in close formation helped keep the boats afloat but left the survivors exhausted.

They were frightened, wet, cold, hungry and thirsty, bouncing and rolling on hard wooden seats while frequent waves broke over them. In Harold Wood's boat those not on watch were dozing in a state of semi-conscious exhaustion when someone yelled 'ship ahoy'. They had spotted a ship's lights. Hope soared. The ship seemed to be heading straight for them. Some struggled to open water-tight tins with numb fingers, desperate to get their flares and matches. Nothing was going to stop them now. They took turns to burn the flares and wave them, while others rowed hard towards the approaching lights, leaving the two other boats trailing. As the gap closed, they yelled harder and burned more flares. At last, after about 20 minutes more, a vessel loomed out of the darkness and an unmistakably English voice called out:

'Hello you fellows! We've got the other boat all right. Come along the starboard side, will you?'

Second Officer Wood directed actions to avoid smashing the boat against the ship and soon they were alongside. It was just after 7.00 pm. They had been adrift for about 30 hours.

HMS *Mallow* had been cruising alone looking for mines and U-boats, not following a specific course. She had encountered the chief officer's lifeboat by good fortune and taken its people aboard. They then sailed on to find the other boats. Once survivors had boarded from all three remaining boats, the crew fed them and gave them hammocks. Most tried to get some sleep. *Mallow*'s wireless operator sent an immediate message to Alexandria, probably the first news of the loss of SS *Persia*. Though the survivors had mixed and vague information about a possible fifth lifeboat, the message requested another ship to look for other survivors. HMS *Mallow* made all speed to Alexandria, where she arrived at 3.00 pm the next day, 1st January 1916. There the 158 survivors were transferred to HMS *Hannibal*, an 1896 battleship then serving as a depot ship, where the crew treated them very well. They must have presented a sorry spectacle; dirty and bruised, worn and haggard, many with cuts and wounds, but all happy at their rescue. Some went ashore and made the more immediate purchases necessary for

Royal Navy Acacia Class sweeping sloop HMS Mallow which rescued over 150 survivors and carried them to Alexandria
By kind permission of David Riley, Product and Licensing Manager, Museum of New Zealand Te Papa Tongarewa

their comfort and stayed that night aboard the *Hannibal*. On 2nd January they were moved to the Savoy Hotel[115].

Survivors were able to send a cable to a family member to let them know of their survival and welfare. Captain Berryman cabled his mother from Alexandria addressed to 'Berryman Delaford Guildford Surrey' with the cryptic but adequate message: *'Saved = Ted'*.

The survivors from the four lifeboats then transferred ashore to the Regina Palace Hotel. On 2nd January, Ted Berryman wrote a long letter to his fiancée Nell, with a request for her to copy it and send it to family members[116]:

'No one saw the submarine, though the officer on watch on the bridge saw the track of the torpedo for about the last few yards, but she had struck before he could give any orders. She struck almost amidships, just under the funnels, bursting a boiler and killing I'm afraid all the engine room staff who were on duty at the time.

---

115 Royal Navy Log Books of the World War 1 Era, HMS Hannibal: Edited by Pat Marcus: https://www.naval-history.net/OWShips-WW1-01-HMS_Hannibal.htm
116 Letter from Ted Berryman to his fiancée Nell, 2nd January 1916

Only one boat was lowered in an orthodox way. The Chief cut away 3 [boats] and the 2nd Officer 2 more. These latter two, however, full of passengers and crew were caught by the davits as the ship heeled over and were swamped.

I'm afraid nearly all the first-class passengers (there were only 14 I think, saved out of 80 and only one lady first-class passenger*) were caught up on the port side when she heeled over and were carried down with her.

The behaviour of the ladies was just priceless, they bore their sufferings wonderfully and did all they could to help. There was no panic on board, but the whole thing was over in 5 minutes and gave little time for thought. Some people had marvellous escapes. Two second-class passengers, (sisters, one married with a little boy) when she was struck, went to opposite sides of the ship. All three went down with the ship and came up again side by side in the water, though they were on opposite sides of the ship when she sank; they were all three rescued.**

As the ship heeled over a huge blast of ashes etc came out of the funnels just as they were level with the water and several of the rescued were coal black, including the Chief Officer, who also got a nasty knock on the head from one of the funnels.

All the Christmas mails for India, China, Aden, British East Africa and Egypt went down, terrible isn't it? No one saved a thing except what they stood up in. The sensation of walking solemnly over the side of the ship into the water is indescribable. For myself (and the others tell me the same) I felt no fear, more annoyance than anything else; but I know I shall funk it now. Everybody's nerves seem to have gone a bit. It seemed so deliberate but was the only thing to do of course. I'm afraid a great many people didn't leave the ship, or jumped too late and so were drowned.

The engine kept going to the last and when she was lying on her side the propeller was racing round, half out of the water and causing a tremendous stir, splashing up the water to a tremendous height.

The Chief Engineer*** on hearing the explosion went down to the engine room to turn off the steam and was last seen down there disappearing into a cloud of steam. A very plucky thing to do, but it was hopeless and he was never seen again.

---

*   Mrs Penn Gaskell
** Mrs Agnes Shanks and Mrs Eulalie Hutchinson and her son David
*** Ernest Jeffery, Southampton

The Captain was not rescued. I saw him on deck just before she sank, tying a life-belt on to a lady. He had not got one on himself. He must have gone down with the ship. Fortunately, she was an empty boat as regards passengers. Only about 80 first class and few 2nd. The horrible part is the number of women missing and children too, but I think that all that was possible to rescue were rescued.

I hope I never go through such a terrible experience again. A pal of mine, one Fisher of the Indian Army, [Lieutenant Gerald Thomas Fisher] summed it up by saying "It was worse than any attack" and I think he is right. I have tried to give you a comprehensive account of this awful business. Please forgive the many literary shortcomings, but it's a hard thing to write about, but I know you would like to know all about it, as I don't suppose you'll get much from the papers.'[117]

Despite lingering doubt over numbers, it seems that HMS *Mallow* had collected up to 158 survivors. Given the almost impossible circumstances in which attempts to launch lifeboats floundered, saving this number from only four boats was incredible.

P and O Official Statements

Daily Express, 3rd January 1916 under the headline
'Murder of Innocents: Glad New Year for the Huns'.

'The P&O Company regrets to state information has been received from the Admiralty that the steamship "Persia", 7,974 tons, which left London on December 18 and Marseilles on December 26, carrying his Majesty's mail and bound for Bombay, has been sunk off Crete and that only four boats got away from the ship. These boats were picked up by a steamer bound for Alexandria. It is feared that the loss of life among the passengers and crew has been heavy.'

In a second statement, the company announced 'on Admiralty authority' that:

'the Persia was torpedoed. The vessel was heavily laden with parcel post and mail. There was very little cargo on board and certainly no war material'.

---

117 Nesham, Félicité (Ed) (1987). Socks, Cigarettes and Shipwrecks- A Family's War Letters 1914-1918. Gloucester: Alan Sutton Publishing and Benedicta Makin/Family Letters www.familyletters.co.uk

Note the phrase *Admiralty authority* used above. The Defence of the Realm Act ensured tight control over the news to ensure that it was thoroughly sanitised and often almost content-free. In 1916, David Lloyd George, is reputed to have said in confidence to C P Scott, Editor of the *Manchester Guardian*:

> *'If the people really knew [the truth] the war would be stopped tomorrow. But of course, they don't know and can't know.'*

Half-Afloat

Lord Montagu later described his struggles and those of others in a badly damaged lifeboat that lost contact with the others. When he first surfaced, he saw the sea covered with struggling people but very little wreckage and could see only three boats. There was no sign of a submarine nor had he seen one when he was aboard the *Persia*. He swam towards a locker floating in the distance and found the ship's surgeon, Dr Everett, clinging to it, apparently stunned by a head injury. The locker could only support one person, so he left the doctor clinging to it and swam to a capsized boat about fifty yards away. Indian seamen crowded her hull, maybe too many for it to support, but he scrambled astride the keel, from where he saw another boat a short distance off picking up people. He shouted for them to come and help, but they rowed away. An hour after the sinking there remained four Europeans and about twenty Indian and Goan crew on the upturned boat. Others had dropped off as they became too weak to hold on. The boat righted on a big wave and they managed to get into her with great difficulty. Montagu noticed that she had a large hole in her hull and a split bow and was unstable because her buoyancy tanks were either smashed or perforated. Any weight on the starboard side tended to capsize her.

About sunset, most aboard were sitting with their knees in water. There remained thirteen Indian seamen and firemen, two Goan stewards, one Italian passenger, one Scotchman (sic), an English steward named Martin and Montagu; only nineteen men. Had it not been for Alexander Clark, the Scottish passenger, and Martin, the steward, who both helped him back aboard each time the boat capsized, Montagu felt he would have had no chance of survival. He managed to stand up for a look round and saw only one boat to the east about a mile away and one or two survivors clinging to the wreckage to the south. Although there was only a gentle wind there was a considerable swell with the sea breaking over them.

Through the night several exhausted Indian crewmen died. Those surviving lowered the bodies overboard to reduce weight and instability. About 8.00 pm a steamer passed a mile to the south with all her lights glowing. They tried to attract attention by shouting and saw two red flares to the east. Despite their efforts, the ship passed by, possibly suspecting the ruse of an enemy submarine. When the moon rose at about 2.00 am, one or two more had died, including the doctor's Goan servant who had been sitting on the gunwale of the boat next to Montagu.

About three hours after sunrise they saw a two-funnelled steamer to the south, raising their hopes again. They hoisted a piece of a torn flag on the one oar left in the boat and saw a lifeboat to the east of them do the same. The ship passed about three miles away but either did not see them or saw them, but as bait in a U-boat trap. About noon, one of the Indian crew managed to open a tin of biscuits from a locker in the boat, so they all ate a little. By then, they had been nearly thirty hours without food or water.

They gave up hope of salvation. Lord Montagu found it a great struggle to stay awake and hold on. They capsized again about 7.00 pm and lost the tin of biscuits and the red flares they had hoped to use that night. Then, at about 8.00 pm, they saw the masthead lights of a steamer far away to the east. Montagu could see from her lights that she was heading towards them. As she sailed closer, they started shouting in unison and when about half a mile away, she stopped. Like other ships, she may have feared a trap and did not approach until she had time to be sure. She drew closer and at about 8.30 pm they heard a shout and she blew her whistle. When even closer they shouted that they had no means of manoeuvring alongside. Eventually, the ship gently and skilfully drifted close to them, threw down lines and hauled them alongside. The crew lowered ropes to haul them aboard. She was the Alfred Holt and Co SS *Ning Chow*, bound from China to London under Captain Allen.

Mr Allan MacLean, the third officer of the *Ning Chow* and officer of the watch, had heard their cries and was the man responsible for saving them. Once aboard, the survivors recovered slowly from exposure and injuries and eventually arrived back in Malta, at dawn on Monday, 3rd January 1916. They went to St Paul's Bay for examination and were then taken to Valletta, where Captain Andrews, the P&O company agent, met them and was considerate and kind. Lord Montagu believed that their rescue was a miracle. He felt that they had all been fast approaching a state of complete exhaustion in a boat barely afloat and the chance of the SS *Ning Chow* passing close enough to hear them was small. He believed that the captain, officers and crew of the SS *Ning Chow* had done everything possible during the crisis.

Alfred Holt and Co SS Ning Chow which picked up eleven survivors from the badly damaged fifth lifeboat and took them to Valletta

Reports of the sinking and survivors had arrived in London from Alexandria two days earlier and excluded all the men in this lifeboat. Lord Montagu's friend, Lord Northcliffe, had even written Montagu's obituary and published it in *The Times*. The eleven survivors landed at Valletta were passengers Lord Montagu, Alexander Clark and Italian citizen Benvenuto Mafessanti, and crew members steward Charles Martin and seven unnamed members of the Indian and Goan crew. Mr Clark had been travelling with his brother-in-law Thomas Burns and his wife Cecilia, both of whom he would later learn had died.

Sadly, some men had perished in the barely floating boat. More might have survived if they had not separated from the other boats where they might have had chances to transfer and get access to water, biscuits and shelter. The reality is that they were never close enough. The westerly breeze may have caught the undamaged boats, all floating higher in the water, and pushed them eastward, while the damaged boat, barely afloat had much less surface area to catch the breeze, so its drift would have been slower, leaving it further behind by the hour. It is possible that some aboard gave in to the temptation to drink seawater, which could have led to dehydration and death[118]. Others may have died from injuries sustained during the attack and sinking, or even from existing frailties worsened by extreme physical effort as they fought to escape and stay afloat.

---

118 http://oceanservice.noaa.gov/facts/drinksw.html

Though he had survived, Lord Montagu grieved over Eleanor's loss. He had last seen and clung to her as they tried to reach their boat, only to be torn apart by the surge that swept over the deck. He wondered whether one of the four distant lifeboats had picked up his beloved 'Thorn', but would soon learn that her name was not on any list of survivors. Long after he would remain hopeful and optimistic that, one day, he would find her.

The Lottery of Life and Death

It was only possible to learn what happened to *Persia* and her people from those survivors who told later of their escapes and the fate of those they knew, both winners and losers in the battle for survival. Some brief accounts speak for those who were never able to tell their own stories.

Colonel 'the Honourable' Edward Stuart St Aubyn (General Staff) serving as a King's Messenger, died at the age of 57. There is a memorial to St Aubyn at St Michael's Mount Castle, Cornwall, where his family had lived since about 1650[119], and the Chatby War Memorial in Alexandria, Egypt, also commemorates him.

Reports of the death of Lieutenant Colonel Henry Backhouse, one of the last passengers to board SS *Persia*, appeared in the *Macclesfield Times* of 14th January 1916 and *Macclesfield Courier* of 15th January 1916:

> '*The news, received from official sources on Saturday, that Lieutenant-Colonel Henry Backhouse, who commanded the 1/7th Batt. Cheshire Regiment in the Dardanelles, had been drowned through the torpedoing of the P&O liner Persia, came as a painful shock to Macclesfield. It was not known, even among the members of his own family that the gallant officer was on the ill-fated vessel.*
>
> *Towards the end of the year, the Colonel fell victim to sciatica and rheumatism. He was removed to hospital at Malta in November. He left the hospital on December 12th for a rest camp and it is presumed that when he boarded the Persia on December 28th at Malta it was with the intention of proceeding to Egypt to re-join his regiment.*

---

119 http://www.unofficialroyalty.com/december-1915-royalty-and-world-war-i/ and http://thepeerage.com/p47943.htm#i479422

Lt. Col. Henry Backhouse has no known grave and is commemorated on stone no. 4B on the Chatby Memorial in Egypt. Locally, he is commemorated on the Macclesfield Park Green, Town Hall, St Michael's Church, King's School, Park Green Club and Macclesfield Golf Club war memorials and on the Sutton St James' Church and Sutton Walker Lane war memorials.'

Ted Berryman rescued Marie Derogez after *Persia* sank and she subsequently continued to India to her wedding. Her husband, M Bonnand, wrote to Captain Berryman from Calcutta to thank him. Later M and Mme Bonnand wrote to the Royal Humane Society recommending Ted for an award and he received the Society's medal for saving a life at sea. Years later, when asked by his children why he wore a blue medal ribbon on the right breast of his uniform, Ted, modest throughout, made light of it by replying that a lady in the sea was so large he had clung to her and used her as a float.

Thomas Burns and his wife Cecilia were both lost in the sinking. The tragic loss of his infant daughter to meningitis had delayed Cecilia's brother Alexander Clark's return to India and he rebooked to travel with Thomas and Cecilia on the SS *Persia*. Alexander's luck improved in the few minutes of mayhem when *Persia* sank. He was one of the even luckier small group of survivors found by SS *Ning Chow* in the badly damaged lifeboat and landed at Valletta.

Rose Burcombe, her daughter Helen of 2 years and 2 months and her son Edward, only 10 weeks old, all died in the attack on SS *Persia*. They were on their way to join husband and father, Sergeant Edward John Burcombe, in India. Novice traveller Edith Smith, Rose's cousin acting as the children's nurse, survived the sinking. She later married Rose's

Rose Burcombe with baby Edward and daughter Helen.
The caption reads 'Sister Rose and baby at Home. Were torpedode (sic) by the Germans.'
By kind permission of Rachel Rudkin

widower Edward. Sadly, there was to be no happy ending for the new Burcombe family. Edward died in hospital in Colaba, Bombay, in 1921, never to see his and Edith's newly born daughter.

Marjorie Doris Penn Gaskell, who would later be known as actress Ann Codrington, was the only woman first-class passenger to survive the sinking, despite being six months pregnant. Sadly, she and her mother, Mrs Helen Maude de Burgh Codrington, became separated during the sinking and her mother died. Marjorie recovered in Alexandria and continued to Quetta.

In Deansgrange cemetery in the suburban area of Dún Laoghaire-Rathdown, part of the former County Dublin, Ireland, an inscription on a headstone in memory of Elizabeth Kathleen Dawson reads:

'Also Major W. O. C. Dawson
her eldest son
who lost his life through enemy action
on S.S. Persia Dec. 30 1915.'[120]

Captain William Henry Selby Hall, RNR, went down with his ship and his body was never found. He and his wife Mary had a son in 1891, who died aged only 21 and is buried in Portslade cemetery, East Sussex. On this now-worn headstone, close to a seemingly derelict chapel, it is difficult to read:

'In tender and loving memory of Charles Ottley Hall
Only son of Captn W H Selby Hall and Mary his wife
Who fell asleep in Jesus On 20th July 1912 Aged 21 years.'

This brief mention of William Hall predates the *Persia* sinking. Did Mary still believe she was his wife in 1912? His name is on the memorial at Tower Hill. Southampton Seamen's Society commissioned a commemorative tribute to him, made from part of a ship's wheel mounted on an oak plinth with a plaque in gilt:

'In Memory Of Capt. W. H. S. Hall of The P & O Liner Persia. Sunk by enemy torpedo Mediterranean – 30th December 1915'.

This is now on display in the Maritime Museum in Buckler's Hard.

---

120 http://www.igp-web.com/IGPArchives/ire/dublin/photos/tombstones/1headstones/deansgrange-sw2.txt

Following her dive into the sea from *Persia*'s companionway, Doctor Elizabeth Impey never reappeared. Her Quaker family were naturally heartbroken but comforted by the kind words received from many people about Elsie and her death. One of the women, whom Elsie had helped on the ship, wrote to her father:

'Your daughter was a brave woman; we all consider she died a heroine's death'.

Another wrote:

'It was very generous of Dr Impey to give me the assistance she did when practically all were looking after themselves'.

At a meeting on 8th February 1916, someone spoke of *'the courage and self-sacrifice shown by our friend at such a dread moment'*.

Words in a book by H Winifred Sturge and Theodora Clark titled *The Mount School, York*, (Elsie's school) record that:

'her calming the fears of the others; then standing at the head of the companionway to help the women and children on to the slippery deck; all the time thinking last of herself and her own safety' – 'truly as they said, "a brave woman" and one of whom we may be well proud'.

Elizabeth's name is also recorded in St Michael and All Angels churchyard, Cofton Hackett, Bromsgrove, on her father Frederic's gravestone, reading:

'Elizabeth Stephens Impey MB Ch. B
Elder daughter of F & EC Impey
Who perished nobly on the torpedoing
Of the SS Persia in the Mediterranean
In her 39th year
Whilst on her way to be Medical Officer
To the Dufferin Hospital for Women
At Lahore India December 30th 1915'

and on memorial panels at York Minster to women of the British Empire who died in World War 1 and on a memorial stone at Longbridge Meeting

House that records the time and manner of her death. The stone is next to that of her mother who had died on 6th March 1914[121].

The other woman doctor who jumped from the sinking ship, Dr Lilian Cook, was one of those rescued by HMS *Mallow* and taken to Alexandria from where she and other survivors travelled to Bombay on the P&O liner SS *Medina*, arriving on 19th January 1916. The next day Lillian married The Reverend John Warnshuis in the United Free Church of Scotland Mission House.

Gladys Enid MacDonald was also heading to her wedding but died during the attack. Her fiancé, Rowland Hatt-Cook, must have waited anxiously for her joyful arrival in Bombay, only for his hopes and plans to be dashed. They had planned their marriage in the city in January 1916, so the chosen date must have been almost too painful for him to bear. For Enid's parents, the attack doubled their grief, having already lost Gladys's brother to a previous U-boat attack. Lieutenant Donald MacDonald, RN, died when U-9, under Otto Weddigen, sank HMS *Hawke* in October 1914.

Robert N McNeely, the ambitious young American, had wanted to marry his sweetheart Wilma and take her with him on the posting to Aden, but her parents' veto inadvertently saved her life but condemned her to grieve over what might have been. Robert perished alone, his love for Wilma unfulfilled. His body was later washed up near Alexandria and recovered by the collier *Sterling*. He had written a letter to his mother from Tilbury on the day *Persia* sailed, telling her that the ship was a very good steamer conveyed by cruisers and destroyers all the way, so he understood that passage on this steamer was entirely safe. Which arrived first – his optimistic letter or the notification that he was missing?

Captain Humphrey Richard Locke Lawrence died aged only 27 and his body was never found. On the day that he died, his temporary captaincy in the 34th Sikh Pioneers appeared in *The Gazette*. His name appears on the Chatby Memorial in Alexandria. His brother died in service with the Royal Flying Corps in January 1917.

Edwin and Frank Herbert were cousins hailing from an Oxfordshire farming family and both working aboard SS *Persia*. It is believed that Edwin was the ship's carpenter who survived, while Frank was steward-in-charge and sadly lost[122].

---

121 https://mounthistoryroom.files.wordpress.com/2014/07/elizabeth-impey-story.docx
122 The News, Portsmouth, Thursday, 16th June 2016

Some survivors reported that Captain John (Jack) Thornton Lodwick, DSO, met his death standing on the deck of the sinking ship, flinging chairs and anything that would float to women and men struggling in the water, working alongside Second Lieutenant John Lionel Miller-Hallett. Captain Lodwick was known as an excellent swimmer and could have saved his own life by plunging into the sea, and witnesses tell that he gave his life for others without hesitation. The Government of Bombay presented a tablet recording his services, attached to the memorial to his grandfather, General Lodwick, at Lodwick Point, in the Sanatorium of the Bombay Presidency[123]. The following is an extract from a letter from Colonel Ormsby, dated 18th January 1916, about Jack Lodwick:

> '*Captain Lodwick's loss as a regimental officer is incalculable. In the course of thirty years' service, after intimate knowledge of many hundreds of officers, I have not come across half a dozen of his equals and it is a melancholy pleasure to be able to remember that during the six years I have commanded the battalions, the terms I have used in my annual reports on him are such as I have seldom been able to use in their entirety to any other officer. He possessed a peculiar knack of getting the best and most willing work out of his men and there was no man I would sooner have had with me in a tight place than him. I am perfectly certain that he died as he lived – calm and collected and doing his best for those around him.*'

Jack's widow Kathleen gave birth to their son, John Alan Lodwick, on 2nd March 1916, only sixty-four days after his father's death in the *Persia* sinking.

Maharaja Sir Jagatjit Singh Bahadur, his family and those of his party who disembarked from *Persia*, travelled to Genoa by train to board the Dutch ship SS *Prins Der Nederlanden* for Port Said. At Port Said he changed back to the P&O line, boarded SS *Medina* and continued to Bombay and home in Kapurthala. Of those in his entourage who remained aboard, some were lucky and others not. The fortunate included Inder Singh, a strong swimmer. His unconfirmed story has him boarding a large raft-like wooden structure on which he survived for three days until picked up by a searching vessel. Mlle Guyot, his servant, also survived but B Mangal Singh, B Partab Singh and governess Kathleen Reed all died. Inder Singh eventually made his own way to Kapurthala, arriving by train and making his way into the city on foot. Everyone thought it was a miracle that he had risen, because they had believed him dead.

---

123 http://lib. Militaryarchive.co.uk/library/Biographical/library/The-VC-and-DSO-Volume-II/files/assets/basic-html/page390.html

Second Lieutenant Lionel Miller-Hallett arrived in Alexandria on HMS *Mallow*, where survivors stayed in the Regina Palace Hotel. He received an advance of £15 to kit himself out and was assured that P&O was paying hotel bills. He was keen to get on to Bombay. In the letter to his mother, he told her that he was writing with the pen she gave him and told her that his ring, cigarette case and pipe were all right, but that his camera was the worse for wear. He signed himself off:

Very best of love to all,
Ever your very loving son,
LION.

When he arrived back at the Cantonment in Dehra Dun, he seems to have felt a sense of duty to a few people, friends made and lost in the space of a few days. He wrote a letter to a Mrs Crossley, the mother of Mrs Smith who died in the sinking with her husband. Note that I have inferred a few illegible words from their context:

Dehra Dun Cantonment
6/3/16

'Dear Mrs Crossley

I am afraid that it will seem a very long time before you see this letter.

I was at the same table as your daughter Mrs Smith — and had just sat down beside her when the explosion occurred. That moment and the ensuing ones on deck made me prouder than ever before to be British. None of the ladies showed any sign of fear at all, although you could see they knew the danger. I did not hear a word spoken in the saloon following the explosion. Mr & Mrs Smith went for a boat on the port side & mine was just opposite on the other. After the Captain had sent all women and children on my side down to the port side, I went down there and while throwing tables and chairs overboard saw Mr & Mrs Smith standing quietly together: soon afterwards the boat turned on its side. Death must have been practically instantaneous: our officer who was caught and washed out at the last moment said he felt nothing except a vague surprise at the greatness of the forces about him.

Just after we had come on deck – Gardiner* [sic], a 2nd Lieut. who was also at our table and was from the same lifeboat as Mr & Mrs Smith gave the latter his lifebelt as Mr Smith had apparently been unable to reach his cabin which was amidships. Mrs Smith had been unwilling to take it, saying that it was not fair to him – but he assured her that he was a very good swimmer, as indeed he was and she eventually consented; later the Captain threw a lifebelt down from the upper deck to Gardiner & he was saved.

He is a great athlete and possesses many trophies gained in sport. At his last school sports at Durham in 1913, he won six first prizes and gained the record for the highest number of points ever obtained at the school sports. He was a great Rugby footballer, having played for Richmond. When the Hunts. Cyclist Battalion was inaugurated, he became one of the first Lieutenants and was subsequently promoted to the rank of Captain. He reverted to a Lieutenant to join the regular army and he was on his way to his regiment in India when the Persia was sunk.[124]

The voyage had been such a good one all the way and our table was by far the cheeriest on board. At Marseilles, Mrs Smith took us all out to tea and we were making great plans as to what we would do at Port Said the following days. A friend of Mrs Smith's – a Mrs Graham who I think she knew at Chittagong also came aboard later from Marseilles onwards – Robertson of our table, of the Indian Police and in the 4th Cavalry looked after her after the explosion & the last I saw of them was they were standing quietly together on deck.

It is on those at home that the greater load falls and has fallen throughout the years, but I hope that those three children who lost parents in this disaster will someday know how pluckily they behaved. All the ladies on board realized the dangers & yet when it came all faced it calmly; higher courage than that it is impossible to find anywhere –

I have not put down in a letter to you all that the officers who were saved said and felt about the conduct of the ladies on board and after such an experience; they came from a deeper source than at other times. I hope in years to come that I may meet your grandchildren when I am home on leave. I expect I shall always be able to find their address from Mrs Hill. I am afraid that this is a

---

124 Hunts County News, 7th January 1916

* Lieutenant JMS Gardner was the third son of the Reverend W R Gardner, vicar of St Mary's and rector of All Saints, Huntingdon. He went to Durham School, obtained an exhibition and studied at St John's College, Cambridge, where he had some military training in the University Officers' Training Corps.

very short letter but I hope that it may do something in the way of sharing what people thought & did during those few moments.

I am yours sincerely

J. L. Miller-Hallett'

Marcel and Hilda Conran-Smith had left their six-year-old son Louis at school in England before returning to India together. They were both killed. Orphaned Louis grew up to become Lieutenant Commander Louis Conran-Smith, RN, awarded the DSC in December 1943 for *'steadfast courage and skill in command of HMS Hazard in a dangerous and important minesweeping operation'*[125].

Joyce Minnitt was returning to India with her baby, Christine Joy, born in March 1915. Joyce and Christine, then aged 10 months, both died.

Lieutenant Colonel Alfred Ralph Nethersole died in the attack leaving behind a widow in Sydenham, Kent, Mrs Marian Alfreda Cairns Nethersole.

Stewardess Mary Pennington, 'The Duchess', survived the attack and landed at Alexandria.

William Orr Orr drowned in the sinking but his nephew and travelling companion, James B Dickie, escaped in one of the lifeboats and landed in Alexandria. He later continued to his planned destination in Burma, but never fully recovered from the ordeal and died there a few months later. As William was the last male of that Orr line, ownership of the Kaim passed to his half-sister Margaret. Her husband, another James Dickie, later became known as 'Dickie of the Kaim'. On William's mother's gravestone an inscription reads:

'William Orr Orr
Who died when the SS Persia
Was torpedoed in the Mediterranean Sea
30 December 1915 aged 49 years
I am the resurrection and the life'[126]

Lieutenant John Alexander Tower Robertson died in the attack on SS Persia, aged 29. He was born at Berwick's Ravensdowne Barracks and educated at The Grammar School of Anthony Browne, Serjeant at the Law,

---

125 *The Times,* Tuesday 22nd August 1944
126 http://www.lochwinnoch.info/history/local-people/the-last-william-orr-of-kaim

in Brentwood and then at Uppingham College[127]. He served in the Old Berwick Volunteers as a subaltern and made time to take part in activities of the Boy Scout movement in Berwick. While working in Calcutta, he became Assistant Chief Commissioner of the Scouts in India and received a decoration from the Chief Scout, General Baden Powell. He gained a commission in the Indian Army Reserve of Officers in March 1915 and became attached to the 2nd Battalion, 3rd Queen Alexandra's Own Gurkha Rifles. His unit transferred almost immediately to the Western Front, first to France and later to Flanders. His battalion was one of the many Indian Army units then sent to Mesopotamia and John had home leave before heading back on SS *Persia* to rejoin them. His commanding officer later wrote:

> *'During the time he served with us in France, he proved himself time after time to be an invaluable officer – cool brave and cheery and self-reliant, thoroughly reliable in every way, in fact, we could have not picked a better anywhere. We had all been looking forward so to getting him back and to lose him this way is a bitter grief. I feel certain that he died cool and cheery, with all of his wits about him and doing his best to save others.'*

Another officer said:

> *'He was very popular with all ranks. An enthusiastic volunteer – by his death the Commandant has lost a personal friend and the corps the services of one of the best of officers and a good comrade.'*

Lieutenant John Alexander Tower Robertson's name appears on the Chatby Memorial, Alexandria, on a plaque in the Church of the Holy Trinity and St Mary's and on the war memorial in the Guildhall, both within very short strolls of his Ravensdowne birthplace in the historic border town of Berwick-upon-Tweed.

Arthur Twining Roch was an engineer lieutenant in the Royal Navy. Late in 1915, his ship HMS *Prosperine* sailed to support the British intervention in Mesopotamia. Arthur went home on leave prior to this and boarded the SS *Persia* to rejoin his ship. Arthur was among those lost. He was 42 years old and is commemorated on panel 8 of the Chatham Naval Memorial in Kent and in St Mary's Church, Warren, a parish in the hundred of Castlemartin which dates from the thirteenth century. The church contains a marble memorial to him[128].

---

127 North East War Memorials Project at http://www.newmp.org.uk/article.php?categoryid= 99&articleid=1476&displayorder=49
128 Information by kind permission of Steven John, West Wales War Memorial Project

Homer Russell Salisbury, president-elect with the Seventh-day Adventist Church was travelling to take up his appointment. He had sailed from New York to join the SS *Persia* in Marseilles, bound for India but was never to arrive.

Captain Arthur Freer Spreckley (Gurkha Rifles) was drowned in the attack, aged only 27. Also lost with him were his wife Ada Blanche Celina Spreckley and their infant daughter Pamela. The last sighting of the family was Mrs Spreckley frantically seeking their infant daughter and Captain Spreckley seeking both. Their infant son, David, too ill to travel, had remained behind and became an orphan.

There is a cross near the entrance to Holy Trinity Church, Old Town, Stratford-upon-Avon. Part of it is a memorial to Mrs Kathleen Stoehr. The inscription reads:

> *'In loving memory of Kathleen Stoehr born August 12 1894,*
> *entered into life December 30 1915.*
> *She perished in the sinking of the SS Persia off Crete by a German submarine.*
> *Wherever she went she brought light and joy.*
> *She was beloved by all who knew her.*
> *"His servants shall serve him and they shall see his face."*
> *The wife of Felix Stoehr, Captain Royal Engineers*
> *and the daughter of Reginald Hudson, Stratford-upon-Avon.'*

From the *Northampton Daily Echo*, Monday, 3rd January 1916:

> *'The news of the sinking of the P. And O. Liner Persia, received in Northampton on Saturday, gave rise to considerable anxiety, for among the passengers on the boat were four Y.M.C.A. Workers, bound for Egypt, two of whom were Northampton young men, while in charge of the party was Mr A. H. Johnson, Y.M.C.A. Divisional Secretary. Happily, definite news has been received this morning that Mr Johnson and the two Northampton men are safe. Up to eleven o'clock this morning no news had been received of Mr Hopkins, the fourth member of the party. The two Northampton men are Mr Reginald W. Heams, son of Mr and Mrs W. J. Heams, of Kettering Road and Mr Leonard W. Gascoigne, son of Mrs Moss, who keeps a provision dealer's shop in Hunter Street. "Reg" Heams, as he is familiarly known to a wide circle of friends in Northampton, is 24 years of age. He had been employed as a clerk at J. Sears and Co.'s factory, but in March last left to take up work*

among the troops with the Y.M.C.A. He had worked for a time at Tring in the Divisional Office with Mr Johnson. When the National Council of the Y.M.C.A. appointed the latter to go to Egypt to supervise the work there, Mr Heams volunteered to accompany him and was accepted. Mr Heams is well known in cricket and football circles as he has been secretary of the Mount Pleasant Football Club and was captain of the Prince's Street Cricket Club. He has done extremely valuable work for the Y.M.C.A. and is held in the highest esteem by his colleagues. Leonard W. Gascoigne reached 19 years of age on Christmas Day, spending his birthday on board ship. He was formerly apprenticed with Mr J. E. Partridge, of Sheep Street and from the outbreak of the war did voluntary work among the troops for the Y.M.C.A., giving up his holidays for the purpose. Since November he had been on the permanent staff and was delighted at being one of the men selected to accompany Mr Johnson to Egypt. Mr A. H. Johnson is one of the best-known men in the Y.M.C.A. Movement. He was formerly a commercial traveller and was unpaid secretary of the Wednesbury Y.M.C.A. He did such good work in that capacity that he was given a permanent appointment and for some time past had been a Divisional Secretary. Since the outbreak of war particularly he had shown possession of remarkable organising ability. Mr Hopkins is not a local man, but he did excellent work in connection with the Y.M.C.A. Hut at Bedford. Mr H. G. Reynolds (secretary of the Northampton Y.M.C.A.), who has succeeded Mr Johnson as divisional secretary, had an anxious time during the weekend and has kept in close touch during the whole time by telephone and telegraph with the P. And O. Company's office in London. The company's representatives have shown every courtesy and consideration in the matter and have done their best to obtain every information possible. Another local passenger on board the vessel was Mr W. Everett*, the eldest son of Mr R. M. Everett, proprietor of the George Hotel, Kettering. Mr Everett was on board the vessel as a surgeon and New Year's cards posted at Marseilles have been received by the family. No news has been received concerning Mr Everett and much sympathy will be felt with the father and the brother (Captain F. Everett, of the Northamptonshire Regiment) and the other members of the family in their painful anxiety.

Ayah Mary Fernandez, travelling home without a child in her care, probably died alone, as she had lived for months before. The Four Sisters of the Congregation of Daughters of the Cross, returning from the convent at

---

*   Mr Everett was on the crew list of SS *Persia* as Surgeon. He was spotted by Lord Montagu clinging to a floating locker and suffering from a head wound but was not among the rescued.'

Carshalton House to Karachi, were all lost, while Miss Maysie Markwick, under their care as chaperones, somehow survived.

Finally, what became of George Walton, *Persia*'s stand-in second saloon chef, who had not been on *Persia*'s original crew list? He had sacrificed Christmas at home and deputised for another chef who was then able to stay with his wife for the birth of their child. Sadly, George died as a result of his kindness, leaving his widow Ruth to sorrow over his Christmas generosity.

Warm and comfortable on board but women's clothing must have made escaping and staying afloat extremely difficult in the rushing sea water
© P&O Heritage Collection
www.poheritage.com

Why *Persia*?

Some blame P&O for the sinking of SS *Persia* because the company continued to publish and advertise dates and times of sailings, but so did all the other shipping companies. I eventually discounted this theory on the grounds that communications and technology of the time were inadequate to locate any specific ship in the open sea, particularly when the Admiralty advocated route variations and zigzagging during daylight. My belief grew that the SS *Persia* was doubly unlucky firstly because her course inadvertently carried her close to the waiting U-38 and secondly because the commander of that U-boat was the angry Max Valentiner. There are no reasons to believe that he was looking for SS *Persia* – any enemy or neutral ship would have done, but a big liner would add thousands of tons to his tally.

Just as Godfrey Herbert had launched a 'take no prisoners' vendetta from HMS *Baralong* after the *Lusitania* deaths, I believe that Max Valentiner had become embittered by the loss of his cousin, Bernd Wegener, in an alleged British war crime, and the death of his best friend, Claus Hansen, in a Q-ship ambush. He had then grown angry with his own government which had ordered U-boats from their potentially war-winning campaign around the British Isles to appease the United States. He was hostile because the ongoing British blockade was starving his own family and millions more. Valentiner would write about his service in U-38 later, styling himself as a Viking[129], one of those highly capable and well-armed seamen and fierce warriors known for swift and often cruel attacks. Perhaps he was pursuing Viking-style vengeance. In modern times they might have checked Max Valentiner and Godfrey Herbert for stress disorders and the psychological transformations these can bring. Both seem to have been exhibiting several of the symptoms, including aggressive, reckless and destructive behaviour.

---

129 Valentiner, Max (1934). *U38. Wikingerfahrten eines deutschen U-Bootes*. (U-38. Viking voyages of a German U-boat). Berlin: Ullstein

So, it seems that this had become payback time, with SS *Persia* simply in the wrong place at the wrong time. Valentiner probably wrote '*assume* (her) *to be a troop transporter*' in his logbook to justify sidestepping international law and his own government's orders. When he viewed SS *Persia*'s sparsely populated decks through his periscope, he would have seen that *Persia* could not have been a troopship, but reasoned that if ever called to account for sinking her, any evidence would have been beyond reach. However, fate took hidden and ironic vengeance on Valentiner – he chose to sink rather than stop and search the SS *Persia*, destroying an incredibly valuable prize ship later thought to have been carrying the Maharaja's millions in jewels, watches and bullion. As it was, the SS *Persia* became a lonely statistic, just one of over 760 allied ships attacked by U-boats since the outbreak of war 17 months earlier, 45 per month on average.

Luck later improved for some of *Persia*'s passengers because HMS *Mallow* had been out 'looking for submarines and mines', more in hope than expectation, when she stumbled across *Persia*'s lifeboats. The Royal Navy did not have the means to find or fight U-boats, nor the ability to escort merchant ships and, until 1917, there was no improvement in this dire situation. Britain's Dreadnought warships stayed home to avoid the U-boats they expected their merchant marine colleagues to face every day. The valour of merchant seafarers who kept Britain fed, fuelled and supplied with raw materials throughout the war is inestimable, but crude numbers show they suffered seventeen thousand deaths and 3,305 lost ships[130], a dreadful waste, and just another statistic.

Looking back over 1915, the *Baralong* incident marked a low point in the history of the Royal Navy, but it didn't happen in isolation. It was as much a human failing as a naval one, seemingly provoked by the infamous sinking of RMS *Lusitania* without warning by Walther Schwieger, commander of U-20. It shook the world after she unexpectedly turned towards the submerged U-20 and into such cataclysmic consequences. Of her 1,959 passengers and crew, 1,195 died, including 27 of 33 infants. Six hundred people became 'the missing'. The sinking that caused outrage in Britain, America and much of the world, was celebrated in Germany and for a while was the subject of a commemorative medal. Red mist had then descended across some British naval eyes. HMS *Baralong* ambushed U-27, exactly as the promoters of Q-ships intended, but then took murderous revenge for *Lusitania* by wiping out the U-boat crew – euphemistically referred to as 'taking no prisoners', which news was then censored in Britain.

---

130 Commonwealth War Graves Commission (CWGC)

Whatever might have been a brotherhood of the seas had descended into bloody murders and revenge, when civilian lives seemed less important than tonnage sunk. SS *Persia* was caught in this murderous downward spiral simply because her approaching smoke caught Valentiner's eye. He was not waiting just for her, nor could he have interpreted P&O sailing times to find her or any other named ship. U-38 was more like a spider waiting patiently for the first insect to happen along.

In the latter half of 1915, two ordinary men, Max Valentiner and Godfrey Herbert, experienced and committed appalling wrongs. Both had trained to kill as part of their patriotic duties, but were unprepared for dealing with the consequences. Instead, they probably found it less troubling to turn their backs on the morals and principals of civilisation, at least while far beyond its sight.

> *'The most shocking fact about war is that its victims and its instruments are individual human beings and that these individual human beings are condemned by the monstrous conventions of politics to murder or be murdered in quarrels not their own.'*
>
> Aldous Huxley – Words and Behaviour (1936)

Germany alleged war crimes by McBride (Lieutenant Commander Godfrey Herbert) of HMS *Baralong* and Britain made similar allegations against Kapitänleutnant Max Valentiner of U-38. Neither case ever came to court. Both men received decorations for their exploits, Herbert with the DSO and Valentiner with the Pour le Mérite – heroes in their own countries, criminals elsewhere. What would the future hold for each of them?

What Became of Godfrey Herbert?

Herbert was awarded the Distinguished Service Order on 10th September 1915[131], only twenty-one days after the euphemistically named '*Baralong* incident'. The citation referred to submarine actions during operations in the Sea of Marmora, the inland sea that opens out at the eastern end of the Dardanelles. Given that naval operations there commenced with an attack on 19th February 1915, it is difficult to see how Herbert could have served there and then. He served as liaison officer aboard the French steam-powered submarine *Archimede* from 16th December 1914, then went to HMS *Maidstone* at Harwich and to SS *Antwerp* in early 1915. He was on that Q-ship when it encountered Weddigen's U-29 on 12th March 1915, but could not get close. Weddigen had sunk three British ships that day, the *Andalusian*, the *Headlands* and the *Indian City*, but when *Antwerp* appeared, the U-boat lingered on the surface to see what might happen, then slipped beneath the surface and disappeared, much to Herbert's frustration. He took command of the *Baralong* on 17th March, followed by weeks of cruising to tempt a U-boat without any contacts. How he could have served beyond the Dardanelles at that time is difficult to understand.

Late in 1915, he became captain of the new E-class submarine E22. This lasted for only eight months but, with no successes against enemy ships, he transferred back to Q-ship duty, replaced on E22 by his friend Lieutenant Commander Reginald Dimsdale on 24th April 1916. The following day, Dimsdale died along with thirty of his crew when UB-18 under Kapitänleutnant Otto Steinbrinck torpedoed E22. Only two survived to become prisoners of war. In tragic circumstances, Godfrey Herbert had escaped with his life once again.

---

131 https://www.naval-history.net/WW1NavyBritishLGDecorationszzDSO.htm HERBERT, Godfrey, Cdr, RN, DSO (29292) (31483)

Herbert had chosen to marry on the day the E22 sinking appeared in the newspapers. His wife was Elizabeth, the widow of a Royal Marine friend killed in February 1915. Herbert next captained Q-ship *Carrigan Head*, also known as Q4 and carried out patrols for weeks without sighting a single U-boat. All was quiet until, on 9th September 1916, UB-18, still under Otto Steinbrinck, ordered *Carrigan Head* to stop 60 miles off the Lizard. At 1,500 yards, the U-boat hit *Carrigan Head* with two shells. *Carrigan Head* returned fire but missed with all seven rounds as UB-18 submerged. Herbert dropped a depth charge which exploded so close to his own ship that one of its guns discharged accidentally, causing severe self-damage. The U-boat that had killed his friend Dimsdale made a successful getaway.

After this, Herbert moved back to submarines, his first love, in time to take part in sea trials for steam-powered K-class submarines, envisaged as high-speed (21 knot) giants, larger than the destroyers of their day. Their role would be to steam at speed ahead of the Grand Fleet then submerge to attack an enemy battle fleet. The Navy appointed Herbert commander of K13 undergoing trials in Gareloch on 29th January 1917 with a crew of 55, plus 25 Admiralty and dockyard workers and Lieutenant Commander Francis Goodheart, who was preparing to take command of K14. She had just completed a measured course at 23 knots, making her the world's fastest surfaced submarine.

However, diving had been troublesome in the new K-class, complicated, slow and taking at least five minutes, during which boilers had to be shut down and the funnel and all vents sealed. This had resulted in unwanted visits to the seabed in earlier trials and, on this day, it happened again. A flickering warning light went unheeded so four boiler room inlets stayed open. She took in water and went down quickly, landing on the bed 9 fathoms down (54 feet, 15.5 metres). Darkness was approaching, so the rescue could not start until the next day. Herbert ordered the engine room sealed and the thirty-two trapped men drowned immediately. The remaining crew could not evacuate but they were safe while the air lasted. Herbert and Goodheart then devised a scheme for both to escape in turn from the conning tower and direct operations from the surface. Goodheart was to go first, then Herbert would close the hatch behind him. Goodheart escaped but Herbert was unable to close the hatch and shot to the surface. There was no sign of his colleague. Rescuers made slow progress but fed air and supplies down to the stricken submarine. Fifty-five hours after the initial mishap, 48 survivors emerged and rescuers recovered 32 bodies. Yet again, Herbert had managed to survive when others around him had died. They found Goodheart's body, his skull shattered during the attempted escape. His award of the Albert Medal in Gold, made posthumously[132] by King George V, is equivalent to today's George Medal[133].

The tragic accident ended Herbert's submarine days. He took over four armed trawlers in March 1917 to seek submerged U-boats by turning off his engines and drifting silently while listening on hydrophones for noises from the U-boats' electric motors. On 12th June 1917, one of Herbert's trawlers, the *Sea King*, dropped a random depth charge to see if she could stir up any U-boat movement below. She did better than that, by chance blowing up UC-66 and her load of mines, leaving oil and debris, but no bodies on the surface. The Navy did not credit Herbert with his sinking until May 1919, but when eventually recognised he earned a bar to his DSO.

Herbert spent the rest of the war in a staff role, where he had time to mull over his very mixed experiences, his several failures and narrow escapes during which others died. Particularly irritated by the lack of any reward for his crew for sinking U-27 and perhaps conveniently forgetting the merciless killings, he raised the request again and the crew of *Baralong* eventually received an award of £1,000 in June 1918, followed by another £185 from an Admiralty Prize Court in November 1919. The total value of these awards was equivalent to about £60,000[134] in 2015, boosting Herbert's esteem in the eyes of his crew. He was their hero. Potential evidence against him in any court regarding crimes during the *Baralong* Incident would have met with an overwhelming rebuttal. However, it seems that nothing would convince senior officers that the now Commander Herbert, DSO and Bar, would ever wear the four rings of a captain on his sleeve.

Commander Godfrey Herbert retired from the Navy in 1919 and took up a sales post for the Birmingham Small Arms Company Limited (BSA), well-known for manufacturing military and sporting guns, motorbikes, cars, buses, steel, iron castings, tools, coal-handling machinery and other industrial products. He became managing director of the Daimler Car Division before moving to live and work in South Africa, his wife's birthplace, and later in Beira, Portuguese East Africa (now Mozambique).

On the outbreak of World War 2, the Navy recalled him to the command of 11,136-ton HMS *Cilicia*, an armed merchant cruiser, pendant number F.54, escorting convoys along the West African coast. While on these duties, Lord

---

132 The official citation for the award of the Albert Medal in Gold to Goodhart (Gazetted on 23rd April 1918) provides a graphic account of what happened
133 https://www.greatwarforum.org/topic/254451-francies-herbert-h-goodhart/
134 Historical UK inflation rates and calculator: http://inflation.iamkate.com/

Haw-Haw, the American-born Irish propaganda broadcaster to the United Kingdom during World War 2, singled him out for attention, naming him in a broadcast, referring to the *Baralong*, his McBride pseudonym, naming his current ship and boasting that they knew its exact position. He reminded Herbert that a £10,000 reward (perhaps £500,000 in 2015 values) for him, dead or alive, still existed and ended with:

'*We will get you, Captain Herbert.*'

They, the Nazis, did not, but the threat worried the Admiralty. Herbert only served aboard *Cilicia* from 2nd September 1939 to 15th March 1940 and then went ashore for a while before his last command, that of HMS *Kelantan*. He left the Navy in 1944 aged 60 and returned to Beira and his job with a shipping agent where he became managing director. He later moved to his company's office in Salisbury, Rhodesia (now Zimbabwe), before retiring to Umtali (now Mutare) close to the Mozambique border. Here, Herbert used to meet socially with Commander Patrick Cochran, a retired naval officer and friend. They would sometimes stay overnight in the British Club, where Cochran told that he sometimes heard screams during the night from Herbert's room. Herbert told his friend that he was not ashamed to admit that he had recurring nightmares about his time on *Baralong*[135], perhaps ongoing signs of stress disorder.

Godfrey Herbert died of leukaemia on 6th August 1961 in Umtali. He was seventy-seven. Officers from HMS *Dolphin* scattered his ashes off Nab Tower, out where the Solent meets the English Channel. The tower was to have been part of England's anti-submarine defences during the first war, in which he had served, but was in place too late, the problem that recurred for Herbert during his anti-submarine days and which appears to have frustrated and angered him to extremes.

---

135 Coles, Alan (1986). *Slaughter at Sea?: The truth behind a naval war crime.* p 190. London, Robert Hale Ltd. ISBN 978-0-7090-2597-9

What Became of Max Valentiner?

Is it permissible merely to carry out orders and commit one's conscience to someone else's keeping?[136]

On 1st January 1916, two days after the sinking of SS *Persia*, Valentiner was awarded the Iron Cross 1st class and on 14th May, the Knight's Cross with Swords of the Royal House Order of Hohenzollern, an order of knighthood awarded to military officers and civilians of equivalent status.

During 1915, he had attacked 75 vessels, sinking 179,685 tons and causing the deaths of 1,356 people, but in 1916 he attacked only 56 vessels for 116,871 tons, 19 ships fewer than in 1915, their tonnage down by sixty-two thousand. Deaths caused by U-38's guns and torpedoes plummeted by 1,342 when compared with 1915. Perhaps he had exorcised some demons? Did the weight of one thousand three hundred lost souls in 1915 lie heavily on the pastor's son?

One of his noted attacks in 1916 took place on 3rd December when he sank three ships in Funchal Roads or Funchal Harbour, Madeira. Photographs show a large sweeping bay in which visiting ships anchored offshore. It was after this attack, seemingly made on becalmed and unprotected ships, that he earned Prussia's highest military award, the Orden Pour le Mérite, known also as the 'Blue Max', awarded to officers for repeated and continual gallantry in action. Of the 498 German and Austrian U-boat commanders in World War 1, only 29 are known to have received this honour, of which Valentiner was the sixth. Whatever the entente allies thought of Max Valentiner, some people in Germany and Schleswig and his senior officers appear to have

---

136 Solzhenitsyn, Aleksandr (1973). The Gulag Archipelago, 1918-1956: An Experiment in Literary Investigation, Books V–VII

held him in high regard, confirmed when on 5th January 1917, he became an honorary citizen of his home town, Sønderborg. At sea, success at the level he had enjoyed in 1915 again eluded him aboard U-38, despite the announcement by Germany on 9th January that unrestricted submarine warfare had resumed. In January he sank one vessel, February three, none during March and April, four in May, none in June, five in July and one in August.

Valentiner finally left U-38 in Kataro on 15th September 1917 and travelled to Kiel to take command of U-157. The Imperial Navy had built two large cargo-carrying U-boats, *Deutschland* and *Bremen*, to help beat the blockade of Germany by carrying cargo from the United States while submerged, but plans for more ended once America joined the war. Cargo U-boats under construction were reconfigured as Class 151 U-boats. While similar in length to Valentiner's previous U-38, the 151 class was larger in every other dimension, displacing 1,512 tons when surfaced compared with only 685 tons. They could carry eighteen rather than six torpedoes, treble the number of rounds for deck guns and had a range of 25,000 miles compared with only 8,790.

Christian August Max Ahlmann Valentiner wearing some prestigious decorations including Pour le Merite

In what would become Valentiner's final voyage as a U-boat commander, he took U-157 down the west coast of Africa and around the Canary Islands. He boosted his supplies by capturing the *SS Norefos*, a Norwegian freighter, on 11th January 1918 and used her as a supply ship until she outlived her usefulness and he sank her on 1st March. On this voyage, Valentiner sank only seven ships, returning to Kiel after 130 days, the longest mission ever by a submarine at that time. His relieved parents arrived in Kiel to welcome him home after he had been out of radio contact for two months. He left his post as commander of U-157 in July 1918 to help oversee the completion of U-143 and to train new U-boat commanders in attack methods, a subject in which he was both qualified and experienced. All Germany's shipyards were building U-boats, with plans for 40 every month, so the need for well-trained officers and men was considerable. If each new U-boat was to have a 30-man crew, 1,200 men would need training every month. When the Kaiser visited to find out about submarine training, Max Valentiner was a guest at the imperial lunch table.

A few days after the Kaiser's visit, Valentiner received a message that his father had died. The Imperial Navy provided him with a steam torpedo boat to hurry home to Sønderborg to be with his grieving mother and to pay his respects to his father. His senior officers clearly held Valentiner in the highest regard.

By the autumn of 1918, the war was going badly for Germany. The German Admiralty made an order on 24th October for the Kaiserliche Marine to provoke a decisive battle with the British Grand Fleet in the southern North Sea. This angered German sailors who had spent extended periods in harbour, their political masters unwilling for them to confront the British Navy. The men had grown frustrated doing menial and unnecessary chores just to keep them busy, particularly repetitious and pointless parade-ground drill. Resentment of their officers had grown. The elite still seemed to be enjoying the good life, while ratings felt angry and humiliated.

On 29th October, an order to prepare for the battle was issued. The sailors foresaw this as a suicide mission and were unwilling to risk their lives when they already realised that Germany was losing the war. The Kaiserliche Marine rescinded the order but the genie was out of the bottle. During the night of 29th to 30th of October, sailors aboard ships of the Third Navy Squadron mutinied as they lay at anchor off Wilhelmshaven. Some sailors travelled across Germany spreading the news and seeking support. The lives of naval officers appeared to be at great risk with threats made to kill them, as in the Russian revolution. A report that a British flotilla was heading for Kiel roused senior officers to leave the area, particularly those named as war criminals by the British, which included Valentiner. He left with his wife and child for Hamburg where his wife's family lived.

The situation was desperate. The population was starving and the army retreating. On 9th November 1918, Kaiser Wilhelm II abdicated and left for Holland in the hope of avoiding civil war. Max Valentiner's name disappeared from the official list of German naval officers. He adopted the name Carl Schmidt and vanished into the chaos of post-war Germany, after becoming the third most successful U-boat commander of that war measured in gross registered tons sunk, in his case 299,482 tons. Only Kapitänleutnant Lothar von Arnauld de la Perière (455,869 tons) and Kapitänleutnant Walther Forstmann (391,607 tons) headed him.

In 1920, citizens voted in a referendum for Schleswig to reunite with Denmark and the official Anschluss of Nordschleswig took place on 15th June. The city council then debated how a likely war criminal could be an honorary citizen of the city of Sønderborg and Valentiner resigned the honour with reluctance.

During the inter-war period, Valentiner ran a small company in Kiel, dealing in engines and spares, and tried his hand as a shipowner. He also worked for both Drägerwerke which made diving and breathing equipment and for Adeltwerke which built ship lifts and cranes. In January 1940, soon after the outbreak of World War 2, he became Group Commander for the U-boat Acceptance Commission, a position he held until March 1945. On 1st January 1941, the Kriegsmarine promoted him to Kapitän zur See and then on 31st March 1945, he retired from the Kriegsmarine. At some time his family emigrated to South America but he he lived at Sønderborg until his death aged 65 on 19th July 1949, possibly caused by engine fumes inhaled in his early career when serving aboard gasoline-powered U-boats U-3 and U-10. His grave is in Sønderborg cemetery, Denmark. During house-clearance someone found his honorary citizenship certificate and since 2014 it has been on permanent loan to the Deutsches Museum, Nordschleswig.

His decorations were:

Lifesaving Medal
Order of the Crown
Iron Cross 2nd class
Iron Cross 1st class
Royal House Order of Hohenzollern
Pour le Mérite
Order of the Iron Crown
Iron Half Moon
Liakat Medal
Empire Silver Medal Imtiaz with Scimitars
Hanseatic Cross

What Became of Survivors?

While the names of many who perished aboard the SS *Persia* appear on well-known memorials such as those on Tower Hill in London, in Alexandria and Mumbai, the names of many others are on modest memorials in towns, villages, local churches and family headstones. We must not forget all those who endured the trauma of the attack and survived, but only a few of their stories remain.

Marjorie Doris Penn Gaskell continued her journey back to Quetta in good time to give birth to a daughter, Patricia Maud, on 14th March 1916. This daughter would become known as the actress Patricia Hilliard and survive until 2001. Marjorie's mother Helen died in the sinking and her only known memorial is an inscription on the grave of her father-in-law, Colonel Edward Christopher Codrington in Littleham near Exmouth, Devon. The younger brother Kenneth never talked about the sinking but it seems that he secretly blamed Marjorie for insisting on going to Quetta at short notice to have her baby, leading to the death of their mother[137].

Dr Lilian Warnshuis (Dr Lilian Cook when she boarded SS *Persia*) and her husband John would have two daughters, Joan and Lois. They moved to the United States in 1925 where Lilian worked as a doctor in New York. From 1949 she was the medical head of Connecticut College and they later named the Infirmary at the College after her. She was the first woman appointed to the staff of Staten Island Hospital and won New York Infirmary's Elizabeth Blackwell Award for Outstanding Women Physician in 1955[138]. She died at the Episcopal Church Home, Wilmington, Delaware, in 1985 at the age of 98.

---

137 Family history by James Crowden, June 2016
138 Connecticut College, Connecticut College Alumnae Magazine, Spring 1984

Once safely home, on 25th January 1916 the Maharaja Sir Jagatjit Singh Bahadur wrote to a Mr Wood, Political Secretary to the Government of India[139], about a recent discussion the two of them had shared with the Viceroy of India, Lord Hardinge. The conversation touched on 'the heavy material loss' sustained by the Maharaja in 'the disaster to the ill-fated SS *Persia*'. This related specifically to his Knight Grand Commander of the Order of the Star of India insignia, awarded to reward conspicuous merit and loyalty, and three other medals commemorating events in the British royal family. He added that the losses had not occurred through any lack of care on his part but through the gross and wanton act of His Majesty's enemies. He asked for replacements in time for a Durbar he planned, and learned that he had to pay. This raises again the question as to why anyone warned about a possible attack on a ship on which he had planned to travel would disembark with his family, make other travel plans and leave aboard a fortune in jewellery, bullion and cherished decorations[140]. Were his riches ever loaded? Did they remain on board when he decided not to board the SS *Persia*? If so, are they scattered across the seabed or somewhere inside the sunken ship? If not, where are they?

The Maharaja later divorced Prem Kaur. He arranged a pension for her and she returned to live in Malaga, dying in Madrid in 1962. In 1942, in his late sixties, he married Tara Devi, the actress daughter of a Czech count. She seems to have tired of living with a declining elderly man and probably committed suicide by jumping off the 73-metre minaret, Qutb Minar, in the Mehrauli area of Delhi, in 1946, clutching her two poodles. The Maharaja represented India at the League of Nations General Assembly in Geneva in the late 1920s and died aged 76 in 1949, his huge losses in the wreck of SS *Persia* apparently still a mystery.

Edward Berryman continued to write regular letters after he survived the sinking. In one, written on 7th January 1916, he tells:

> *'Last night we dined the officers of the Mallow, our rescuers; awful nice chaps. The skipper, one Roberts, lived at Chobham & knows Guildford well & confesses to having been in love with Betty Neville once! So, if any of the girls meet Betty, they may tell her that a former flame of hers rescued us & we owe him much more than we can ever repay.'*

---

139 Letter from the Maharaja of Kapurthala to Mr Wood dated 25th January 1916
140 Notes from Elisa Vázquez de Gey, author of *Anita Delgado – Maharani de Kapurthala*

Captain Berryman rejoined the 39th Garhwal Rifles near Suez, at a place he described as 'close by the place where Moses struck the rock' and returned to his regimental duties. He thought often of those he had known and lost on SS *Persia*. In March 1916 he wrote home from SS *Muttra* on a voyage to Bombay, where he had hoped to spend 'a couple of days'. Instead, he had to join the first train to Kohdwara railhead. From there, he made a 25-mile (40 km) march to Lansdowne, Uttarakhand, where the British had developed the Recruits Training Centre for the Garhwal Rifles. He settled back into routine and letter writing and it was there he learned of the sinking of another P&O liner, SS *Arabia*, which he knew to be carrying a friend back to England, a Mrs Proctor who had lived in Lansdowne. He would later learn that she had survived. The regiment next deployed to Delhi for largely ceremonial duties. This brought an uncomfortable period for him during which he played tennis and attended regular parties, but he suffered survivors' guilt and exasperation at the lack of military action. Early in 1917, the Garhwalis redeployed once again to Mesopotamia to help gain control of the Arabian Peninsula with its oilfields and to help protect the short sea route to India via the Suez Canal.

When the war ended, there was still no return home. Now a Brigade Major, Ted ended his war after the Mesopotamia campaign suffering extreme exhaustion and perhaps from influenza that had started to ravage much of the world. Back in England, his fiancée Nell's 21st birthday fell on 11th November 1918. She spent that day nursing her family through the dangerous epidemic and was washing dishes in the sink when she heard the news on the wireless that the war was over. Ted's thoughts had been about some home leave and an early wedding until he learned that he would have to stay in 'Mespot' on 'Post-bellum' duties. He eventually arrived back in England in May 1919, gaunt and worn down after three-and-a-half years away. He and Nell married in June and went together to India during the 1920s where he was one of the more senior officers and she was one of the youngest wives. They had two children, Martin and Félicité, who spent their first six or seven years with Ted and Nell in India before returning to schools in England. Ted retired in the mid-1930s as colonel of the regiment and he and Nell built a home in Guildford. Martin joined his father's regiment and was killed in Malaya in 1942. Félicité, who later edited her father and uncles' wartime letters, worked in Bletchley Park. Their father, the 'Ted' in our story, died aged 80 in 1964, remembered as an avuncular figure, full of games, verses and picture delights for children and for his heroic part in saving life.

What Became of Some Survivors?

Lionel Miller-Hallett had a short attachment to the 1st Battalion, 6th Gurkha Rifles in 1917, followed by an appointment as Commandant of the Gilgit Scouts. He then rejoined his Regiment in command of the 1st Battalion Depot. He attended the Senior Officers' School, Sheerness, in 1935–36 and represented his Regiment at the funeral of King George V, before becoming Lieutenant Colonel Miller-Hallett in August 1940 and transferring to the No.1 Training Battalion, Nepalese Contingent, where he served until 1945. He earned the Star of Nepal 3rd Class for his services. 'Lion' married Miss Ruth Simpson in 1925 and had two daughters. He retired to Shirley Holms, Sway, in the New Forest, where he enjoyed gardening and sailing and was active on Boldre Parish Church Council and as a church warden at St John the Baptist Church. He died on Easter Day 1971 aged 75 and lies in the peace of Boldre churchyard in the New Forest, almost 56 years after he survived two wounds on the Western Front and the destruction of SS *Persia*.

Lionel Miller-Hallett studio portrait for the occasion of his engagement
By kind permission of Richard Lander

Stewardess Mary Pennington, 'The Duchess', returned to work as a stewardess for P&O caring for the rich and famous in first class until around the outbreak of World War 2. Among those she looked after were Mary Pickford, who gave her a signed photograph. When serving aboard the SS *Rajputana*, she met Mahatma Gandhi when he sailed for London in 1931 on his historic mission: *'going to England to realise the dream of my life – the freedom of my country.'*[141] In 1939, Mary married a much younger man and became Mrs Rogers. He worked as a musician on P&O and after the war became bandleader on the SS *Canberra*. He outlived Mary.

---

141 Chronology of Mahatma Gandhi's life, England 1931, written by Mohandas K Gandhi

Although he was never aboard, David Spreckley was a victim of the sinking, losing both parents and a sister. Adopted and eventually educated at the Royal Naval College, Dartmouth, and the Royal Military Academy, Sandhurst, he resigned from the Army at the age of 21, becoming a pacifist and member of the Peace Pledge Union. He chose to serve time in jail instead of paying fines for breaching public order and wilfully obstructing a footpath and was jailed again in November 1944 for failing to comply with conditions of being a conscientious objector to the war. In 1952, he met Anne, the woman who was to become his life-long partner, who was 18 years his junior. He may have been the first factory owner in Britain to have handed a company over to its employees. He stood as a parliamentary candidate three times without success but had more success in district council politics before leaving to join the Campaign for Nuclear Disarmament. Mr Spreckley died in July 2013 aged 98[142]. He had clearly made a strong recovery from whatever ailed him in 1915.

Reg Heams, of the YMCA party in Kew Gardens
By kind permission of Jeremy Kidd

Arthur Johnson was later appointed Secretary of the Trading Department of the YMCA in Egypt. In the *London Gazette* supplement of 17th June 1918, he received an OBE for his war work with the YMCA. He became the chairman of the Ridgeford Trust Ltd., exempted dealers in securities, and of Jay Securities, as well as a director of several companies including the Wolverhampton Steam Laundry, the Ulster Spinning Company Ltd. and the Old Bleach Linen Company Ltd. In the mid-1930s he founded Ridgeford Industrial Investments, which specialised in small company flotations on the stock market, and helped bridge the so-called MacMillan Gap created after the war when the 'big five' British clearing banks

---

142 Hywel Barrett, Hywel (2013). *Hunts Post*, Friday, 16th August

declined to loan money to small and medium-sized enterprises[143]. Arthur's death announcement appeared in *The Times* on Saturday, 3rd May 1952. Reginald Heams continued to work with Arthur Johnson after the war and became his company secretary. He never spoke about the *Persia* and it was many years after Reg's death in June 1969 that his family learned of his fortunate escape from the sinking, when his grandson, Mr Jeremy Kidd, chanced upon a passenger list on the internet.

Agnes Lees subsequently travelled on to Biladia, Gujarat, where she served from 1916 until 1928. While there she wrote a booklet on the sinking of SS *Persia*, entitled *The thrilling experience of a passenger by the SS* Persia *on the 30th and 31st December 1915 in her own words*. She published this anonymously in India, though she added her name like a signature at the end of the short text. She left Biladia for Kotra in 1928 where she served until 1935, when she moved on to Lusadia, Gujarat. Agnes retired to England in 1947 after 31 years of missionary service.

When back in England, Lord Montagu criticised the government over bombing raids by twin-engine Gotha aircraft which, in their first raid on London, killed 160. For his pains, the press and political opponents turned on him. He had two more trips to India and a temporary promotion to brigadier general in between. During his last time in India, he completed a fourteenth visit to the war-worn North-West Frontier. When he said his final goodbye to India, in April 1919, Lord Montagu's legacy was the army's possession of 4,000 motor vehicles, 7,000 trained motor transport personnel and a thousand miles of strategically important roads including the Khyber Pass. For his services to India, he became a Knight Commander of the Indian Empire.

His return to Beaulieu should have enabled him and Lady Cecil to spend more time together, but this was not to be. She had not enjoyed good health since suffering from rheumatic fever as a girl and died on 13th September 1919, aged only 53, forty-eight days before he retired from the army. She left John with two daughters, Helen and Elizabeth, but no male heir. For a peer and owner of an 8,000-acre estate aged 53, this sad event would also leave a cause for concern.

Early in 1920, Lord Montagu holidayed in the south of France, where he met the Barrington-Crake family and he subsequently visited them in their London home. On 10th August 1920, he married their daughter, Alice Pearl Crake, who became Baroness Montagu of Beaulieu[144].

---

143 Scott, Peter and Newton, Lucy (2006). *Jealous monopolists? British banks and responses to the Macmillan Gap during the 1930's*. Economics & Management Discussion Papers em-dp2006-36, Henley Business School, Reading University
144 The Peerage: http://www.Thepeerage.com/p2595.htm#i25945

Lord Montagu started to campaign for improved roads and motor transport in Britain and, after a tour across the country, in 1921 he wrote a series of articles for *The Times*, the last of which ended:

'We must make ready for the needs of the future, for the value of road power to the nation will increase with every succeeding year.'

After advocating overhead roads to reduce London's traffic congestion in 1923, he became chairman of a company with the aim of building:

'a great motorway, about 226 miles long, from London to Birmingham, Manchester and Liverpool at an estimated cost of £15 million'.

It would be another 35 years before the 8¼-mile Preston bypass, the first part of the M6, opened. Britain's motorway network grew from this modest start.

John and Pearl had had two daughters, Anne and Caroline, but he still did not have a male heir. Then on 20th October 1926, their third child, son Edward John Barrington Montagu, was born, followed in 1928 by a third daughter, Mary-Clare.

In October 1928, Lord Montagu received treatment for an enlarged prostate, but pleurisy inhibited his recovery. He spent Christmas resting at home with his family and wrote some articles for the *Observer*, including one on road building to create jobs, another on a channel tunnel and a scheme to turn unprofitable railways into toll roads. In March he underwent an operation on his prostate. This was followed by pneumonia, a lung abscess, another operation and a chest infection. He died, aged 62, on 30th March 1929, having survived in a half-sunken lifeboat just over thirteen years earlier.

His family followed his funeral instructions written in the first of two letters he left when returning to India in 1916. The second letter had instructions for no one to open it until after his death when it went to Joan Eleanor Thornton, by then a 26-year-old teacher. The letter told her that he was her father, not her uncle as she had understood. It described the parts of his life that mattered; of his meeting and falling in love with her mother and of their devotion to each other. He wished her that someday she may experience the joy produced by the great love that he shared with her mother and hoped that she may see Beaulieu, *'my beloved Beaulieu, which she loved so much too'*. He described a bequest, named its trustees and her guardian and hoped that she would marry '*a gentleman-like and good man who really loves you*'. He signed the letter:

'Goodbye darling Joan.
God bless you always.
Your loving father,
Montagu of Beaulieu'.

How the Montagu family and Joan finally met and how she became one of the family is beyond the remit of this story, but Paul Tritton describes it in his book *John Montagu of Beaulieu, Motoring Pioneer and Prophet*.

Montagu had written to his friend Lord Northcliffe after his return from the sinking of SS *Persia*:

'I had a hard time but lived through it by the grace of God – for a good purpose I hope.'

His good purposes served India, its transport infrastructure and its army extremely well, guiding them through great strides into the twentieth century. When he finally returned to Britain, his imagination and energy collided with the same resistance to new ideas that may have let Britain down in the war, particularly at sea. His battles in the House of Lords and beyond to overturn dated ideas and vested interests in military flying eventually led towards the formation of an Air Ministry that lasted 46 years, from 1918 until 1964, under the political control of the Secretary of State for Air. His ideas for a south-to-north motorway were almost four decades ahead of their time, but are now long-established and, as he forecast, road transport has taken over from railways as Britain's primary method of carrying vast quantities of every cargo imaginable. He probably drove himself into the ground in pursuit of his ambitions for British transport, but his thinking was often too far advanced for his contemporaries.

William Dowling had been rescued by HMS *Mallow* and this turned out to be the first of several close escapes in his career at sea. On 6th November 1916, he was serving aboard SS *Arabia*, one of SS *Persia's* sister ships, when she was torpedoed by UB-43 in the Mediterranean on a voyage from Sydney to London. In October 1918 he was aboard the troopship *Kashmir* when it collided with the troopship *Otranto* off the Isle of Islay with great loss of life. Then, in 1920, he was aboard the SS *Graf Waldersee* which had been surrendered to the United States before it came into British ownership. She and several other impounded ships were anchored in the Thames estuary when her anchor failed and she drifted into the smaller Austrian vessel, SS *Kleist*, causing considerable damage. Crew aboard the *Graf Waldersee* were invited to jump off the ship to be picked up by Southend lifeboat but declined. The 12,300 GRT ship was eventually taken in tow by six tugs but then ran down and sank a collier. *Graf Waldersee* was beached in mud off Gravesend near the Ship and Lobster pub and William crossed the river to Tilbury and caught a train home for the night. He survived all these adventures and recorded them almost fifty years after the *Persia* sinking in a document headed '*A True Story, an account of the sinking of the "Persia", December 1915,*' which I acknowledge and appreciate. In this document he also mentioned his shipmates in the purser's department aboard SS *Persia* and added that '*all were equal in God's eyes*'.

War Crimes or Warfare?

History has demonstrated that only countries who lost wars seem to have had war criminals in their ranks or governments. The Paris (Versailles) Peace Conference in 1919 set terms for the countries of the Central Powers to satisfy. The main outcome was the Treaty of Versailles in which Section 231 placed the guilt for the war on the aggression of Germany and her allies and set high reparation payments. Articles 227 to 230 of the Treaty specified arrest and trial of German officials alleged to have been war criminals. Article 228 gave Allied governments the right to try German war criminals in their military tribunals and required the German government to comply with extradition orders. The Allied powers submitted a list to the German government naming nine hundred alleged war criminals.

The number of U-boat captains suggested as war criminals by Britain after the war varies between five listed by Edwin Gray and eighteen by John Terraine. Max Valentiner was one of five U-boat commanders listed as a war criminal by the British government according to Gray[145]:

Max Valentiner (U-38 and U-157)

Walther Schwieger (U-20 and U-88)

Claüs Rucker (U-34 and U-103)

Konrad Gansser (U-33 and U-156)

Wilhelm Werner (U-55)

However, making lists was as far as this ever progressed. There was no trial of any U-boat commander. Not Schwieger for *Lusitania*: nor Valentiner for *Persia*, nor for shelling and torpedoing the liner *Ancona* as she tried to

---

145   Gray, Edwin A (1994). *The U-boat War 1914-1918*, Appendix Two, German Submarine Aces. London: Leo Cooper

disembark passengers and crew into lifeboats: not Rücker for an attack on 1st June 1915, when trawler *Victoria* tried to escape and had sustained heavy damage and one death. *Victoria* stopped and surrendered but Rucker's U-34 closed to 200 yards, continuing her bombardment and killing five more seamen. Once she surrendered, the shelling that followed was unnecessary and almost certainly a punitive and unlawful act of murder[146]. Gansser in U-33 attacked the 4,796-ton SS *Clan McLeod* east of Malta on 15th December 1915, on passage from Chittagong to London. The Clan Line steamer tried to escape but the U-boat pursued and shelled her until she stopped and surrendered. While disembarking her crew into lifeboats, U-33 reopened fire killing twelve[147]. Wilhelm Werner, commander of U-55, sank the 5,597-ton SS *Torrington* 150 miles south-west of the Scilly Isles on 8th April 1917, with the loss of 34 lives. When 22 of these clambered onto the U-boat's deck, she then submerged leaving them to drown. Members of Werner's crew apparently revealed that this was not the only occurrence of this behaviour. *Torrington* was in ballast at the time, so had no cargo of any sort to help the allied cause.

Germany refused to extradite any German citizens and proposed that they should face trial within German's justice system, at the Reichsgericht, the supreme criminal and civil court in Germany, based in the city of Leipzig. Only three months on from the issuing of a 900-name list, the Allies accepted the proposal and reduced the list to 45 names, not all of whom they could trace. Only 12 faced trial for offences such as ill-treatment of POWs. The courts convicted six men and gave sentences typically in numbers of months, not years. Only three naval officers faced trial. Leutnants Ludwig Dithmar and John Boldt of U-86 had sunk the hospital ship HMHS *Llandovery Castle*. Sadly, 234 people including doctors and nurses of the Canadian Army Medical Corps, soldiers and seamen died in the sinking and subsequent machine-gunning of lifeboats on 27th June 1918. The commander, Oberleutnant zur See Helmut Patzig apparently left the country and never stood trial. After the court convicted the two men, it sentenced them to four years with hard labour but they escaped on their way to prison. Later, the court overturned the convictions on the grounds that the submarine's commander, the absent Patzig, was solely responsible. The third man to stand trial, Kapitänleutnant Karl Neumann of UC-67 faced a charge of sinking the hospital ship HMHS *Dover Castle* on 26th May 1917, but the court acquitted him. His defence? He was following orders.

---

146 Wreck Site: http://www.wrecksite.eu/wreck.aspx?154284
147 Gray, Edwin A (1994). *The U-boat War 1914-1918*

By 1922 it was clear that the trials were a waste of time, effort and money and those remaining prisoners should be handed over to the Allies to face trials. This never happened and the whole mess was swept discretely under the carpet. Valentiner was free to continue a normal life. Britain, as one of the victorious nations, did not have war criminals.

In 1934, long after any thoughts of pursuing alleged war criminals had been set aside, Max Valentiner told some of his story. His account of some of his service on U-38, entitled *U 38. Wikingerfahrten eines deutschen U-Bootes* – (U-38. Viking rides in a German U-boat), was published by Ullstein, Berlin. On page 11, Max refers to Klaus Hansen as his 'best friend'[148] and describes with warmth their billets together in a dilapidated palace in Wanzenbug. The SS *Persia* and other 1915 attacks did not merit any mention in the book, presumably because a candid account might have adversely affected his reputation.

Perhaps Britain committed crimes against international law by its naval blockade of Germany during World War 1 as some scholars suggest, and thus might be to blame for the deaths of many Germans through starvation. However, those who look back can see that in 1914 Germany exported much of its harvest of rye to Russia and had long pursued industrialisation leading to urbanisation and large-scale migration of jobs from farming to factories. As the war approached, over one-quarter of Germany's foodstuffs already needed to be imported, much of them from Russia and the United States, a big change since the 1870s when Germany had been a net exporter of grain[149]. Germany seems to have put more thought into its war plans, particularly the Schlieffen Plan, than it did into maintaining its food supplies and seemed confident that food supplies from the Netherlands, Scandinavia, and Romania would continue, unaffected by any naval blockade. The advent of their U-boat blockade seems to have some of the characteristics of an afterthought, but once it got under way it increased in effectiveness. While the aims of the two blockades seem to have been broadly similar, the operations differed widely. Britain's armed merchant ships provided the main effort in Britain's successful blockade, conducted by using stop, examine and escort to be searched in port to remove any contraband found, then allowing them to proceed with minimal casualties. Germany's blockade was initially to stop, search and sink if justified, but degenerated

---

148 Valentiner, Max (1934). *U38 Wikingerfahrten eines deutschen U-Bootes.* (U-38.Viking voyages of a German U-boat). p 11, p 136 & p 137. Berlin: Ullstein
149 Davis, Belina (2014). https://encyclopedia.1914-1918-online.net/article/food_and_nutrition_germany

into 'sink without warning' irrespective of casualties to British and other nations' merchant seamen and civilian passengers. Information on over 15,500 civilian merchant seafarers killed by enemy action in the World War 1 is on the Commonwealth War Graves Commission (CWGC) website. Of these, over 12,000 have no known graves[150].

As for SS *Persia*, years drifted by and when U-boat successes in World War 2 recaptured the headlines, she sank further into obscurity but for a few treasured memories, medals and documents held by families, friends and descendants of her passengers and crew. More recently, the Honourable Mary Montagu Scott put her considerable energies and resources into the creation of 'The SS *Persia* Story' at the Buckler's Hard Maritime Museum, on the banks of the Beaulieu River in Hampshire. The Museum tells the story of SS *Persia*, her passengers and crew and of her grandfather, John Walter Edward Douglas-Scott-Montagu, 2nd Baron Montagu of Beaulieu, KCIE, CSI, DL – Colonel Lord Montagu, whose survival has kept *Persia*'s story alive in the museum.

---

150 cwgc.org

SS *Persia* Remembered – 1966 and 2016

An act of remembrance was held in 1966, believed to have been suggested by William Dowling, former head saloon waiter and supported by the third Lord Montagu. The desire of one survivor to remember his shipmates and passengers in such a way remains very moving. The liner SS *Iberia* sailed close to the site of the sinking and wreathes were cast on behalf of P&O by Staff Captain G Terry and Purser C Hare and on behalf of Edward, Third Baron Montagu of Beaulieu, as a tribute to Eleanor Thornton, his father's private secretary, lost in the sinking.

Staff Captain G Terry and Purser C Hare cast SS Persia memorial wreaths from SS Iberia off the coast of Crete in 1966, including a tribute from Edward, Third Baron Montagu, for Eleanor Thornton, his father's secretary who was lost in the sinking
By kind permission of Richard Dowling

Buckler's Hard Maritime Museum became home to the first permanent memorial to all those lost in the *Persia* tragedy. It takes the form of a striking wall-mounted sundial created by Harriet James. Descendants and relations of passengers and crew on *Persia*'s last voyage attended a Remembrance Service at Buckler's Hard on 15th June 2016. This included readings from survivors' accounts, including one by Lord Montagu retelling his grandfather's survival struggle. P&O Captain Alistair Clark read the poem *In Waters Deep* by Eileen Mahoney. The Reverend John White, Parish Priest of Beaulieu Abbey and St Mary's Chapel, Buckler's Hard, conducted the service, with music performed by the Beaulieu Band.

Paul Ludlow, P&O Cruises Senior Vice President unveiled the memorial sundial which was blessed by John Attenborough, Chaplain of the Port of Southampton. Lord Montagu, grandson of the Colonel Lord Montagu who survived the sinking, then led a wreath-laying ceremony. After the service, families whose relations had lived and died together aboard the *Persia* mingled, sharing stories, smiles, hugs, handshakes and just a few tears. There was a display of the SS *Persia* Jewellery Collection, showing a range of limited-edition designer jewellery made from gems recovered from the wreck, sold to raise funds for the Mission to Seafarers and Smiletrain charities.

Among those who attended the service were several descendants and relations of those who were aboard SS *Persia* including:

A relation of Lieutenant Colonel Henry Backhouse

A niece and two granddaughters of Captain E R P (Ted) Berryman

A grandson of Thomas & Cecilia Burns and nephew of Alexander Clark

A granddaughter of Thomas & Cecilia Burns and niece of Alexander Clark

A great-grandson of Thomas & Cecilia Burns & great-great-nephew of Alexander Clark

A great-granddaughter of Helen Maude de Burgh Codrington and a great-nephew of Kenneth de Burgh Codrington

A grandson of Henry Eves

A daughter and a grandson of Reg Heams

A great-granddaughter and family members of Edwin Herbert, cousin of Frank Herbert

A granddaughter of Ernest Howell

A son of Charles Martin

Two nephews and two great-nieces of Mary McGinn

A grandson of Joyce Minnitt

Three grandsons and a granddaughter of Colonel Lord Montagu

Relations of Mary McMinn connected to the Spreckley family

A relation of William Orr Orr and James Bulloch Dickie

A great-grandson of Mary Pennington

A great-granddaughter of Mr & Mrs Marcell Smith

A relation of the Spreckley family

A grandson of John Thomas

A son of Joan Thornton, grandson of Eleanor Thornton

A grandson of George Walton

During interesting discussions that followed, some present raised a question that has lingered for over a century. Could crew members have saved more lives? Even after my early research I felt that this was unlikely. The damage from two explosions was so serious that *Persia* sank in five minutes; her decks had ruptured and her entire engine room crew probably died instantly. To bring the ship to an emergency stop needed the rotation of her propeller to be reversed, that is for her to go from 'full ahead' to 'full astern' but with no one alive in the engine room to respond to such an order even if it could have been given, SS *Persia* would have continued at her cruising speed, gradually losing momentum over a relatively long distance, subject to wind, current and capsize. Safe lifeboat launching in those days assumed kindly conditions, such as when a ship had stopped and was not listing heavily. Neither of these conditions benefited the SS *Persia* and those aboard.

Could the captain and crew have done more? Many of the watch-keeping crew would have been asleep in their confined cabin spaces and would have had little time to save themselves, let alone aid passengers. Some crew members and passengers made valiant, even self-sacrificial efforts to help others. Survivors commended their courage. Captain Hall was later criticised for his directions to women passengers, who were already disadvantaged by their clothing. With hindsight and more time to think, he might have given different instructions, but from torpedo strike to sinking took only five minutes, an overwhelming and fast-moving tragedy with hundreds suddenly facing death. The heavy death toll was unavoidable and might have been even higher in the absence of acts of valour and self-sacrifice, or if the watchkeepers on HMS *Mallow* and the SS *Ning Chow* had not been so alert and their skippers unafraid to stop in dangerous waters.

This day of remembrance showed that memories of the SS *Persia* live on, thanks to the work of Colonel Lord Montagu's granddaughter and her team at the museum, to descendant relations and friends, and a few articles and websites. However, the families still had unanswered questions.

Why was a P&O liner left to her own devices in this dangerous zone? What else occupied the French, Italian and Royal navies? Why had Valentiner ignored international law and his own government's recent '*Arabic*' Pledge? Why did seven of every ten people aboard die? Why had this U-boat attack, like many others, been so easy, like shooting fish in a barrel? What could it achieve for the German war effort? Why has SS *Persia* no place in nautical history, a forgotten metal coffin, deep beneath the eastern Mediterranean?

The Gallipoli Campaign had involved many warships – over 100 British and 15 French – while the successful and clandestine evacuation of over 100,000 men from Anzac Cove and Suvla Bay took place between 10th and 20th December 1915. This was followed by the withdrawal of 35,000 men from Helles from late December 1915 until 9th January 1916. SS *Persia* was just one of many merchant ships alone in the Mediterranean while navies directed their priorities elsewhere.

Persia's large death toll was a consequence of the rapid sinking, far quicker than most could have envisaged, perhaps resulting from Valentiner's incredible skill with his torpedo and the direct and doubly explosive strike on her boilers. She turned on her side very quickly washing away both boats and people. As for what it achieved for the German war effort – very little except outrage. The great irony is that a cruiser rules 'stop and search' ought to have found the Maharaja's vast fortune and saved many lives.

At that stage in the war, U-boat mistrust gripped Britain and many neutral shipping nations. *Persia* and her probable 334 losses were just more un-needed statistics. After a brief flurry of press interest, she, like hundreds of other merchant ships, simply died away as attacks by U-boats surged to 3,724 in 1917[151].

The living owe it to those who no longer can speak to tell their story for them.
Czeslaw Milosz, Nobel Prize in Literature 1980

---

151 Ship losses by month: https://uboat.net/wwi/ships_hit/losses_year.html

Names in the lists that follow were sourced from the Buckler's Hard Maritime Museum's memorial, updated with new information gathered during the research and writing project. Crew lists were believed originally sourced from The National Archives, Kew, BT99/3112/25H and BT99/3112/211

Passengers Lost

Claire Marie Adins, Missionary age 32, Belgium, known as Sister Francois Xavier

H L Ainsworth, Captain

Henry Backhouse, Lieutenant Colonel

Mancherji Nanabhoy Bananji, Student, age 21, India

Florence Barratt, Miss, Child's Nurse, age 21, England

Maurice Gordon Bean, Captain Indian Army

Walter Beer

Lal Behari, Salesman, age 35, India

Pheroze Behram, Student, age 21, India

Alice E Benson, Mrs, age 37, England

Dorothy Benson, age 11, England

Kathleen A Benson, age 5, England

Emma Isabel Bilby, Miss, Church Worker, age 47, England

Birch, Miss, Mrs Tresham's Nurse

May E Bliss, Mrs

Adelaide Helen Rebecca Bull, Miss, Missionary

Rose Burcombe, Mrs

Helen Burcombe, age 2 years 2 months

Edward Burcombe, age 10 weeks

George Burgess, Cotton Mill Manager, age 53, England

Ann Burgess, Mrs, age 55, England

Thomas Burns, age 49, Scotland

Cecilia Burns, Mrs, age 49, Scotland

G Carboni

Thomas Alexander Carlaw, Insurance Secretary, age 25, Scotland

Helen Maude de Burgh Codrington, Mrs, age 45.

Arthur Morris Coleman, age 16, son of Frank Coleman

Frank Morris Coleman, Proprietor, *Times of India*

Marcell Francis Conran-Smith, Superintendent of Telegraphs, age 39, England

Hilda Conran-Smith, Mrs, age 38, England

W Campion Cooper, Lieutenant

W O C Dawson, Major

A De Guili

E De Guili

F De Guili

John De Renzy, Merchant, New Zealand

Sadashiv Maninarayan Dikshit, Lawyer, India

S Dolumal

Lily Duncan, Mrs, age 39, England

William Edward Edgecombe, Locomotive Superintendent, age 41, England

Grace Ethel Edgecombe, Mrs, age 37, England

Mary Fernandez, Ayah, age 30, India

Gabour, Mrs

Gabour, Infant

M Ganz

S Gaudillon, Madame

James Ponsonby Gilbert, Captain, 6th Jat Light Infantry, Indian Army

Gilbert, Mrs J P

Gopalkrishma R Gokharkar, Doctor, age 28, India

Owen Gough MC, Lieutenant

Beryl Graham, Mrs, age 32, England

Alexander Colquhoun Grant, Clergyman, age 31, Scotland

Christian Maitland Grant, Doctor, age 29, Scotland

George Hoggan

Harry Alfred Hopkins, age 32, England

Ernest Alfred Russel Howell, age 47, Lieutenant Colonel Indian Army

Elizabeth Hoyle, Mrs, age 38, England

Hoyle, Daughter, age 3, England

SS Persia Remembered 30th December 1915

H F M Hughes, Miss

Margaret McCall Hutchison, age 15 months, Scotland

Elizabeth Stephens Impey, Doctor, age 38, England

J R Jonaja

George H Keddy, Staff Sergeant, India S T Corp, England

Keddy, Mrs, England

Keddy, Son, age 6, England

Keddy, Son, age 3, England

Chuni Lal

Humphrey Richard Locke Lawrence, Lieutenant, 34th Sikh Pioneers, England

Mary Eliza Leather, Mrs (née Robinson)

John (Jack) Thornton Lodwick DSO, Captain 39th Garwhal Rifles

Gladys Enid MacDonald, Miss, age 30, England

Edward Waters Harbin Marsh, Captain, The 13th Rajputs (The Shekhawati Regiment)

Mary Elizabeth McGinn, Mrs

Quintilla McGinn, boy, age 4 months, born 15/8/15

McGinn family un-named Ayah

John Jamie McHardy, Jute Mill Overseer, age 44, Scotland

Robert Ney McNeely, US Consul designate, Aden, age 32, United States

Julia Anna Anson Minnitt, Mrs

Christine Minnitt, age about 10 months (born March 1915)

E F M Mitchell, Miss

Marie-Josephine Molhaut, Missionary, age 28, Belgium, known as Sister Xavier Marie

Alexander MacDonnel Montgomery, age 3, England

Alfred Ralph Nethersole, Lieutenant Colonel, Indian Army, age 48, England

Andree Nicholle, Miss

Sybil O'Reilly, Mrs

William Orr Orr, Scotland

H Page, Mrs, age 37, England

G B Papasian, Merchant, age 29, Armenia

Neramal Parmanand

Frederick F Pickard, Chief Engineer

Nasserwanji Sorabji Pudumjee, Cambridge Law Graduate, Student, age 25, India

Sita Ram, Student, age 16, India

Marguerite A T Raulin, Missionary, age 24, Belgium, known as Sister Julie Anna

Kathleen Read, Miss, Maharaja's Party

Wilfred Herbert Rigg, Mining Engineer, age 38, England

J A Robertson, Lieutenant, 2nd Battalion, 3rd Queen Alexandra's Own Gurkha Rifles

William Adam Robertson, 2nd Lieutenant, Indian Army

Arthur Twining Roch, Engineer Lieutenant, RN

C E Ross, Mrs, age 35, Scotland

Elizabeth B Ross, age 2 months, Scotland

R V Russell, Indian Civil Service, England

J N Sahai

H R Salisbury

Susanne Scholer, Missionary, age 34, Luxembourg, known as Sister Gerard Majella

Goumal Shamdas

V G Shilston

B M Singh

B P Singh

Arthur R Smijth Windham

Arthur Freer Spreckley, Lt. 2/9th Ghurkha Rifles, Captain Indian Army, age 27

Ada Blanche Spreckley, Mrs (née McMinn), age 24, England

Pamela Spreckley, infant (born 1914)

St Aubyn, Edward Stuart, Colonel

Kathleen Stoehr, Mrs, age 21, England

E R Swiney, Colonel, 39th Garwhal Rifles

Eleanor Velasco Thornton, Miss, Private Secretary to Lord Montagu, England

SS Persia Remembered 30th December 1915

Robert Dunham Tibbs, 2nd Lieutenant, 39th Gauhati Rifles
John Elmsley Bourchier Torkington, Captain, Palamcottah Light Infantry
Tresham, Mrs
Tresham, Infant
H Wilson, Major, King's Own Royal Lancaster Regiment

London Crew Lost

Alcock J,	General Servant
Allen R W,	Refrigeration Mechanic
Allen W,	Able-bodied Seaman
Bellinger E,	Electrician
Berry V G,	Assistant Engineer
Boyd S W,	Third Mate
Brown F O,	Bedroom Steward
Bruce M,	Stewardess
Chant J,	Baker
Cook, E	Bedroom Steward
Coster J,	Stewardess
Cottrell F A,	General Servant and Writer
Croxson, Frederick Charles,	Travelling Chef
Dewey G H,	Marconi Operator
Doughton H,	Able-bodied Seaman
Everett W,	Ship's Surgeon
Fairchild Frederick,	General Servant & Baggage Steward
Gent H,	Stewardess
Graham P,	Seaman
Hall, W H S,	Master
Herbert Frank,	Steward in Charge
Hickingbotham W J,	Third Engineer
Jeffery Ernest,	Chief Engineer
Jones L V,	General Servant
Kane Augustine,	Travelling Inspecting Purser
Lampon J,	Bedroom Steward
Leishman C,	Stewardess
Nelson Charles Rice,	Deck Steward
Parton Harold R,	Fourth Mate
Perrin E,	General Servant
Perry R E,	Barman

SS Persia Remembered 30th December 1915

Pinchen James,	Deck Steward
Preece W,	Linen Storekeeper
Reilly R,	Able-bodied Seaman
Richardson E M,	General Servant
Robertson W,	Boilermaker
Rockett W G,	General Servant
Sargeant Thomas,	2nd Barman
Smith E,	Winchman
Stabler W,	General Servant
Stevenson F J,	Stateroom Attendant & Smoke Room Steward
Stubbington M,	Stewardess
Tarvin F,	Butcher's Assistant
Turner H E	Second Engineer
Wall A S,	General Servant
Walton George,	Second Chef
Wells R,	Assistant Baker
Wilson D A,	Able-bodied Seaman

Bombay Crew Lost

Abdul Ghani Shaikh Yusuf,	Sailor
Abdul Jalal,	Trimmer
Abdullah Mubarak,	Serang
Abdullah Muhammad,	Sailor
Abdullah Sattar Din,	Trimmer
Abdur Rahman Bawa,	Sailor
Abdur Razzaq Daud Haji,	Sailor
Adam Faqir,	Sailor
Adam Ibrahim,	Sailor
Ahmad Abdul Qadir,	Sailor
Ahmad Amir,	Sailor
Ahmad Muhammad,	Fireman
Ahman Khan Pir Khan,	Sailor
Ali Bin Muhammad,	Trimmer
Ali Muhammad,	Sailor
Alla Ditta Ramazan,	Fireman
Allah Ditta,	Fireman
Almeida Pedro,	Steward
Alvares Triphonis,	Steward
Baga Muhammad Qadir,	Fireman
Baghe Ali Husain Bakhsh,	Fireman
Bapu Husain Jina,	Sailor
Barreto Estavas G,	Steward
Barreto John S,	Second Cook
Barreto Jose M,	Steward
Barreto Mathews,	Steward
Barreto Philip,	Steward
Buraq Ali Kallu Khan,	Fireman
Buta Umar,	Trimmer
Cabsal Casme,	Trimmer
Chiraghuddin Alauddin,	Trimmer
Colaco Pedrinho,	Steward

Continho Benedito,	Steward
Continho Sebastias,	Steward
Da Costa Caetano,	Steward
Da Costa Domingo,	Steward
Da Costa Philip,	Steward
Da Silva Francisco,	Steward
Da Silva Francisco,	Sailor
Da Silva Joao,	Steward
Da Silva Julio,	Steward
Da Silva Nicalao,	Pantryman
Dad Muhammad,	Trimmer
Daud Ibrahim,	Serang
Daud Nabbu,	Sailor
Daud Sultan,	Sailor
De S A Juliao,	Steward
De Souza Alcino,	Steward
De Souza Santana,	Steward
Dias Menino,	Steward
Dias Paulo Inacio,	Steward
Faiz Din Chiragh Din,	Fireman
Faizi Ismail,	Fireman
Faqir Abdul,	Sailor
Faqir Ali Akbar,	Trimmer
Fateh Din Azimullah,	Trimmer
Fateh Din Ibrahim,	Trimmer
Fazl Ilahi Mughal,	Fireman
Fazl Ilahi Muhammad Saleh,	Fireman
Fernandes Antonio	Steward
Fernandes Antonio F,	Fireman
Fernandes Constance,	Stewardess
Fernandes Domingo,	Steward
Fernandes Domingo Martin,	Steward
Fernandes Joao,	Steward

Fernandes Manuel,	Steward
Fernandes Minguel,	Steward
Fernandes Santana,	Steward
Firozuddin Badruddin,	Trimmer
Freitas Joaquim P,	Steward
Furtado,	Steward
Gama Francis,	Steward
Gama Laurence,	Steward
George Louis,	Steward
Ghulam Husain,	Fireman
Ghulam Husain Ishmail,	Sailor
Gomes Beneditto,	Steward
Gomes Floriano,	Steward
Gomes Silvestre,	Steward
Gonsalves Sebastiao,	Steward
Gracios Jocaguim,	Steward
Hakim Nuruddin,	Trimmer
Hasan Muhammad,	Trimmer
Husain Fazl,	Fireman
Husain Sultan,	Sailor
Husain Usman,	Sailor
Ibrahim Fazl,	Fireman
Ibrahim Khuda Bakhsh,	Fireman
Ibrahim Sharfu,	Fireman
Ibrahim Umar,	Sailor
Ilmdin Fazldin,	Fireman
Ilmuddin Muhammad Bakhsh,	Fireman
Imamdin Pola,	Fireman
Imamuddin Khuda Bakhsh,	Fireman
Iman Din Kallan,	Fireman
Iman Din Muhammad,	Fireman
Inamidin Hayat,	Fireman
Isa Umar,	Sailor

Jaafar Qasim,	Sailor
Jacques Ferlliano,	Steward
Jacques Jose,	Steward
Jan Muhammad Ibrahim,	Trimmer
Karam Din Bawa,	Fireman
Karam Ilahi Ibrahim,	Fireman
Khuda Bakhsh Jalal,	Fireman
Khurshid Ahmad,	Fireman
Khurshid Muhammad,	Fireman
Khurshidali Naththu,	Fireman
Lobo Arelino,	Steward
Lopes Francis,	Steward
Machado Joseph,	Steward
Manji Balji,	Deck Hand
Martino Caetano S,	Scullion
Mirza Jang,	Trimmer
Mota Kala,	Trimmer
Muhammad Alam Fateh Din,	Fireman
Muhammad Fazldin,	Fireman
Muhammad Hasan,	Fireman
Muhammad Hayat Nasimullah,	Fireman
Muhammad Husain,	Sailor
Muhammad Khamis,	Trimmer
Muhammad Sharifuddin,	Sailor
Muhammad Tayyib,	Sailor
Muhammad Vali Husain Ali,	Fireman
Musa Umar,	Sailor
Nabi Bakhsh Khuda Bakhsh,	Fireman
Namdin Nuruddin,	Fireman
Nazir Mubarak,	Trimmer
Neyk Muhammad Faqir Muhammad,	Fireman
Noronha Jose,	Steward
Nura Vali Dad,	Fireman

Nuruddin Nawab,	Fireman
Pahlwan Dulhe,	Fireman
Pais Isoc,	Steward
Pereira Crispino,	Steward
Pinto Diogo,	Steward
Pir Ditta Ismail,	Trimmer
Polah Imamuddin,	Fireman
Qasim Ali,	Fireman
Rajab Ali Ilahi Bakhsh,	Fireman
Ramos Joaquim,	Steward
Razzaq Husain,	Trimmer
Rebelo Augusto,	Steward
Rebelo Caitano,	Steward
Rodriques Antonio,	Steward
Rodriques John F,	Steward
Rodriques Rozario,	Steward
Sadi Nizamuddin,	Fireman
Safinae Din,	Fireman
Sahib Din,	Trimmer
Sahibdin Nur,	Trimmer
Said Rahmatullah,	Sailor
Saqi Muhammad Karim Bakhsh,	Fireman
Shaikh Mohyuddin Shaikh Jina,	Sailor
Silveira Alexandre,	Steward
Silveira Noscimento,	Steward
Sufi Jumma,	Fireman
Sulaiman Muhammad,	Sailor
Sulaiman Rahmatullah,	Sailor
Tavares Chrysosto,	Steward
Tavares Cipriano,	General Servant
Teresa Estavao,	Steward
Valies Antonio J,	Steward
Valles Pascoal G,	Steward

SS Persia Remembered 30ᵗʰ December 1915

Vicente Henriques,	Steward
Viegas Rozario,	Steward
Yunus Shaik Ibrahim Shaikh,	Sailor
Yusuf Ibrahim,	Sailor

The Bombay 1914–1918 Memorial, Mumbai

The Ambush of SS Persia

Passengers who Survived

J P Bachmann
E R P Berryman, Captain
C Bigham, The Hon
Browne, Mrs
Alexander Clark
L Cook, Miss
Gustadji Muncherji Cooper, Mr
Bombardier Curtis
Marie R Derogez, Mlle
James Bulloch Dickie, Scotland
W J Eathorne, Mr
Manumal Edsardsas, Mr
G T Fisher, Lieutenant
Isabel Fladgate, Miss, Actress
Alfred Gabour, Mr
Gabour, Miss
J M Gardner, Second Lieutenant
Leonard W Gascoigne, Mr
Penn Gaskell, Mrs
Charles H Grant, Mr, Oil Manager[152]
Alan Grave, Mr
Guyot, Mme
John Lionel Miller-Hallett, Second Lieutenant
R A Harkness, Mr
Reginald W Heams, Mr, YMCA
George Hutchison, Major
Eulalie Edith Hutchison, Mrs
David Hutchison, aged 3
G Hyman, Mr
J Jacono, Mr
Arthur Henry Johnson, Mr

---

152   *New York Times*, 2nd January 1916

SS Persia Remembered 30th December 1915

Ernest Knight, Mr
I Knubchand, Mr
Leccore, Mr
Agnes J Lees, Miss
Alfred G Lyell, Captain
Benvenuto Maffesanti, Sig.
Maysie Markwick, Miss
Mondas, Mr
Montagu of Beaulieu, Lord
John J Nelson, Captain
Charles Myles O'Reilly, Major
S Parasram
A C Pegg, Lieutenant
R Ratonchand, Mr
Laurence E P Russ, Mr
Russ, Mrs
H C Salmon, Mr
C W Scott, Second Lieutenant
Agnes Shanks, Mrs, sister of Eulalie Hutchison
Isabel Sharp, Nurse for Hutchison children
Inder Singh, Mr
Slawick, Mr
Slawick, Mrs
Mary Ellen Smith, Mrs
Walter Ernest Smith, Mr
William Smith, Mr
Edith Smith, Miss
Henry Austin Smith or Smyth, Mrs
T G Spinney, Lieutenant
Emile Sutter, Mr
Gepaldas Vishindas, Mr
R Warner, Mr
L Wellington, Gunner
Young, Mr

On 3rd January 1916 *The Times* reported that six other surviving passengers landed at Alexandria. They were Mrs Bardrone, Captain Knibbs, Sidney Lawrence, Leonard Moss, Walter Smith and H J Sloper.

London Crew who Survived

Anderson C W,	Boatswain
Benge, J,	Second Steward
Birchley, G,	Able-Bodied Seaman
Burfoot, A,	Butcher
Butler, A J,	Chef
Carrick, W,	Bedroom Steward
Caulfield, F G,	General Servant & Printer
Clark, Frank	Writer
Clark, Gerald,	Chief Officer
Coughlan, Daniel,	Head Steward
Darlington, H,	Storekeeper
Dowling, William Henry,	Head Saloon Waiter
Eves, Henry Edwin,	Second Engineer
Flinn, C,	Bedroom Steward
Gasper, F,	Bedroom Steward
Godfrey, F,	Bedroom Steward
Hazlewood, T W,	Assistant Engineer
Henri, L,	Barber
Herbert, George,	Carpenter
Ireland, J F,	Third Engineer
Martin, Charles,	Steward
Matthew, H G,	Assistant Engineer
Mollon, W H F,	Assistant Engineer
Pennington, Mary Anne,	Stewardess (The Duchess)
Perry, J,	Bedroom Steward
Petts, C,	Able-bodied Seaman
Pinner, J,	Baggage Master
Preston, A E,	General Servant

SS Persia Remembered 30th December 1915

Price, E,	Able-bodied Seaman
Scrivener, A,	Able-bodied Seaman
Stevens, G,	Deck Steward
Thomas, J D,	Joiner
Toop, C,	Smoke Room Barman
Turk, W,	Second Waiter
Wood, H G S,	Second Officer

Bombay Crew who Survived

Abdool Khim Mohamed,	Trimmer
Abdooramon Hoossein,	Sailor
Ahmed Abdoolla,	Trimmer
Allabux Alladitta,	Tindal
Bakar Hoossein,	Sailor
Dawood Fackeer,	Sailor
Ebrom Chaman,	Sailor
Ebrom Hoossein,	Sailor
Ebrom Mohamed,	Sailor
Fackeer Mohamed Endoo,	Serang
Faiz Allam Neck Mohamed,	Fireman
Jamal Jewa,	Sailor
Macklan Mackia,	Fireman
Mockan Ellamdeen,	Fireman
Mohamed Mohida Koole,	Sailor
Mohamed Oosman,	Sailor
Mohamet Ahmadeen,	Panuwalla
Neck Mohamed Fackeer,	Fireman
Oosman Abdoola,	Sailor
Saidoo Ferroo,	Trimmer
Saidoolla Mohamed,	Panuwalla
Sharofan Peerbux,	Fireman
Manuel Salvadore Tavares,	Pantryman
Estack Fermiano Rodrigues,	Waiter
Benjamin Nazareth,	Waiter
Joas Francisco Leito,	Waiter
Pascoal Furtado,	Bedroom Cabin Steward
Joseph Britto,	Waiter
Joseph Fernandes,	Waiter
Britto Manuel Xavier,	Waiter
J Taveira,	Waiter
Felix Petru,	Waiter

Joas Baptiste Mendonca,	Engineer's Servant
Meniono Dias,	Waiter
Sebastias Fernandes,	Waiter
Minguel Antonio Fernandes,	Curry Cook
Domingo Rodrigues,	Waiter
Manvelino De Costa,	Waiter
Victor Pontes,	Scullion
Luiz Pinto,	Waiter
Phillip Gomes,	Topass
Joaquim Antonio Silva,	Waiter
Antonio Gabriel Tereza,	Scullion
Antonio Gabriel Baretto,	Baker
Custodio Phillip Fernande,	Topass
Caetano Piminto,	Waiter
Joaquim Fernandes,	Topass
Mariano Predade Rodrigues,	Iceman
Vincent Dias,	Scullion
Rogue De Mello,	Butcher
Joseph R Fernandes,	Scullion
Silvestio De Silva,	Waiter
Caetano Nones,	Bedroom Cabin Steward
Joseph Caetano Dias,	Scullion
Francisco Game,	Waiter
Crispiano Correa,	Assistant Cook

Acknowledgements

My wife Sylvia and I paid a visit to the Maritime Museum at Buckler's Hard in 2015 when I first learned that no one had published *Persia's* story. On our short journey home, I mentioned that perhaps I might try to fill this apparent gap. She knew I loved history and that I had written one book on project management and thought it sounded good to investigate further. With no relevant experience, I dived in and although she has had much time to regret my absence from help in running our household, her support and advice have never faded. My children and grandchildren also tolerated my preoccupation and I am deeply grateful for the loving support and tolerance from them all. For those familiar with the wonderfully perceptive '*Love is …*'[153] cartoons, this might have been captioned '*still smiling even after his bright idea became a four-year obsession*'.

I am indebted to many people for their help and advice during my research and writing. My hunt for information started at the Maritime Museum at Buckler's Hard in Hampshire, where the Honourable Mary Montagu-Scott DL has the helm, capably supported by Archivist Susan Tomkins. Both have been wonderfully supportive and enthusiastic throughout and generous with their help on what became a long and convoluted trail. I owe them both immense gratitude for bearing with me.

Along the way I made many contacts and, inspired by their enthusiasm and support, hope that I have remembered them all. They include Caroline de Burgh for input on the Penn Gaskell and de Burgh families; Tamsin Bacchus for information about Captain E R P (Ted) Berryman and a great proofreading job; Tom Bliss for information about Agnes Lees' *Remarkable Story*; Janet Brown about Lieutenant John Alexander Tower Robertson; James Crowden about the de Burgh family; Judith Curtloys

---

153 Kim Casali and Bill Asprey

and Penny Keens of Christ Church, Oxford for information about Lieutenant Humphrey Richard Locke Lawrence; Susan Day, on behalf of the Old Bancroftians' Association, and Jeremy Bromfield, Archivist, Bancroft's School Woodford, about Second Lieutenant Robert Dunham Tibbs; Trevor Deakin for valuable read-throughs and suggestions; Richard Dowling for information about William Henry Dowling, Head Saloon Waiter; Christopher Ecclestone for his SS *Persia* website; Peter and Pip Edwards about Captain E R P (Ted) Berryman; Don Elks and Tim Law about the sinking of SS *Arabia*; Beth Ellis, Curator, Digital Collections & Web Editor, P&O Heritage Collection for extraordinary and enthusiastic help finding images and setting up licensing arrangements; the Everitt family for information about Mary Elizabeth Everitt; Martin Eves for information about Second Engineer Henry Eves; Maciek Florek, author of the *Torpedo Vorhaltrechner Project* for information about Kaiserliche Marine U-boat torpedoes; Suzanne Foster, Archivist at Winchester College for permission to use information about Robert Vane Russell; Elisa Vasquez de Gey, biographer of the Maharani Prem Kaur, for information about the Maharaja and Maharani of Kapurthala; Michael Gallaher, Manager PR and Historian at Cunard; Michael Hamill for translations from Max Valentiner's book on U-38; Erik Hansen, the Max Valentiner historian; Gudmundur Helgason for his amazing website uboat.net; Kit Hether for information about Joyce Minnitt, and her baby Christine/Joy; Rosemary Hubbard about Mary Elizabeth McGinn; Adrian Hughes, proprietor of the Home Front Museum, Llandudno, for in-depth knowledge of the prisoner-of-war break out from Dyffryn Aled; Susan Burns about Thomas and Cecilia Burns and Alexander Clark; Steven John for information about Engineer Lieutenant Arthur Twining Roch RN; Chris Johnson for information about the Spreckley family; Jeremy Kidd about Reginald Heams and the YMCA party; Brian May about Berthon folding boats; Tim Law and Don Elks about the sinking of SS *Arabia*; Barbara Wiseman about William Orr Orr and nephew James B Dickie; Benedicta Makin about Captain E R P (Ted) Berryman; John Thorold Masefield, CMG and Robin Masefield, great-nephews of J L Miller Hallett for family letters shared and Richard Lander for photographs of and information about John Lionel Miller Hallett; The Alexander Turnbull Library for a newspaper report on the *Baralong* Incident; David Riley, Product and Licensing Manager, Museum of New Zealand Te Papa Tongarewa, for the quality image of HMS Mallow; Rosie Rowley and Macclesfield Reflects – the Great War Commemoration Group; Sukey Roxburgh of Deep Tek; Rachel Rudkin for information about Rose, Helen and Edward Burcombe; Catherine Smith, Charterhouse Archivist, for words about and photograph of Arthur Morris Coleman; Mark Smith for information about Mary Pennington, 'The Duchess'; Ralph Spreckley about David Spreckley; Joyce Stevenson of Thurlby Village together with Northorpe about Frederick Fairchild; Martyn Taylor for information about William Orr Orr and James Dickie; Katherine Thompson of the Churchill Archives Centre about Sir Archibald Hurd and for establishing contact with Mr John Willmer; Thurlby Village together with Northorpe about Frederick Fairchild; Roy Walton for information about George Edward Walton; Sam Warwick re P&O shipwrecks and Commodore W H S Hall and his family; Judith Webb about Henry Backhouse; Adrian Wilkinson of Lincolnshire Archives for information about Frederick Fairchild; David Williams for William Orr Orr and James Dickie; Viv Williams of Flintshire War Memorials about Guy Lesingham Spreckley; John Willmer, grandson of Sir Archibald Hurd and copyright holder, for permission to use extracts from his grandfather's extraordinary books; Angela Wren for translations from Max Valentiner's book on U-38; my brother, Keith Wren, Lieutenant Commander RN (retd.) for his enthusiasm, professional knowledge, valuable read-throughs and suggestions.

Claire Waring edited and proofed my text with incredible thoroughness, patience and professionalism. Her input guided me through vital corrections and improvements and the process became an enjoyable and very worthwhile learning experience. Mike (Bernie) Levens, a friend from days at Keswick School, proofread my text as did Tony Barnett, Tamsin Bacchus, Trevor Deaking, Susan Tompkins and Keith Wren. What a wonderful team! Finally, I would like to thank Duncan Beal of York Publishing Services for sharing experience, wisdom, enthusiasm and guidance over the last year.

Maritime Epilogue

Finding SS Persia

It was 2001 before searchers found the wreck of SS *Persia* off Crete at a depth of 10,000 feet (3,000 m). Deep Tek Limited, of Newport-on-Tay, Fife, is a company at the forefront of underwater technology that develops, manufactures and commissions complete solutions to undertake remote, heavy-duty work in deep and ultra-deep water. It designed and built a revolutionary winder system and fibre rope winch allowing a massive extension to deep-sea operations. SS *Persia* had seemingly loaded an immensely valuable cargo in her strong room, so Deep Tek also fabricated a range of equipment for cutting down through five decks to access the strong room and made a self-loading system for the recovery of its contents. The salvage operation was a technical success, with the decks removed down to the strong room and its contents recovered to the surface. Without the winch and winder technology, the SS *Persia* would have been beyond workable reach.

Moya Crawford, Chairman and Director of Technology Implementation at Deep Tek commented:

> '*Working with synthetic filament rope in 3,000 metres water depth, accessing the Bullion Room of the SS Persia, gave us the unparalleled experience of watching braided soft rope work on a drum winch. This hands-on experience, coupled with the technical and financial discipline of "No Cure/No Pay", led us to thoroughly understand what was needed to transfer soft-rope technology into the oil and gas sector. Our machinery was able to cut into the Persia's strong room from where we recovered more than 200 rubies and other precious stones. We did not find gold – someone will have to go back for that, but the real value to us lies in showing that no part of the seabed is now beyond reach.*'[154]

---

154 http://digital-silver.co.uk/TimeGun/fate-sspersia.html

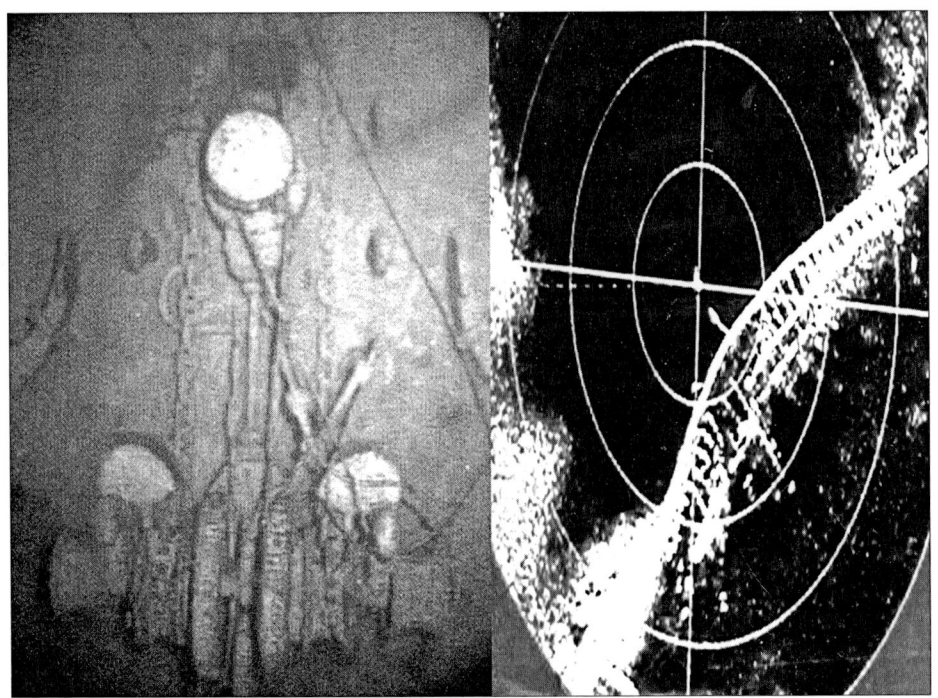

Images of SS Persia on the sea bed when found by Deep Tek
By kind permission of Alex and Moya Crawford, Deep Tek Limited

In 2003 Deep Tek recovered jewels and artefacts, but found nothing of the Maharaja's vast fortune, perhaps worth over £35m in 2002 values. The Buckler's Hard Maritime Museum displays the recovered bullion room door and many personal items from the wreck. These include pipes, cutlery, boots, thimbles, razors, banknotes and, perhaps the most poignant, a tiny pair of baby shoes. What happened to the Maharaja's fortune if it wasn't in *Persia*'s strong room? Was it ever aboard the *Persia*? Was it dispersed across the ship in secure cabins such as those of the captain and other officers? Perhaps the Maharaja never loaded his treasure, or loaded and then unloaded it? It seems that Max Valentiner reached an early decision to sink SS *Persia*, giving no warning and making no search. Perhaps he never learned that in his haste he may have destroyed a floating El Dorado, or that if he had followed the cruiser rules, he, his crew and the German war effort might have been richly rewarded and over three hundred lives perhaps spared.

Maritime Epilogue

If SS Persia had been a troopship, who would have worn these?
© *Beaulieu Enterprises Ltd.*

U-38

U-38 had three further commanders after Max Valentiner. They were Wilhelm Canaris, Hans Heinrich Wurmbach and Clemens Wickel. She carried out a total of 17 patrols before her crew surrendered her to France on 23rd February 1919 and the French broke her up in 1921.

HMS *Baralong*

After the '*Baralong* Incident', she was renamed HMS *Wyandra*, then deleted from Lloyds Register and renamed *Manica*. She was sold to Japan and renamed *Kyokuto Maru* in 1923[155].

MacCallum More

This iron sailing ship was dismasted and abandoned while in ballast between New York and Rotterdam on 23rd January 1917[156].

---

155 The Ships List – Ellerman & Bucknall Line: https://www.theshipslist.com/ships/lines/ellerman6.shtml
156 Scottish Built Ships: http://www.clydeships.co.uk/view.php?ref=5591

HMS *Mallow*

On 14th July 1918, HMS *Mallow* rescued passengers from the 3,761-ton French mailboat *Djemmah* carrying 754 passengers and crew after UB-105 torpedoed her (Kapitänleutnant Wilhelm Marschall)[157]. The ship sank in two minutes with the loss of 436 lives. Those rescued by HMS *Mallow* included the future acting Governor General of Madagascar, M Joseph Guyon. *Mallow* later received letters of commendation from the Admiralty and Guyon[158]. She was transferred to the Royal Australian Navy in July 1919, dismantled in July 1932 and sunk as a target off Sydney on 1st August 1935.

HMS *Monmouth*

Escorted Godfrey Herbert's epic submarine voyage from Portsmouth to Hong Kong. Sunk with all hands (735) on 1st November 1914 in the Battle of Coronel[159].

SS *Nicosian*

Nicosian's crew were issued with new discharge books that omitted her voyage in August 1915. This was a precaution in case the Germans ever captured any of her crewmen. Her owners renamed her SS *Nevisian* in order to protect future crews and her work ended in a breaker's yard in 1933[160].

SS *Ning Chow*

She continued in service with Alfred Holt and Company and served them for 30 years until scrapped in 1932.

SMS *Rostock*

Missed by Godfrey Herbert's torpedoes from D5 in 1914, she was badly damaged during the Battle of Jutland and scuttled by her escaping crew on 1st June 1916.

---

157 https://www.uboat.net/wwi/ships_hit/1666.html
158 https://ipfs.io/ipfs/QmXoypizjW3WknFiJnKLwHCnL72vedxjQkDDP1mXWo6uco/wiki/HMS_Mallow_(1915).html
159 Massie, Robert K (2003). Castles of Steel: Britain, Germany, and the Winning of the Great War at Sea. pp 233–234. London: Jonathan Cape. ISBN 0-224-04092-8
160 The Ships List – Leyland Line: https://www.theshipslist.com/ships/lines/leyland.shtml

SS *Arabia* – *Persia*'s Sister

The authorities seemingly learned some lessons from losses at sea. UB-43 torpedoed *Persia*'s sister ship SS *Arabia* some ten months later, on her voyage from Australia to London. The human outcome was very different. Before departing Port Said she had loaded and fitted one of the temporary 4.7" defensive guns shared by ships travelling in alternating directions between Port Said and Gibraltar. Three gunners had joined the ship and practised firing once they put to sea on the morning of Saturday 4th November 1916. She had a naval escort for the first two days of her voyage towards Malta. The escort left her at 9.00 pm on Sunday, having arrived in what the Navy must have thought to be a less dangerous part of the sea after the narrower passage south of Crete.

Fourteen hours after the escort detached, the morning of Monday 6th November was clear and warm. A torpedo struck *Arabia* and exploded at 11.00 am and 11 engine-room crew lost their lives. *Arabia* sank slowly, stern first, but all the 439 passengers and the rest of the crew escaped in lifeboats. One of the passengers was Mrs Paula Scotland[161] travelling with her 9-month-old daughter, Norah. Australia's 10th Light Horse Regiment had evacuated Paula's husband to England for treatment from where he cabled Paula asking if she would bring Norah, the daughter he had never seen. Paula escaped into a lifeboat with her tiny daughter. The U-boat that claimed the sinking was UB-43 under Kapitänleutnant Hans von Mellenthin.

Four Royal Navy minesweepers came to *Arabia*'s rescue 90 minutes later, by which time the U-boat had disappeared. Fortunately, Ellerman Lines passenger liner SS *City of Marseilles* also took part in the rescue[162] and landed its contingent at Port Said, while survivors picked up by the minesweepers, including Paula and Norah, landed in Malta, almost replicating the aftermath of *Persia*'s sinking. The provision of an escort, the closeness of a fleet of minesweepers, the gunners' practice and improved emergency evacuation procedures had contributed to a less harmful outcome for SS *Persia*'s sister ship – improved but clearly still far from perfect.

Things changed for the better in an unexpected way for Mrs Scotland when she received a cable from England. It read *'Await my coming – be there first opportunity'*. Her husband arrived in Valletta by troopship, to rejoin his wife and cradle his daughter for the first time[163]

---

161 http://www.peoplehelp.com.au/stories/arabia.html
162 'Arabia 1898'. Fact Sheet. P&O Heritage: http://www.poheritage.com/Upload/Mimsy/Media/factsheet/95400ARABIA-1898pdf.pdf
163 Emails and documents from Tim Law and Don Elks

SS *Adenwen*

After surviving an attack by U-29 in March 1915, SS *Adenwen* was torpedoed and *sunk* by UC-65 in March 1917

Postscript

One of my aims was to create a modest memorial to all those aboard the SS *Persia* when the torpedo struck. The 'official' death toll and that shown on the memorial at Buckler's Hard and quoted widely elsewhere is 343, while those named as lost total 334. Perhaps an early transcription error passed into history, unseen in the fog of war. While a number gives scale to a death toll, it is only a statistic. A single name represents a life ended on that fateful day, or one person who survived unimaginable trauma. I hope that the names lists are complete but accept that their spelling may vary from family records and other sources and I apologise for errors and omissions.

I remain acutely aware that some aspects of my SS *Persia* story are based on a hypothesis, closer to probable than possible, but beyond proof given the passage of time and the secrecy and censorship that prevailed to hide much of what happened from the public. This takes us back to David Lloyd George who once said:

> 'If the people really knew (the truth) the war would be stopped tomorrow. But of course, they don't know and can't know.'

Over 100 years later, it would be gratifying if my modest attempts stimulate the emergence of more information on the sinking of this P&O liner. Those who can add more and are willing to share, or who want to identify errors, please email me at ss.persia@yahoo.com

Alan Wren December 2019

Glossary

Abaft	Behind (on a ship) – towards or beyond the stern
Admiralstab	Imperial Admiralty Staff
Bhandary	Cook
Boat deck	The deck on which a ship's lifeboats are stored and operated (winched down to the next lower deck for ease of boarding)
Bombay	The city and port on the west coast of India, now known as Mumbai
Bosun (Boatswain)	In charge of deckhands and responsible for supervising deck operations
Bunker(ing)	Load(ing) fuel (usually coal in 1915)
Cable	From 'cablegram' – telegram transmitted via an undersea cable
Cantonment	Permanent military camp or a large military training camp in India
Central Powers	The alliance between Germany and Austria-Hungary and later the Ottoman Empire and Bulgaria
Coal trimmer	See Trimmer
Companionway	A stairway or ladder leading from one deck to another in a ship

Decks aboard SS *Persia* (Top-down)	Boat Hurricane Spar Main Lower Orlop
DEMS	Defensively Equipped Merchant Ship
Dreadnought battleship	In 1906 Portsmouth Dockyard launched a revolutionary British battleship, HMS *Dreadnought*, whose design, specification, armament and speed heralded a powerful new type. All battleships built to replicate the new specification were classed as 'Dreadnoughts' irrespective of their country of origin. Ships built earlier became known as Pre-Dreadnoughts.
DSO: The British Distinguished Service Order medal	Instituted during Queen Victoria's reign and awarded to officers who had performed distinguished or meritorious service during wartime, typically during combat
Entente	The alliance of Britain, France and Russia at the outset of World War 1
Durbar	Reception held by an Indian prince or a British governor or viceroy in India
FdU	Führer der Unterseeboote (Commander of U-boats)
Fireman	Ship's crewman responsible for shovelling coal into the furnaces and spreading it evenly to burn efficiently, maximising heat to the boilers and keeping the ashes cleared to maintain airflow for the same purpose

GCSI	Knight Grand Commander of the Star of India
Gross register tonnage (GRT)	Size of a ship expressed as its enclosed volume/capacity where 1 grt = 100 cubic feet (2.83 m3): the total permanently enclosed capacity/volume of a vessel used for harbour and canal transit fees
Handelskrieg	Commercial warfare (sinking cargo vessels to cut off supplies to the enemy)
Hexanite	An explosive charge used in German WW1 torpedoes – 60% TNT and 40% hexanitrodiphenylamine, first developed in 1907 and about 7% more powerful than 100% TNT (http://www.navweaps.com/Weapons/WTGER_Main.php)
HMHS	His Majesty's Hospital Ship
HMS	His Majesty's Ship
HNoMS	His Norwegian Majesty's Ship
Hurricane deck	The upper deck on some ships. On SS *Persia*, the deck below the boat deck. Crews needed to lower lifeboats level with this deck so that passengers could step rather than climb in
Kaiserliche Marine	The Imperial German (Kaiser's) Navy between 1871 and 1919
	Officer Ranks Junior to Senior
	Leutnant zur see
	Oberleutnant zur see
	Kapitänleutnant
	Korvettenkapitan
	Freggatenkapitan
	Kpitan zur see
Knot	A ship's unit of speed equal to one nautical mile (1.852 km) per hour, approximately 1.15 mph

Glossary

Kriegsmarine	The navy of Nazi Germany 1939–45
Lascar	(Archaic) A sailor from India or South-East Asia; early seventeenth century: from Portuguese *lascari*, from Urdu and Persian *laškar* 'soldier', from the laškar army, now seen as pejorative (*Oxford English Dictionary*)
Line-astern	Ship formation following a leader in line, each one at a set distance and directly astern
Long Forties	An area across the North Sea east of Aberdeen consistently 40 fathoms (240'/73 metres) deep
Lyddite	Filling in early British high-explosive shell with thick steel case designed to splinter into large and small shrapnel fragments flung at high velocity all around
Maharaja / Maharajah	Sanskrit word meaning 'Great Ruler' or 'High King' which term spread across much of India. A female ruler or the wife of a Maharaja was known as Maharani or Maharanee
Merchant raider	Warship or submarine used to seize or sink enemy or neutral merchant ships
Mespot	Soldiers' slang for Mesopotamia
Nautical mile	Unit of length/distance derived from the circumference of the earth at the equator divided by the minutes in that circle (360 degrees each of 60 minutes = 21,600) then determined to be 1.1508 miles or 1.852 kilometres. (It was standardised in 1970 and since then 1 nautical mile = 1.852 kilometres)
Orlop deck	The lowest deck in a ship, often where cables are stowed, usually below the water line

Painter	A line attached to the bow of a boat for tying up or towing
Point	One of the 32 subdivisions of a compass, each of 11.25 degrees which enable reference to headings in a general fashion, without computing degrees. A lookout aboard SS *Persia* first spotted the approaching torpedo '4 points on the port bow' that is 45° from straight ahead.
Poopdeck or Poop	A deck formed as the roof of a cabin built on the rear or after-part of a ship
Post-bellum	The period after a war
Pour le Mérite	Germany's highest military medal awarded during World War 1 – also known as Der Blaue Max (The Blue Max)
Promenade deck	An upper covered deck for the use of passengers
Quarter (deck)	The portion of a ship close to the stern
Queenstown	Port in County Cork, Ireland, known as Cobh since 1920
RMS	Ship prefix – Royal Mail Steamer or Royal Mail Ship
Scout Cruiser	Small (2,900 ton), fast (25 knots), more lightly armed and armoured cruisers for work with destroyer flotillas, leading their torpedo attacks and backing them up when attacked by other destroyers (1903–1910)
Scullion	(Archaic) Similar to kitchen porter
Sea anchor	Device to keep a boat stable in heavy weather and minimise broaching (turning side-on to the waves) which can be thrown over bow or stern on a rope so the boat pitches (end-to-end) rather than rolls (side-to-side), improving comfort and safety

Serang	Senior Indian seaman (Bosun equivalent)
Six-pounder	Gun of 2.2" calibre firing explosive projectile weighing approximately 6 lb (2.7 kg)
SMS	Seiner Majestät Schiff – 'His Majesty's Ship', abbreviated to SMS – ship prefix used by the Prussian Navy, the Kaiserliche Marine (Kaiserliche Marine) and the Austro-Hungarian Navy
SS	Ship prefix – Single-screw steamship
Spar deck	Light upper deck of a vessel
Thwart	Narrow seat across a boat for rowers or passengers
Tindal	Senior Indian seaman (Bosun's Mate equivalent)
Topass	Indian apprentice equivalent
Trimmer	A crew member in the engineering staff who moved coal from the bunkers to the furnaces to keep the firemen supplied with fuel while maintaining the ship's trim and optimising her speed and economy. Also helped firemen to clear and remove ashes and dispose of them into the sea
Tunnel	A tubular structure through which the propeller shaft of a ship extends from the engine room to the stern.
Vizeadmiral	Vice Admiral, Kaiserliche Marine

Bibliography

Books and Websites

Ackerley, J R et al (1932). *Escapers all: being the personal narratives of fifteen escapers from war-time prison camps 1914-1918*. London: Bodley Head.

Adams, T M (n.d.). *The BARALONG Affair*. Retrieved 2016 from Historical RFA: http://historicalrfa.org/archived-stories2/1280-the-baralong-affair-17

Allen, Charles (Editor) (1985). *Plain Tales from the Raj*. London: Century Publishing. ISBN 0-7126-0715-3.

Anon (n.d.). *British Naval Policy – 1890-1920*. Retrieved 28th February, 2019, from Global Security: https://www.globalsecurity.org/military/world/europe/uk-rn-policy2.htm

Anon (n.d.). *The P&O Empire*. Retrieved in 2019 from ships-worldwide.com: http://www.trains-worldexpresses.com/webships/400/406.htm

Anon (n.d.). *The Royal Navy in the Great War*. Retrieved 27th February 2019, from Global Security: https://www.globalsecurity.org/military/world/europe/uk-rn-policy3.htm

Anon (1900). The SS *Persia*. *The Shipping World & Herald of Commerce*, Vol. XXII, No. 367, 31st October.

Aujla, G (2001, 27th May). *The saga of Maharaja's sunken treasure*. From the *Tribune*: https://www.tribuneindia.com/2001/20010527/spectrum/main1.htm

Bainton, Roy (2015). *Honoured By Strangers: Captain Cromie's Extraordinary First World War*. Constable and Robinson.

Bönker, D *Naval Race between Germany and Great Britain, 1898-1912.* Retrieved from International Encyclopedia of the First World War: https://encyclopedia.1914-1918-online. net/article/naval_race_between_germany_and_great_britain_1898-1912

Boyle, F A (1999). *Foundations of World Order: The Legalist Approach to International Relations, 1898–1922.* Duke University Press.

Bridgland, T (1999). *Sea Killers in Disguise: Q Ships and Decoy Raiders.* ISBN 978-0-85052-675-2. Leo Cooper.

Buckley, C, Harley, Simon, Jellicoe, Nick and Lovell, Tony (Editors) (2018). *Dreadnought Project: Tenth Cruiser Squadron (Royal Navy).* Retrieved from Dreadnought Project: http://www.dreadnoughtproject.org/tfs/index.php/Tenth_Cruiser_Squadron_(Royal_Navy)#Composition

Canadian Centre for Occupational Health and Safety (2019, 22nd February). *Combustible Dust.* Retrieved from: https://www.ccohs.ca/oshanswers/chemicals/combustible_dust.html

Carradice, P (2014, 28th August). *The Colditz of the Denbigh Moors – and some great escapes: Wales.* Retrieved from: http://www.bbc.co.uk/blogs/wales/entries/3a87832f-650b-302d-acc1-39deed2f0246

Chatterton, E K (1922 [Reprinted 2010]. *Q-ships and Their Story.* London: Sidgwick and Jackson

Chatterton, E K (1935). *Amazing Adventure – A Thrilling Naval Autobiography.* London: Hurst & Blackett Ltd.

Clarke, Christopher M (2009). *Kaiser Wilhelm 11: A Life in Power.* Penguin Books UK. ISBN 978-0-14-103993-0

Coles, A (1986). *Slaughter at Sea? The Truth Behind a Naval War Crime.* London: Robert Hale Ltd.

Compton-Hall, R (1991). *Submarines and the War at Sea, 1914-1918.* Macmillan.

Declaration of Paris (1856) and the Hague Conventions (1899 and 1907) sea (Cruiser Rules).

Craig, L A (2013). *Josephus Daniels: His Life & Times* (p.300). University North Carolina Press.

DiGiulian, Tony (2019). *Torpedoes of Germany Pre-WWII.* Retrieved from NavWeaps: http://www.navweaps.com/Weapons/WTGER_PreWWII.php

Ecclestone, C (n.d.). *The Sinking of the SS Persia.* Retrieved, 2016, from: https://sites.google.com/site/thesinkingofthesspersia/

Faulkner, Marcus (2015). *The Great War at Sea. A naval atlas 1914-1919.* Barnsley: Seaforth Publishing. ISBN 978-1-84832-183-0.

Florek, M (1916). *Torpedo attacks during WWI.* Retrieved from Torpedo Vorhaltrechner Project: http://www.tvre.org/en/torpedo-attacks-during-ww1

Friedman, N (2014). *Fighting the Great War at Sea: Strategy, Tactics and Technology.* Naval Institute Press.

Frothingham, A L (n.d.). *Handbook of War Facts and Peace Problems 1919. Chapter 8: Illustrative Extracts. The Allied Peace Terms of January, 1917.* Retrieved from National Security League: http://net.lib.byu.edu/estu/wwi/comment/WarFacts/wfacts4b.htm

Gibson, R H & Prendergast, M (2002). *The German Submarine War 1914–1918.* Penzance: Periscope Publishing.

Grace's Guide (2017, 1st August). *Caird and Co.* Retrieved from *Grace's Guide to British Industrial History*: https://www.gracesguide.co.uk/Caird_and_Co

Greentree, D (2014). *Q Ship vs U-Boat 1914-18.* Duel (Book 57). Oxford: Osprey Publishing.

Gröner, Erich, Jung, Dieter and Maass, Martin (1991). *German Warships 1815–1945. Volume 2. U-boats and Mine Warfare Vessels.* Translated by Thomas, Keith & Magowan, Rachel. London: Conway Maritime Press. ISBN 0-85177-593-4.

Halpern, P G (2015). *The Naval War in the Mediterranean: 1914-1918.* Routledge library editions: Military and naval history. London: Routledge.

Hankel, G E (2016, 21st October). *Leipzig War Crimes Trials.* Retrieved from International Encyclopedia of the First World War: https://encyclopedia.1914-1918-online.net/article/leipzig_war_crimes_trials/2016-10-21

Hansen, E (n.d.). Retrieved 1915, from Max Valentiner: http://www.max-valentiner.dk (Site no longer available)

Helgason, G (n.d.). *WWI U-boat Types – Type U31*. Retrieved from uboat.net: https://uboat.net/wwi/types/?type=U+31

Helgason, Gudmundur (n.d.). *U-boat War in World War One*.

His Majesty's Stationery Office (1916). *Memorandum of the German Government in regard to Incidents alleged to have attended the Destruction of a German Submarine and its Crew by His Majesty's Auxiliary Cruiser "Baralong" on August 19, 1915, and Reply of His Majesty's Government thereto*. Retrieved from WWW Virtual Library – www.vlib.us/wwi/resources/archives/texts/t050925/Baralong.html

Hogg, I V and Thureston, L F (1972). *British Artillery Weapons & Ammunition 1914-1918*. London: Ian Allan.

Hurd, A (1921). *History of the Great War, The Merchant Navy, Volume 1*. London: John Murray.

Hurd, A (1924). *The Merchant Navy, Volume 2*. London: John Murray.

James, A D (2001). *Leaving Cheltenham and all that was dear – re Colonel Ernest Robert Rainier SWINEY*. Retrieved from Commemorations of the Great War: http://www.remembering.org.uk/leckhampton_indiv_comm.htm

JSTOR (n.d.). Submarine Warfare – Austria: Case of the "Ancona". Retrieved from: https://archive.org/stream/jstor-2212351/2212351_djvu.txt

Kan, V (2009, 22nd August). *RMS Lusitania: The Fateful Voyage*. Retrieved 2016, from https://www.firstworldwar.com/features/lusitania.htm

Lake, D (2006). *Smoke and Mirrors, Q-ships against U-boats in the First World War*. Stroud: Sutton Publishing Ltd.

Lees, A (n.d.). *The Thrilling Experience of a Passenger by the SS Persia on the 30th & 31st December 1915 in her own words*. Lucknow: Murray's Press.

Loss of HMS Aboukir, Cressy and Hogue (n.d.). Retrieved 28th February, 2019, from World War 1 Naval Combat: http://www.worldwar1.co.uk/cressy.htm

Lusitania U-Boat Sinks Another Passenger Liner *(SS* Hesperian*).* (2015, 4th September). Retrieved 2015, from Today in World War I: http://today-in-wwi.tumblr.com/post/128337187048/lusitania-u-boat-sinks-another-passenger-liner

Makin, Benedicta. *Letters home from five brothers during the First World War.* Retrieved 2015 and frequently from **www.familyletters.co.uk** . Note that Captain ERP Berryman's letters are also available at https://www.iwm.org.uk/collections/item/object/1030021700

Marcus, P (Editor) (1916, 1st January). Royal Navy Log Books of the World War 1 Era; HMS *Hannibal.* Retrieved 2017, from Naval History: https://s3.amazonaws.com/oldweather/ADM53-43712/071_1.jpg

Massie, R K (2007). *Dreadnought – Britain, Germany and the Coming of the Great War.* London: Vintage Books.

McCarthy, J (2015, 19th April). *The Colditz of North Wales – how Denbighshire stately home became a POW camp for 100 German soldiers (sic).* Retrieved from North Wales Live: https://www.dailypost.co.uk/news/north-wales-news/colditz-north-wales-how-denbighshire-9074558

McMullen, C (2001). *Royal Navy 'Q' Ships.* Retrieved from The World War 1 Document Archive: http://www.gwpda.org/naval/rnqships.htm

National Archives (n.d). *Clan Macfarlane; Official number: 108742.* Retrieved 2019, from the National Archives: http://discovery.nationalarchives.gov.uk/details/r/C14699498

National Maritime Museum. *Crew list document for vessel 'PERSIA'. Official number: 109258.* Retrieved from National Maritime Museum: https://1915crewlists.rmg.co.uk/document/108744

Naval-History. Net (n.d.). *Introductions To The Royal & Empire Navies In World War 1.* Retrieved from World War 1 1914-1918: http://www.naval-history.net/Index0-1914.htm

Nesham, Félicité (Editor) (1987). *Socks Cigarettes and Shipwrecks – A family's war letters 1914-1918.* Gloucester: Sutton Publishing.

Nico, V (2009, 12th June). *Wrecksite Clan MacFarlane.* Retrieved from Wrecksite: https://www.wrecksite.eu/wreck.aspx?58047

The Old Bancroftians Association (2019). *Robert Dunham Tibbs*. Retrieved from The Bancroftian Network: http://www.bancroftians. net/cgi-bin/bancms3pl?id=5829&im=Y

P&O Steam Navigation Co (n.d.). *PERSIA (1900)* Retrieved 28th February, 2019, from P&O Heritage: http://www.poheritage.com/Upload/Mimsy/Media/factsheet/94239PERSIA-1900pdf. pdf

Pocock, M W (2008, 30th December). *Daily Event for December 30, 2008*. Retrieved from Maritime Quest: http://www.maritimequest.com/daily_event_archive/2008/12_dec/30_ss_persia_and_ss_clan_macfarlane.htm

Radcliffe, J (Editor) (2010). *Egypt of the Magicians*. Retrieved from *The New Readers' Guide to the works of Rudyard Kipling*: http://www.kiplingsociety.co.uk/rg_seatravel1.htm

Rare Historical Photos (2013, 25th November). *Inside the German submarine SM UB-110, 1918.* Retrieved from: https://rarehistoricalphotos.com/u-boat-control-room-1918/

Smith, G (n.d.). *French Navy*. Retrieved 6th May, 2017, from Naval-History. Net, WW1 at Sea: http://www.naval-history.net/WW1NavyFrench.htm

The *Sunday Star* (1915). *20 on lost ships reported missing: Italian liner Firenze sunk by submarine.* (1915, 14th November). *The Sunday Star, Washington*, page 16. Retrieved 2019, from Chronicling America: https://chroniclingamerica.loc.gov/lccn/sn83045462/1915-11-14/ed-1/seq-16/

Tritton, P (1985). *John Montagu of Beaulieu, Motoring Pioneer and Prophet.* London: Golden Eagle/George Hart.

Valentiner, M (1917). *300.000 Tonnen versenkt! – Meine U-Boots-Fahrten* (300,000 tons sunk! My U-boat trips). Berlin und Wien: Ullstein.

Valentiner, M (1934). *U 38. Wikingerfahrten einesdeutschen U-Bootes* (U-38. Viking voyages of a German U-boat). Berlin: Ullstein.

von Bethmann Hollweg, T (Translated by Young, G) (1920). *Reflections on the World War.* London: T. Butterworth.

War and Security (2015). *Allegations of War Crimes at Sea in 1915.* Retrieved from The Royal Navy in the First World War: https://warandsecurity.com/tag/u27/

White Star History (2007–2012). *RMS Arabic (II).* Retrieved from White Star Line History Website: http://whitestarhistory.com/arabic2

Wylie, James and McKinley, Michael (2015) The Codebreakers, The secret intelligence unit that changed the course of the first world war (London: Ebury Press) ISBN 9780091957728

Zenzmaier, Jakob (2019). *The Leipzig Trials (1921-1927). Between national disgrace and juridical farce.* Retrieved from The First World War: https://ww1.habsburger,net/en/chapters/leipzig-trials-1921-1927-between-national-disgrace-and-juridical-farce

Index

Aberdeen, 30, 67, 72, 105
Admiralty Prize Court, 144
Alexandria, 63, 66, 90, 92, 96, 100, 117, 118, 120, 124, 126, 128, 130, 132, 134, 135, 150,
Alfred Holt Line, 123, 124, 193
American Missionary Society in Bombay, 71
Anderson, CW, 56
Anschluss of Nordschleswig, 149
Arabic Pledge, (chapter) 41
Armed Merchant Cruisers, 16, 21, 22, 44, 57, 144, 161
Armoured Motor Units (AMUs), 85
Arsenal Football Club, 59
Austria, 45, 48, 91, 146, 158, 197, 206
Austro-Hungary, 9, 15, 52
Austrian flag, 48, 51, 52, 91
Ayah's House, Hackney, 70

Backhouse, Henry, 90, 91, 126, 127, 164
Baden Powell, General, 135
Bancroft's School, Woodford Wells, 76, 188, 208
Baretto, Antonio Gabriel, 58, 64
Battery charging (in U-boat), 94
Bernstorff, Johann Heinrich von, 42
Berry, Victor, 57
Berryman, Edward (Ted) Rolleston Palmer, 77, 78, 79, 106, 111, 113, 118, 127, 151, 152, 207
Berryman, Martin and Félicité, 152
Berthon folding boats, 5, 109
Bertie, Sir Francis, 2

Berwick-upon-Tweed, 76, 134, 135
Bethmann Hollweg, Theobald von, 18, 99, 208
Bhil Mission, 66
Birmingham, 66, 67, 71, 156
Birmingham Small Arms Company Limited (BSA), 144
Black soul, 109
Blockade, 2, 6, 7, 8, 9, 15, 16, 20, 31, 43, 45, 47, 139, 147, 161
Board of Trade, xii, 5, 104
Boiler explosion, 100
Bombay (Mumbai), x, 5, 53, 54, 55, 56, 68, 70, 73, 75, 76, 84, 90, 92, 120, 128, 130, 131, 132, 152
Bombay-Express, 64, 73
Bonnand, M, 127
Boyd, Stuart W, 56
Briones, Anita Delgado, 87
British declaration of war, 14
Britannia Brewery at Barbourne, 70
Buckler's Hard Maritime Museum, 94, 128, 162, 163, 164, 168, 187
Bull, Adelaide, 66, 97, 108, 111
Burcombe, Edward and Rose, 68, 127, 128
Burns, Thomas and Cecilia, 72, 73, 124, 127
Butler, AJ, 58, 64

C-class submarine, 25
Caird and Company of Greenock, 3, 4, 205
Caird, John, 3

Calcutta (Kolkata), 68, 71, 72, 73, 76, 127, 135
Cape Helles, 167
Cape Matapan, 48, 93
Capo Carbonara, 50
Car Illustrated, 81
Carrigan Head, Q-ship (aka Q4), 143
Cattaro (now Kotor, Montenegro), 12, 45, 46, 53
Charterhouse, 73, 188
Chatby Memorial, Alexandria, 126, 127, 130, 135
Chatham Naval Memorial, 135
Christmas Day 1915, 62, 64, 74, 79, 81, 88, 137
Churchill, Winston, 11, 13, 19, 21
Clan Line, 113, 160
Clark, Alexander, 73, 91, 122, 124, 127
Clark, Gerald, 56, 92, 115
Cobh, x, 201
Cochran, Patrick, 145
Codrington, Helen Maude de Burgh, 69, 128
Codrington, Marjorie Doris, 128
Coleman, Arthur, 73
Coleman, Frank Morris, 73
Collins, Corporal, 39
Colomb, Sir John, 1, 21
Commonwealth War Graves Commission (CWGC), 140, 162
Congregation of Daughters of the Cross, 65, 137
Conran-Smith, Marcel and Hilda, 68, 134
Contraband, 8, 9, 10, 16, 23, 37, 162
Cook, Dr Lilian, 71, 96, 105, 130
Cooper, Gustadji Muncherji, 75
Coughlan Daniel, 58
Crete, xi, 46, 94, 95, 110, 120, 136, 166, 190, 194
Crossley, Mrs, 69, 132
Cruiser / Prize Rules, xiii, 8, 9, 10, 15, 20, 31, 37, 42, 49, 167, 191, 204
Cruiser Force C, 17
Curtis, Bombardier, 60

Daily Mirror, 53
Dawson, William Orford Charles, 79
de la Perière, Lothar von Arnauld, 149

Deck cricket, 95, 112
Declaration of London, 9, 11, 22, 37
Deep Tek, 190, 191
Defence of the Realm Act 1914, 24, 121
Defensive gun, 19, 22, 59, 97, 194
Defensively Equipped Merchant Ships (DEMS), 21, 22, 59
Dehra Dun, 76, 132
Derogez, Marie Renée Rosalie, 71, 111, 127
Dewey, George, 56
Dickie, James Bulloch, 74, 134, 189, 190
Dimsdale, Reginald, 142, 143
Distinguished Service Order, 40, 77, 142, 198
Dorothy Gray, Trawler, 36
Dover Patrol, RN, 16
Dowling, William Henry, 58, 64, 97, 98, 116, 157, 163, 166
Dufferin Hospital for Women, Lahore, 67, 129
Dyffryn Aled, 36, 37

Eckardstein, Baron Hermann von, 2
Empire Run, 3, 6, 55, 97
Escobar, Narciso Díaz de, 88
Eugenie Besal, steamer, 52
Everett, William, 60, 122, 137
Everitt, Mary Elizabeth, 68
Eves, Henry Edwin, 56, 100, 102, 164

Fairchild, Frederick, 58
Fastnet, 46
Ferdinand, Archduke Franz, 13
Fernandez, Mary, (Ayah), 70, 91, 137
Fielding, Ellen Pauline (Nell), 79
Finch, William, 41, 42
Firenze (steamer), 52
First and Second Naval Laws (Germany), 2, 3
First Sea Lord, 'Jackie' Fisher, 8, 11
Forstmann, Walter, 46, 149
Funchal Roads, 146
Furbringer, Gerhardt, 30

Gabour, 112, 113
Gallipoli Campaign, 166
Gansser, Konrad, 46, 160

Gareloch, 143
Gascoigne, Leonard W, 65, 66, 136, 137
Gibraltar, 22, 46, 48, 53, 61, 63, 64, 80, 90, 194
Goodheart, Francis, AM, 143, 144
Gough, Owen MC, 79
Graeff, Ernst, 30, 31
Grant, Alexander (Alec) Colquhoun, 67, 95, 96, 105, 113
Grant, Charles, 105
Grant, Henry, 28
Great Ormes Head, 36, 37, 39
Greil, Dr Cecile, 51, 52

Hague Conventions of 1899 and 1907, 8, 22, 204
Haldane, Justice Viscount, 75
Hall, Amy Aileen Mary Selby, 55
Hall, Charles Otley, 55
Hall, Helen Maud Selby, 55, 56
Hall, Mary née Johnson, 55, 56, 57
Hall, William Henry Selby, Master SS Persia, 55, 128
Hampshire Regiment Reserve Battalion, 83
Hampshire Territorial Brigade, 83
Hansen, Klaus, 43, 139, 161
Hanson, Victor Davis, xii
Hardinge, Lord, Viceroy of India, 81, 84, 86, 151
Hargrave, Helen Monica Maude Mary, 55, 56, 60
Hatt-Cook, Rowland, 130
Haw-Haw, 'Lord ', 145
Hazlewood, Wesley, 57
Heams, Reginald, YMCA, 65, 66, 136, 137, 154, 155
Henderson, David, 85
Hennig, Heinrich von, 36
Henry, Sir Edward, 82
Herbert, Edwin, 130
Herbert, Frank, 130
Herbert, Godfrey, xiii, 24 (chapter), 37, 38, 39, 40, 42, 43, 70, 130, 139, 141, 142
Hexanite, 99, 101, 199
Hickingbotham, Walter, 57
Hilliard, Patricia, 150

Hipper, Konteradmiral, 26
Hoggan, George, 73
Holtzendorff, Henning von, 46, 47, 48
Hooghly (Ganga) River, 72
Hopkins, Harry Alfred, 65, 136, 137
Hutchison, David, 114
Hutchison, Eulalie, 106, 112
Hyderabad, Nizam of, 84

Il Messaggero (newspaper), 52
Impey, Dr Elizabeth Stephens (Elsie), 66, 67, 129, 130
Inder Singh, 88, 131
International Naval Conference, 1908-9, 9
Iron Cross 1st class, 146,149
Italy, 9, 48, 52

Jeffery, Ernest, 56, 102, 119
Johnson, Arthur, 65, 81, 137, 154, 155
Johnson, Claude, 81

K13, steam-powered submarine, 143
Kaiser Wilhelm II, 2, 7, 14, 47, 148
Kaiserliche Marine, xii, xiii, 10, 15, 22, 31, 32, 34, 36, 42, 43, 46, 47, 48, 148, 188, 199
Kaiserliche Marine warships
   SMS Admiral Graf Spee, xiii
   SMS Amazone, 34
   SMS Rostok, 26, 193
   SMS Stralsund, 26
   SMS Von der Tann, xiii
   SMS Vulkan, 32, 33
Kerr, Lady Cecil, 81
Kerr, Lord Mark, 86
Kershaw, Eric E, 55
Kershaw, Lorna Hargrave, 55, 56, 60
Kershaw, Ronald Hargrave, 55
Khyber Pass, 84, 155
King Edward's High School for Girls, Birmingham, 66
King George V and Queen Mary, xiii, 87, 144, 153
King's Messenger, 61, 90, 93, 126
Knight Commander of the Indian Empire, 155
Knight of the Royal House Order of Hohenzollern, 146, 149

Knight, Ernest, 107
Kophamel, Waldemar, 46
Kriegsmarine, 149, 200

Lans, Vizeadmiral, 34
Lansdowne, 77, 152
Lansdowne, Marquess of, 9
Lawrence, Humphrey Richard Locke, 80, 130
Le Calvados (French troopship), 48, 96
Lees, Agnes, 66, 96, 97, 108, 110, 111, 155
Levantine Sea, 95
Lincolnshire Yeomanry, 48
Llandudno, 37
Lloyd-Jones, David, 121, 196
Lodwick, John Thornton, 76, 77, 108, 131
London, numerous pages
London and South Western Railway (LSWR), 81
Lough Swilly, 18

MacCallum More, Iron 3-Masted Sailing Vessel, 55, 192
MacDonald, Donald, 130
MacDonald, Gladys Enid, 71, 130
MacLean, Allan, 123
Mafessanti, Benvenuto, 73, 74, 124
Maharaja Sir Jagatjit Singh Bahadur, 87, 101, 131, 140, 151, 167
Maharani Prem Kaur, 87, 88, 89, 151
Maitland, Dr Christian (Chrissie), 67
Malakand Pass, 84
Marine Nationale (French Navy), 64, 93
Marineschule, 32
Marne, Battle of, 14
Marseilles, numerous pages
Marsh, Edward Waters Harbin, 75
Martin, Charles Leonard, 108, 124
Massardo, Capitano, 50, 51, 52
Matthew, Harold, 57
McBride, William (alias of Godfrey Herbert), 29, 40, 141, 145
McGinn, Quintilla Gustave, 68
McGinn, William George, 68
McMinn, Ada Blanche Selina, 70
McNeely, Robert Ney, 71, 72, 91, 130
Merchant ships
    SS Adenwen, 27, 195

SS Ancona, 19, 49, 60, 159
SS Antwerp (Q-ship), 26, 27, 28, 142
SS Arabic and the 'Arabic Pledge', 19, 30, 40, 41 (chapter), 47, 49, 60, 96, 99, 166, 225
SS Berwick, 25
SS Californian, 46
SS Calvados, 48, 96
SS Clan MacFarlane, 112, 113, 207
SS Dunsley, 41, 42
SS France IV, 50, 60
SS Glitra, 19
SS Hesperian, 60, 207
SS Karmala, 56
RMS Lusitania, xii, xiii, 19, 20, 29, 30, 31, 47, 54, 60, 100, 139, 140, 159, 206, 207
SS Medina 59, 61, 73, 130, 131
SS Natal Transport, 46
SS Nicosian, 37, 38, 39, 193
SS Ning Chow, 123, 124, 127, 165, 193
SS Norefos, 147
SS Persia, numerous pages
SS Rinjdam, 72
RMS Titanic, xii, 46
SS Trafalgar, 46
SS Woodfield, 48
SS Yasukuni Maru, 48
Mesopotamia, 76, 80, 135, 152, 200
Messina, 50
Miller-Hallett, John Lionel (Lion), 75, 76, 108, 116, 132, 134, 153
Minnitt, Joyce, 70, 134
Montagu of Beaulieu: John Walter Edward Douglas-Scott-Montagu (also Colonel Lord Montagu), numerous pages
Montagu, Edward John Barrington, 156
Mooney, Rose, 68

Naples, 49, 50 59
Nasmith, Eric, 24, 25
Naval Defence Act 1889, 2
Naval Prize Bill, 9
Nethersole, Alfred Ralph, 77, 134
New Forest, 81, 83, 153
New Year (1915-16), 93, 95, 114, 120, 137
Northcliffe, Lord, 157

Index

Northern Patrol, RN, 16

Old Head of Kinsale, 37, 41
Oran, 48
Orden Pour le Mérite, 141, 146, 147, 149, 201
Order-in-Council 20th August 1909, 9
O'Reilly, Charles Myles, 77, 108, 112
Orr Orr, William, 74, 134
Ottley, Charles, 8

P and O Official Statements, 120
Paris (Versailles) Peace Conference 1919, 159
Paris, The Declaration of 1856, 8
Parton, Harold Ranger, 56
Peninsular and Oriental Steam Navigation Company (P&O), 3, 54, 92, 98, 128
Penn Gaskell, 69, 119, 128, 150
Pennington, Mary Anne, 'the Duchess', 58, 134, 153
Pen-y-Gogarth, 37
Periscope 'feathers', 95
Piercy, Lieutenant Commander, 27
Pinner, John (Jack), 112
Pluton (French Minelayer), 52
Pohl, Hugo von, 15
Port Said, xi, 22, 73, 74, 80, 86, 91, 92, 93, 97, 107, 131, 133, 194
Presbytery of Aberdeen, 67
Prince Ajit Singh, 87
Prince Charles, Q-Ship, 30, 31
Prince Heinrich, 34
Princip, Gavrilo, 13
Privy Council, 75

Queenstown (now Cobh), x, 29, 41, 42, 201

Ravensdowne Barracks, 134
Regina Palace Hotel, 118, 132
Reichstag, 40
Richmond, Herbert, 31
Robertson, John Alexander Tower Robertson (Jack), 76, 133, 134, 135
Roch, Arthur Twining, 80, 135
Rolls, Charles, 81
Rolls-Royce, 82, 85

Romano's Restaurant, The Strand, 59
Royal Arsenal, 57, 59
Royal Commission on the Supply of Food and Raw Material in Time of War, 6, 18
Royal Humane Society, 127
Royal Navy, numerous pages
  HMS A4, 24, 25
  Q-Ship Baralong, xiii, 28, 29, 30, 36, 139, 140, 141, 142, 144, 145, 188, 192, 203, 206
  HMS Cilicia, armed merchant cruiser WW2, 144
  HMS Dolphin, 145
  HMS Dreadnought, 1, 8, 11, 16, 18, 27, 140, 198, 204, 207
  HMS Garry, 36
  HMS Hannibal, 117, 118, 207
  HMS Hawke, 16, 71, 130
  HMS Kelantan, 145
  HMS Mallow, 116 (chapter), 130, 132, 140, 151, 157
  HMS Mantua, Armed Merchant Cruiser, 16, 22, 58
  HMS Monmouth, 25, 193
  HMS Pathfinder, 17
  HMS Prosperine, 135
  HMS Roxborough, 35
  HMS Thames, 24
  HMT Dunera, 83, 84
  HMT Mercian, 48
  RMS Lusitania, xii, xiii, 20, 29, 30, 31
  Royal Navy College, Greenwich, 55
Rücker, Claus, 46, 92, 159
Russell, Robert Vane, 74

Salisbury, Homer Russell, 66, 136
Savoy Hotel, Alexandria, 118
Scapa Flow, 18, 36, 44
Schleswig-Holstein, 23, 32, 146, 149
Schlieffen, Alfred von, 14, 161
Schmidt, Carl (post-war alias of Max Valentiner), 148
Schneider, Rudolf (Rudi), 42
Secunderabad, 84
Senghenydd Mine, 100
Sinking of SS Persia, 97 (chapter)
Skagerrak, 33, 34

Smijth-Windham, Arthur Russell, 74, 91
Smith, Walter, 107
Sønderborg, 43, 147, 148, 149
Spirit of Ecstasy, 82
Sportsman Pub, Plumstead, 59
Spreckley, Arthur Freer, 70, 136
Spreckley, David, 154
St. Aubyn, Edward Stuart, Serving as King's Messenger, 90, 93, 126
Steele, Gordon, 29
Steinbrinck, Otto, 142, 143
Stoehr, Charles Felix, 71
Stoehr, Kathleen, 136
Stuart-Wortley-Mackenzie, Cecily Susan, The Honourable, 81
Suez Canal, 53, 65, 80, 83, 87, 93, 152
Supernumerary Engineer Officers, SS Persia, 58
Swiney, Ernest, 79
Sykes, Charles, 82
Syracuse, 52

Taranaki, U-boat decoy trawler, 30
Tenth Cruiser (or Training) Squadron RN, 16, 204
Thames, River, 55, 62, 83, 158
Thames Nautical Training College, HMS Worcester, 55
Third Naval Law (Germany), 8
Tholens, Hermann, 36, 37
Thornton, Eleanor Velasco (Nelly), ix, 81 (chapter), 156, 163, 166
Thornton, Joan Eleanor, 140
Tibbs, Robert Dunham, 76
Tiffin, 97, 104
Tilbury, 53, 54, 55, 57, 59, 62, 66, 67, 90, 130, 131
Tirpitz, Alfred von, 47
Torpedo director, 98
Tower Hill Memorial, 112, 150
Troop transporter (troopship), 99, 140

U-3, 32, 33, 34, 35
U-10, 33
U-24, 30, 40, 41, 42
U-27, 30, 37, 38, 41
U-33, 46, 159, 160
U-34, 46, 53, 92, 159
U-38, xiii, 1, 12, 30, 32 (chapter), numerous pages thereafter
U-39, 46, 53
U-157, 147, 148
U-boot Falle (U-boat Trap), 31, 43
University of North Carolina, 72, 204
Unrestricted submarine warfare, 15, 20, 42, 47, 48, 147

Valentiner, Max, xi, xiii, 12, 23, 31, 32 (chapter), numerous pages thereafter
Valentiner, Otto Friedrich, 32
Valletta, 53, 61, 66, 89, 90, 91, 92, 93, 123, 124, 127, 194
Ville de la Ciotat, French Liner, 92

Walton, George, 58, 59, 91, 138
War crime(s), xiii, 26, 31, 139, 141, 145, 159 (chapter), 205, 209
War Zone, 20, 97
Warnshuis, John, 71, 130, 150
Warnshuis, Lilian, Dr (formerly Dr Lilian Cook), 150
Washington Sunday Star, 53, 208
Weddigen, Otto, 13, 16, 17, 27, 71, 130, 142
Wegener, Bernd, 36, 37, 38, 39, 43, 139
Wellington, Lawrence Arthur, 95
Western Approaches, 26, 63, 64, 73
Whitacre, Wilma, 72
Wilhelmshaven, 44, 148
Wilson, Horace Hayman, 80
Wilson, President Woodrow, 42, 66
Wilson, Sir Arthur VC, 11
Wood, Harold, 56, 98, 99, 117
Wyandra, 192

Young Men's Christian Association / YMCA, 61, 65, 66, 136, 137, 154

Zembra Island, 52